Frommer's®

Rio de Janeiro day by day®

1st Edition

by Alexandra de Vries

Wiley Publishing, Inc.

Contents

Published by:

Wiley Publishing, Inc.

111 River St.
Hoboken, NJ 07030-5774

ISBN 978-0-470-88157-6; ISBN 978-1-118-01950-4 (ebk);
ISBN 978-1-118-01951-1 (ebk); ISBN 978-1-118-01952-8 (ebk)
Editor: Jennifer Reilly
Production Editor: M. Faunette Johnston
Photo Editor: Cherie Cincilla and Alden Gewirtz
Cartographer: Roberta Stockwell
Production by Wiley Indianapolis Composition Services

Cover photos: *Left,* © Thomas Cockrem/Alamy Images; *Center,* © Ben Lewis/Alamy Images; *Right,* © Franck Camhi/Alamy Images; *Back,* © Peter M. Wilson/Alamy Images.

For information on our other products and services or to obtain technical support, please contact our Customer Care Department within the U.S. at 877/762-2974, outside the U.S. at 317/572-3993 or fax 317/572-4002.

Wiley also publishes its books in a variety of electronic formats. Some content that appears in print may not be available in electronic formats.

Manufactured in China

5 4 3 2 1

A Note from the Editorial Director

Organizing your time. That's what this guide is all about.

Other guides give you long lists of things to see and do and then expect you to fit the pieces together. The Day by Day guides are different. These guides tell you the best of everything, and then they show you how to see it *in the smartest, most time-efficient way*. Our authors have designed detailed itineraries organized by time, neighborhood, or special interest. And each tour comes with a bulleted map that takes you from stop to stop.

Hoping to tour the best in contemporary architecture, stroll through Ipanema, or lounge on Copacabana Beach? Planning a walk through Santa Teresa, or plotting a day of fun-filled activities with the kids? Whatever your interest or schedule, the Day by Days give you the smartest routes to follow. Not only do we take you to the top attractions, hotels, and restaurants, but we also help you access those special moments that locals get to experience --those "finds" that turn tourists into travelers.

The Day by Days are also your top choice if you're looking for one complete guide for all your travel needs. The best hotels and restaurants for every budget, the greatest shopping values, the wildest nightlife—it's all here.

Why should you trust our judgment? Because our authors personally visit each place they write about. They're an independent lot who say what they think and would never include places they wouldn't recommend to their best friends. They're also open to suggestions from readers. If you'd like to contact them, please send your comments our way at feedback@frommers.com, and we'll pass them on.

Enjoy your Day by Day guide—the most helpful travel companion you can buy. And have the trip of a lifetime.

Warm regards,

Kelly Regan

Kelly Regan, Editorial Director
Frommer's Travel Guides

About the Author

Alexandra de Vries is a freelance writer and translator. Born in Amsterdam to a Dutch father and Brazilian mother, Alexandra made her first trip to Brazil at the ripe old age of 1 month (alas, few of her food reviews from that trip survive). In recent years, Alexandra has returned many times to travel, explore, and live in this amazing country. Alexandra also cowrites *Frommer's Brazil* and *Frommer's South America.* As a translator, she has translated books on Brazilian icons such as Oscar Niemeyer and Burle Marx.

Dedication

For my mother and father who nurtured my adventurous spirit and gave me the confidence to explore the world.

An Additional Note

Please be advised that travel information is subject to change at any time—and this is especially true of prices. We therefore suggest that you write or call ahead for confirmation when making your travel plans. The authors, editors, and publisher cannot be held responsible for the experiences of readers while traveling. Your safety is important to us, however, so we encourage you to stay alert and be aware of your surroundings.

Star Ratings, Icons & Abbreviations

Every hotel, restaurant, and attraction listing in this guide has been ranked for quality, value, service, amenities, and special features using a **star-rating system.** Hotels, restaurants, attractions, shopping, and nightlife are rated on a scale of zero stars (recommended) to three stars (exceptional). In addition to the star-rating system, we also use a **kids icon** to point out the best bets for families. Within each tour, we recommend cafes, bars, or restaurants where you can take a break. Each of these stops appears in a shaded box marked with a coffee-cup-shaped bullet.

The following **abbreviations** are used for credit cards:

AE	American Express	DISC	Discover	V	Visa
DC	Diners Club	MC	MasterCard		

Travel Resources at Frommers.com

Frommer's travel resources don't end with this guide. Frommer's website, **www.frommers.com**, has travel information on more than 4,000 destinations. We update features regularly, giving you access to the most current trip-planning information and the best airfare, lodging, and car-rental bargains. You can also listen to podcasts, connect with other Frommers.com members through our active-reader forums, share your travel photos, read blogs from guidebook editors and fellow travelers, and much more.

A Note on Prices

In the "Take a Break" and "Best Bets" sections of this book, we have used a system of dollar signs to show a range of costs for 1 night in a hotel (the price of a double-occupancy room) or the cost of an entree at a restaurant. Use the following table to decipher the dollar signs:

Cost	Hotels	Restaurants
$	under R$89	under R$17
$$	R$89–R$177	R$17–R$35
$$$	R$177–R$354	R$35–R$53
$$$$	R$354–R$531	R$53–R$71
$$$$$	over R$531	over R$71

How to Contact Us

In researching this book, we discovered many wonderful places—hotels, restaurants, shops, and more. We're sure you'll find others. Please tell us about them, so we can share the information with your fellow travelers in upcoming editions. If you were disappointed with a recommendation, we'd love to know that, too. Please write to:

Frommer's Rio de Janeiro Day by Day, 1st Edition
Wiley Publishing, Inc. • 111 River St. • Hoboken, NJ 07030-5774

16 Favorite **Moments**

16 Favorite **Moments**

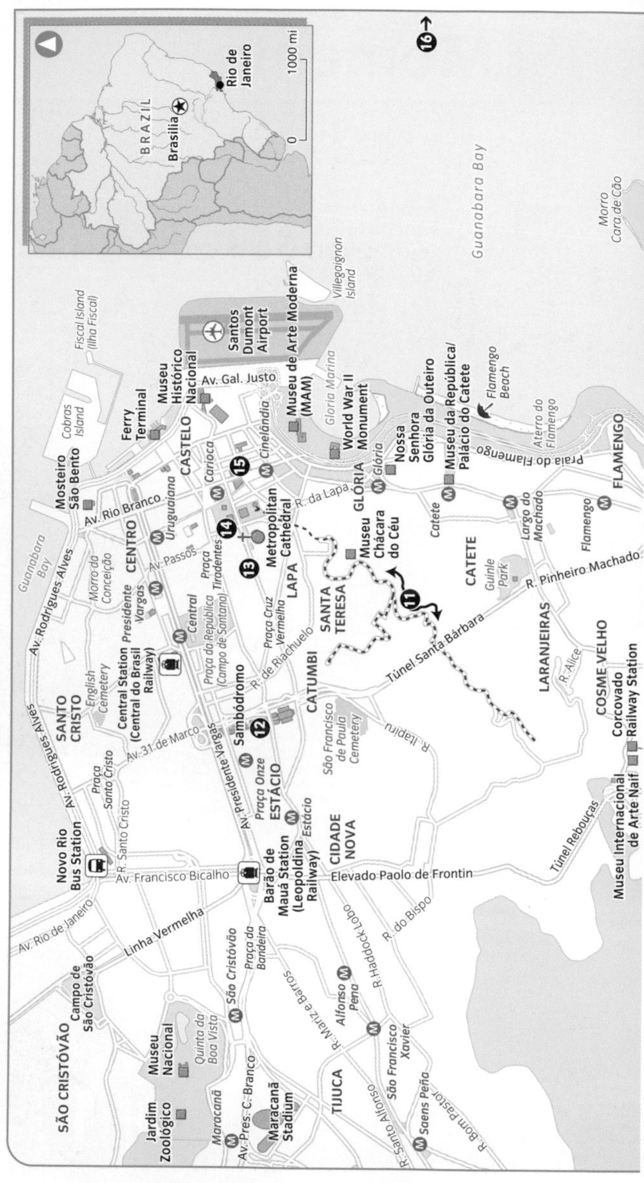

Previous page: The view of Sugarloaf Mountain from atop Corcovado.

16 Favorite Moments

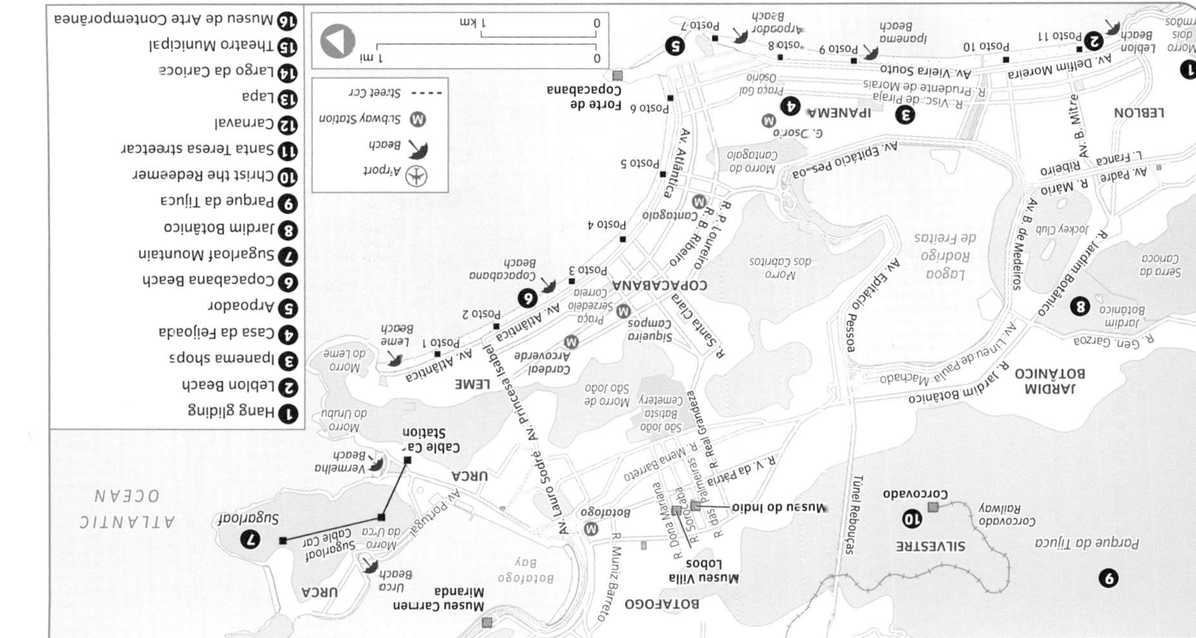

Nicknamed "Cidade Maravilhosa" (the Fabulous City), Rio de Janeiro conjures up images of golden beaches, tropical sunshine, and colorful carnival parades, but the city has much more to offer. Blessed with impressive natural beauty, Rio is nestled between the Atlantic Ocean and steep mountains clad with coastal rainforest. The city's architecture encompasses everything from 18th-century colonial baroque to modern minimalism. A rich cultural scene showcases some of Brazil's most talented musicians and artists. And then there are the people, the friendly, high-spirited Cariocas, who know that they live in one of the most beautiful cities in the world and make sure there is always enough time to kick back and enjoy life; to do otherwise would be disrespectful of the *Cidade Maravilhosa*.

❶ **Spreading your wings and soaring high above the city.** Ever dream you can fly? Now you can, with no experience required! Your hang glider pilot will see to it that you are securely strapped in for take-off from Pedra Bonita, and accompany you on a safe, exhilarating ride through the city's skies. After a 10- to 15-minute flight, you'll land gently on São Conrado Beach. *See p 93.*

❷ **Soaking up the tropical sun on Leblon Beach.** Head to the beach for the quintessential Carioca experience. Just bring some sunscreen and a towel, rent a chair and sun umbrella, and you'll be all set. Soak up the warm rays, go for a swim, meet some locals, have a cold beer or fresh coconut water, and enjoy some fabulous people-watching. *See p 80.*

Ipanema Beach.

❸ **Browsing hip Brazilian fashion in upscale Ipanema.** Ipanema's swanky shopping district is home to some of the most exclusive international and Brazilian labels and designers. But don't expect a stuffy or stuck-up vibe; the shops exude the fun, laid-back atmosphere of this beach neighborhood. *See p 66.*

❹ **Savoring a plate of *feijoada*, Brazil's national dish, at the Casa da Feijoada.** I have never met a Brazilian abroad who wasn't pining away for this rich savory stew of black beans and meat. At Casa da Feijoada, you can try this dish with all the trimmings any day of the week and learn a bit about its history. *See p 103.*

❺ **Watching the sunset at Arpoador.** Time your afternoon stroll so you can walk up Arpoador's rocks just before the setting sun casts a magnificent glow over Ipanema and the silhouette of Dois Irmãos, the peaks just beyond Leblon. *See p 10.*

❻ **Sipping a caipirinha on Copacabana Beach.** Brazil's signature cocktail, made with *cachaça* liquor, lime, sugar, and ice, may have conquered bars across the world, but nothing beats sipping a caipirinha at

Imperial palm trees in the Jardim Botânico.

a beachside kiosk along Copacabana's iconic black and white mosaic sidewalk. *See p 9.*

❼ **Taking the cable car to the top of Sugarloaf Mountain.** A short cable car ride whisks you to the top of Rio's famous landmark granite rock that guards the entrance of the bay. From this unique vantage point you can enjoy magnificent views of the nearby beaches, downtown, the Floresta da Tijuca, and the southside neighborhoods. *See p 11.*

❽ **Strolling underneath the imperial palm trees in the Jardim Botânico.** Clear your head with a relaxing walk through this 200-year-old botanical garden, a green refuge of native and exotic flora that is also home to many birds and even monkeys. A row of elegant Imperial palm trees frames the entrance to the garden. *See p 59.*

❾ **Cooling off under a waterfall in the Parque da Tijuca.** On a hot day, you can beat the tropical heat by seeking cooler climes in the Parque da Tijuca, the largest urban rainforest in the world, and taking a refreshing dip in a waterfall. *See p. 83.*

❿ **Admiring the city spread out at the feet of Christ the Redeemer.** A narrow-gauge train chugs through the rainforest, carrying visitors to the top of Corcovado Mountain and Brazil's most famous monument, the statue of Christ the Redeemer. The views here are truly divine. *See p 13.*

⓫ **Riding the Santa Teresa streetcar.** There is no better way to see Rio's bohemian hillside neighborhood than from a wooden bench onboard this rickety yellow streetcar. It sets out from downtown and travels over the 17m (56-ft.) high Aqueduct before it reaches the cobblestone streets of Santa Teresa. *See p 20.*

⓬ **Donning a costume and joining the biggest party in the world.** All year long, Cariocas look forward to Carnaval, the city's largest and most colorful celebration. Even better than

The Santa Teresa streetcar riding across the Lapa Aquaduct.

Performers at Carnaval.

being a spectator is purchasing a costume and experiencing first-hand *"o maior show da terra"* (the greatest show on earth), to quote the lyrics of a famous samba song. *See p 39.*

⓭ **Dancing the samba in historic Lapa.** Recent urban renewal and renovations have transformed Rio's former red-light district into one of the best nightlife destinations in the city, where you can listen to excellent samba (and other music styles) any given night of the week. *See p 44.*

⓮ **Marveling at the Portuguese colonial architecture at Largo da Carioca.** Amidst a sea of modern office towers lies a small island where time has stood still. Admire the dazzling gilded baroque artwork of the Igreja de São Francisco da Penitência and the lovely colonial architecture of the Convento Santo Antonio, fine examples of 18th-century architecture. *See p 21.*

⓯ **Attending a concert at the neoclassical Theatro Municipal.** Rio's most opulent performing arts venue has been fully restored for its 100th anniversary in 2010. There's no better time to see a concert, and to take in the elegant and impressive gleaming dome, marble stairs, and stained glass windows. *See p 15.*

⓰ **Gazing at the signature curves of Oscar Niemeyer's architecture.** One of the best examples of the work of the 102-year-old modernist architect who left his distinct mark on 20th-century architecture can be seen in Niteroi. His Museu de Arte Contemporânea, with curvaceous lines and reflective pools that mirror the ocean and the sky, is more impressive than any of the artwork on display. *See p 27.* ●

Niteroi's Museu de Arte Contemporânea.

1 The Best **Full-Day Tours**

The Best **in One Day**

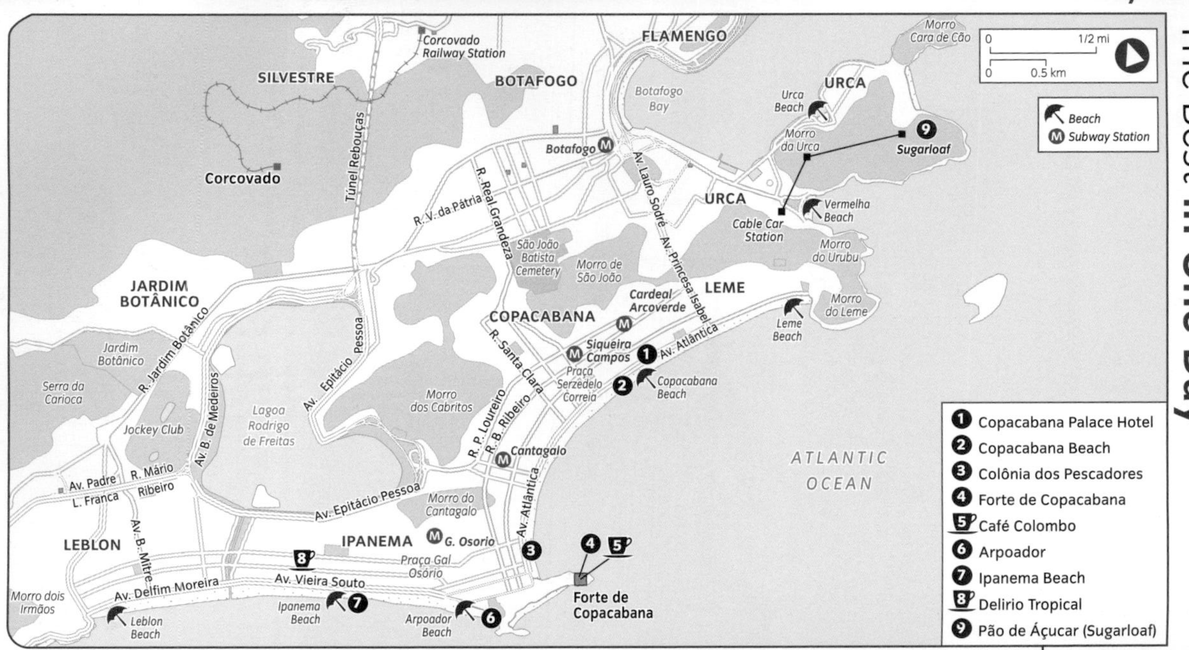

Previous page: Cristo Redentor (Christ the Redeemer).

If you only have 1 day in Rio de Janeiro, experience the spectacular beaches and beautiful vistas that have made the city deservedly famous. Stroll along Copacabana and Ipanema beaches, mingle with laid-back *Cariocas* (residents of Rio), who always find time to enjoy life, and get your bearings from atop Arpoador and Sugarloaf. **START: Metrô to Cardeal Arcoverde.**

❶ **Copacabana Palace Hotel.** This elegant hotel is a favorite among visiting celebrities for its old-world charm and glamour. Built between 1917 and 1923, the Copacabana Palace Hotel was one of the first commercial buildings along this once deserted stretch of beach and dunes. Historic photos lining the wall at the rear of the building (facing Av. N.S. de Copacabana) show how much the city has changed. Start your day with a coffee in Pérgula restaurant, next to the swimming pool. On Sundays, the restaurant serves an excellent, although pricey, brunch with delicious seafood. *15 min. Av. Atlântica 1702, Copacabana. ☎ 021/2548-7070. www.copacabanapalace.com. Metrô: Cardeal Arcoverde.*

❷ ★★ kids **Copacabana Beach.** One of the city's most famous landmarks, Copacabana Beach offers 5km (3 miles) of glorious white sand; it's a true microcosm of eclectic Rio, where tourists and residents meet to swim, tan, flirt, exercise, stroll, and relax. Kids have plenty of space to build sandcastles or kick a ball around. Walk along the boulevard and admire the sea views, watch locals play soccer or volleyball, and sip cold coconut water. *1 hr., or longer. Metrô: Cardeal Arcoverde.*

❸ ★ **Colônia dos Pescadores.** At the end of Copacabana, toward Ipanema, you come to a small fishing community. Early risers may see the boats head out to sea and return with their catch, which is sold at the small fish market on site. In the afternoon, fishermen sit in the shade and mend their nets. *10 min. Av. Atlântica (across from the Sofitel Hotel, around no. 4240), Copacabana. Metrô: Cantagalo.*

❹ ★★ kids **Forte de Copacabana.** Straddling a rocky outcrop between Copacabana and Ipanema, the Forte de Copacabana offers stunning views and a quiet retreat from the hectic city streets. The military buildings and armament date back to 1914 and were constructed to defend Guanabara Bay. The fort houses the **Museu Historico Militar** (Military Historic Museum), an art gallery, and a small gift store, but most visitors come to soak in the panoramic views. Kids will enjoy exploring the cannons and climbing

The sidewalk mosaic at Copacabana Beach.

Hiking Sugarloaf

Guarding the entrance of Guanabara Bay, Sugarloaf Mountain is one of the city's most striking natural attractions. Ever since the first cable car was inaugurated in 1912, visitors have ascended this monolith to enjoy the sweeping views. However, there is another way to reach the top—on foot, along a narrow trail around the back of the steep granite walls that takes you all the way to the viewing platform. Accompanied by an experienced guide, the hike takes approximately 1½ hours and requires a moderate fitness level and no fear of heights. Avid rock climbers may also explore the various rock faces and climbing routes. Contact **Riohiking** (☎ 021/2552-9204 or 9721-0594; www.riohiking.com.br) for hiking or rock climbing tours. See p 93.

up to the strategic viewpoints. 🕘 *45 min. Praça Eugenio Franco 1 (at the end of Av. Atlântica, across from the Sofitel Hotel), Copacabana. ☎ 021/2521-1032. www.fortedecopacabana.com. Admission R$4. Tues–Sun 10am–8pm. Metrô: Cantagalo.*

5 **Café Colombo.** Tucked away inside the Forte de Copacabana, Café Colombo serves outstanding snacks and light meals. This branch of the historic Colombo tearoom in downtown Rio (p 104) may lack old-world glamour, but that's more than compensated by the views of the ocean, beach, and mountains. *Praça Eugenio Franco 1. Cafe only open during fort opening hours (see above) and requires admission ticket. ☎ 021/3201-4049. $.*

❻ ★★ **Arpoador.** Just around the corner from Copacabana and the fort lies Arpoador. Climb to the top of this rocky headland for a fabulous view of Ipanema and Leblon, set against the peaks of Dois Irmãos (Two Brothers). Especially at the end of a long, hot summer day, Cariocas love to gather here to watch the sunset. 🕘 *30 min. Northern end of Ipanema beach. Metrô: General Osório.*

❼ ★★ **Ipanema Beach.** More upscale than Copacabana, Ipanema is Rio's hip and trendy beach, where fashions are created and beautiful people come to see and be seen. When conditions are right, Ipanema is also a popular local surf destination. 🕘 *1 hr. or more. Metrô: General Osório.*

Ipanema Beach with Pedra Dois Irmãos in the background.

8 Delirio Tropical. For a healthy aprés beach meal, try Delirio Tropical. This Carioca institution specializes in fresh salads, pastas, and light meals, including several vegetarian options. *Rua Garcia D'Avila 48, Ipanema. ☎ 021/3624-8164. www.delirio.com.br. $.*

9 ★★★ Pão de Áçucar (Sugarloaf). From its privileged location at the entrance of the bay, Sugarloaf Mountain offers stunning views of Rio de Janeiro. The cable car whisks visitors first to Morro da Urca (220m/722 ft.). Don't waste your time at this stop; head straight to the second cable car that will take you to the very top (396m/1,299 ft.). On a clear day, you can see the beaches of Copacabana and Ipanema, Guanabara Bay, the Parque Nacional da Tijuca, and Corcovado. Time your visit an hour or two before sundown when the city basks in a golden glow and the lights begin to twinkle. *2 hr. Praia Vermelha, Urca. ☎ 021/2461-2700. www.bondinho.com.br. Adults R$44, children 6–12 R$22. Daily 8am–8pm. Bus: 512.*

The Sugarloaf cable car.

Favela Tours

Numerous favelas, or shanty towns, cling to Rio's hillsides and are as much a part of its urban fabric and culture as the beach neighborhoods. One of the first companies to take visitors into the favelas, **Favela Tour** (☎ 021/3322-2727 or 21/9772-1133; www.favelatour.com.br) provides an excellent introduction to the complicated relationship between rich and poor in Brazil. The 2-hour tour costs R$65 and includes a visit to Rocinha, one of the largest favelas in Rio de Janeiro, for an up-close look at how more than 100,000 people live. I often hear travelers say that they feel uncomfortable with the idea of "gawking" at the poor. However, most favela residents actually welcome foreigners who are interested in visiting "their" part of the city, which is often ignored by or discriminated against by wealthier Brazilians. Part of the tour proceeds fund a community school, as well.

A street in Rocinha.

The Best in Two Days

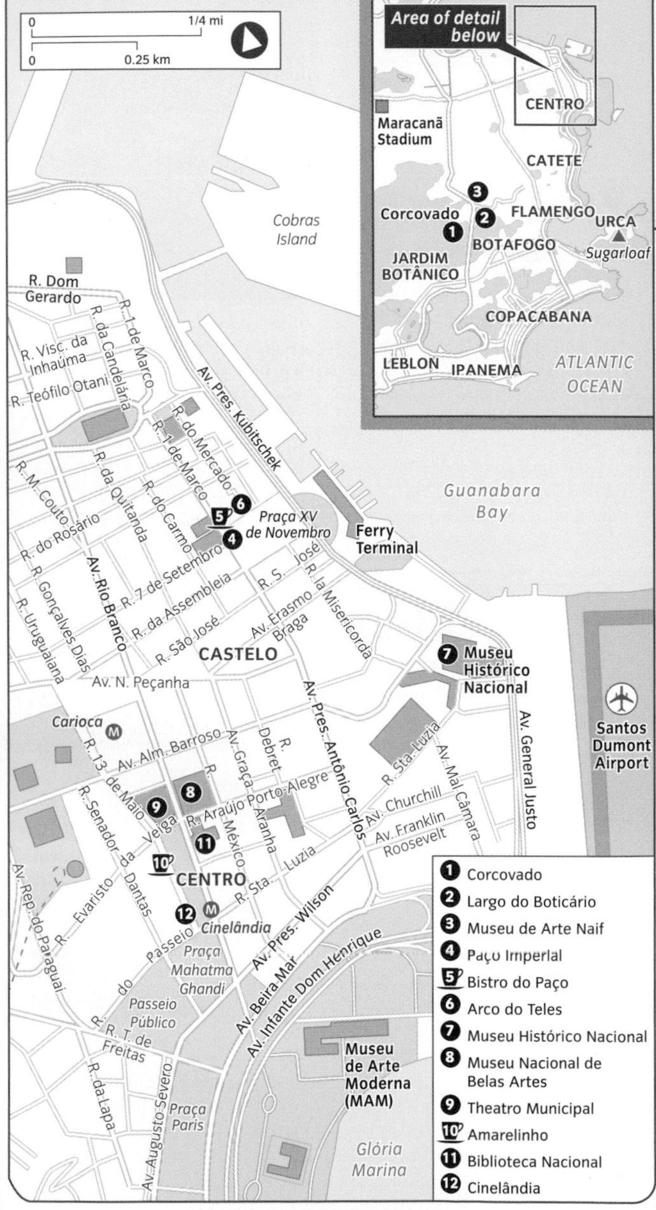
0 1/4 mi
0 0.25 km
Area of detail below
CENTRO
Maracanã Stadium
CATETE
Corcovado
FLAMENGO
URCA
BOTAFOGO
Sugarloaf
JARDIM BOTÂNICO
COPACABANA
LEBLON
IPANEMA
ATLANTIC OCEAN
Cobras Island
R. Dom Gerardo
R. Visc. da Inhaúma
R. Teófilo Otani
R. da Candelária
R. 1 de Marco
R. do Mercado
Av. Pres. Kubitschek
R. M. Couto
R. da Quitanda
R. do Carmo
R. do Rosário
Praça XV de Novembro
Ferry Terminal
Guanabara Bay
R. 7 de Setembro
R. da Assembleia
R. São José
R. S. José
R. la Misericordia
Av. Erasmo Braga
R. Gonçalves Dias
R. Uruguaiana
Av. Rio Branco
CASTELO
Av. N. Peçanha
Museu Histórico Nacional
Santos Dumont Airport
Carioca
Av. Alm. Barroso
Av. Graça Aranha
R. Debret
Av. Pres. Antônio Carlos
R. Sta. Luzia
Av. Mal Câmara
Av. General Justo
R. 13 de Maio
R. Senador Dantas
R. Araújo Porto Alegre
R. México
Av. Churchill
Av. Franklin Roosevelt
Veiga
CENTRO
R. Evaristo da
Av. Rep. do Paraguai
Cinelândia
R. Sta. Luzia
Av. Pres. Wilson
Passeio
Praça Mahatma Ghandi
Passeio Público
R. do
R. T. de Freitas
Av. Beira Mar
Av. Infante Dom Henrique
Museu de Arte Moderna (MAM)
R. da Lapa
Av. Augusto Severo
Praça Paris
Glória Marina
1 Corcovado
2 Largo do Boticário
3 Museu de Arte Naif
4 Paço Imperial
5 Bistro do Paço
6 Arco do Teles
7 Museu Histórico Nacional
8 Museu Nacional de Belas Artes
9 Theatro Municipal
10 Amarelinho
11 Biblioteca Nacional
12 Cinelândia

After spending much of your first day on the beach, it's time to explore farther inland and discover that Rio offers a lot more than sand and sea. Venture into the largest urban park in the world, the Floresta da Tijuca, a green haven of lush Atlantic rainforest, and visit the park's most famous destination, the statue of Christ the Redeemer. Then head downtown, where 18th-century colonial buildings and museums tell the fascinating history of the city. Hard-working Cariocas pack the bustling streets here, but at the end of the day there is always time for a cold beer. **START: Bus 583 to Corcovado train station.**

1 ★★★ **kids** **Corcovado.** It's hard to miss the 38m-high (125 ft.) concrete statue of Cristo Redentor (Christ the Redeemer) on top of Corcovado Mountain (704m/2,310 ft.). Inaugurated in 1931, the statue is reached by a 20-minute train ride through former coffee plantations and lush Atlantic rainforest. Once you reach the top, it's only a short walk and escalator ride to the viewing platform at the feet of the statue. Plan your visit on a clear day to make the most of the divine 360-degree views. *2 hr. Rua Cosme Velho 513, Cosme Velho. ☎ 021/2558-1329. www.corcovado.com.br. Daily 8:30am–7pm. Adults R$36 (children under 5 free). Bus: 583.*

2 ★ **Largo do Boticário.** A 5-minute walk beyond the Corcovado train station takes you to a forgotten jewel of 19th-century Rio, the picturesque Largo do Boticário, a lovely cobblestone square surrounded by colonial houses. The small stream that flows by is the Carioca River that comes down from the Parque Nacional da Tijuca, which now flows mostly underground before draining into Guanabara Bay at Flamengo Beach. *10 min. Rua Cosme Velho 822 (just past the bus stop), Cosme Velho. Bus: 583.*

3 ★ **Museu de Arte Naif.** One of the most colorful and vibrant art collections in the city can be found in this museum, only a few steps beyond the Corcovado train station. Arte Naif is famous for its lively depictions of popular culture. The collection includes works by Brazilian and international artists. *30 min. Rua Cosme Velho 561, Cosme Velho.*

Cristo Redentor atop Corcovado.

A house by Largo do Boticario (p 13).

☎ *021/2205-8612. www.museunaif.com.br. Mon–Fri 1–5pm. Adults R$10, seniors and students R$5. Bus: 583.*

4 ★ Paço Imperial. Dwarfed by modern skyscrapers, the modest Paço Imperial was built in 1743 as the seat of government. In 1808 it was upgraded to a royal palace when the Portuguese royal family arrived, fleeing from Napoleon's troops. It was here that Dom Pedro I declared independence from Portugal in 1822, becoming emperor of Brazil. In 1888 crowds gathered outside to celebrate the abolition of slavery. Today the building serves as a cultural center, hosting concerts, exhibits, films, and theater performances. ⌚ *20 min. Praça XV 48, Centro.* ☎ *021/2215-1622. www.pacoimperial.com.br. Tues–Sun noon–6pm. Free admission. Bus: 121 or 123.*

The Paço Imperial.

5 Bistro do Paço. The thick stone walls of the 18th-century Paço Imperial hide a delightful courtyard cafe, a quiet refuge from the busy city streets. The kitchen serves up delicious sandwiches, quiches, salads, and scrumptious European pastries and desserts. *Praça XV 48, Centro.* ☎ *021/2262-3613. $.*

6 Arco do Teles. A small archway on the north side of Praça XV gives access to the **Travessa do Comércio,** a slice of old Rio with cobblestone alleys, narrow sidewalks, baroque churches, and lovely 19th-century two and three-story constructions. It's a popular lunch and happy-hour destination among downtown office workers. ⌚ *30 min. Travessa do Comércio, Centro (north end of Praça XV). Bus: 121 or 128.*

7 ★ Museu Histórico Nacional. One of Brazil's premier historic museums, the Museu Histórico Nacional gives visitors an overview of Brazil's colonial history. Other exhibits include archaeological artifacts predating the arrival of the Europeans, a 19th-century pharmacy, and several impressive coin collections. The buildings that compose the sprawling museum complex are also worth a visit; the oldest construction dates back to 1762, when it was used by the Portuguese to house military supplies. The museum also hosts major temporary exhibits. ⌚ *1 hr. Praça Marechal Âncora s/n, Centro.* ☎ *021/2550-9224. www.museu*

Artwork on display at the Museu Nacional de Belas Artes.

historiconacional.com.br. Tues–Fri 10am–5:30pm and Sat–Sun 2–6pm. Admission R$6, free on Sun. Bus: 413 or 415. On Sat–Sun a taxi is recommended.

8 ★★ Museu Nacional de Belas Artes. Inaugurated in 1909 as the Academy of Fine Arts, this building was converted into Rio's fine arts museum in 1937. Spanish architect Morales de Los Rios was clearly inspired by the Louvre in Paris when he designed this neoclassical jewel with marble floors, French mosaics, and delicate stained glass. Highlights of the collection include numerous works by foreign artists who visited Brazil, such as eight landscapes painted by 17th-century Dutch artist Frans Post in the northeast of Brazil, and works by Debret, a French painter who lived in Rio de Janeiro from 1816 to 1831 and depicted scenes from everyday life. *1 hr. Av. Rio Branco 199, Centro. ☎ 021/2240-0068. www.mnba.gov.br. Tues–Fri 10am–6pm; Sat–Sun noon–5pm. Admission R$6, free on Sun. Metrô: Cinelândia.*

9 ★★★ Theatro Municipal. Inspired by the Paris Opera, the Theatro Municipal dominates the square with its opulent facade. In honor of its 100th anniversary in 2009, the theater has been completely restored and looks better than ever. It's worth attending a concert here—the city's premier performing arts venue—just to admire the ornate interior. Check the website for concert information. *5 min. Praça Marechal Floriano*

The Theatro Municipal on Cinelândia square.

Amarelinho's terrace.

s/n, Centro. ☎ 021/2332-9191. www.theatromunicipal.rj.gov.br. Metrô: Cinelândia.

10 Amarelinho. A traditional Carioca bar/restaurant, Amarelinho has one of the best outdoor terraces right across from the Theatro Municipal. Stretch your legs and order a *chopp* (draft beer) and a serving of *bolinho de bacalhau* (savory cod snacks). ***Praça Floriano 55, Cinelândia. ☎ 021/2240-8434. www.amarelinhodacinelandia.com.br. $.***

11 ★ Biblioteca Nacional. The monumental neoclassical Biblioteca Nacional contains one of the most important library collections in South America. Inaugurated in 1909, the library also features beautiful marble stairways, bronze sculptures, and French stained glass skylights. ***1 hr. (guided tour). Av. Rio Branco 219, Centro. ☎ 021/2220-9484. www.bn.br. Mon–Fri 9am–8pm and Sat 9am–3pm. Guided tours Mon–Fri 11am–3pm; English-language tour at 1pm. Admission R$2. Metrô: Cinelândia.***

12 ★★ Cinelândia. Cariocas like to think of this square with its lovely neoclassical buildings as their "little piece of Paris," created in the first decade of the 20th century. Inspired by Haussmann's urban renewal of Paris, Rio de Janeiro's mayor Perreira Passos transformed a swampy part of downtown into his vision of a world-class city, with wide boulevards and impressive buildings, like the Escola Nacional de Belas Artes (now the Museum of Fine Arts; p 15, bullet 8), the Biblioteca Nacional (bullet 11), and the Theatro Municipal (p 15, bullet 9). *See mini-tour.*

The Travessa do Comércio (p 14).

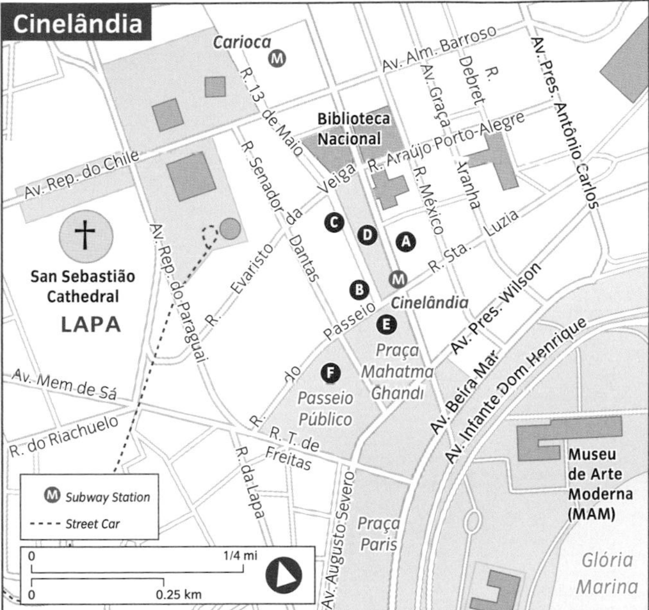

In addition to major attractions like the Theatro Municipal, Cinelândia has a number of smaller sights worthy of a closer look. The **A** **Centro Cultural da Justiça Federal** (Av. Rio Branco 241, ☎ 021/3261 2550, www.ccjf.trf2.gov.br; free admission; Tues–Sun noon–7pm) was originally designed in 1909 and until 1960 housed the federal supreme court. Step inside to admire the colorful stained-glass windows and wrought-iron staircase. In the 1920s, the square earned its nickname Cinelândia when the city's major cinemas were located here. Inaugurated in 1926, the **B** **Cine Odeon BR** (Praça Floriano 7; ☎ 021/2240-1093; www.grupoestacao.com.br) is the last movie theater to survive from that era. The 1920 French-inspired building **C** **Palacio Pedro Ernesto** (Praça Floriano s/n; ☎ 021/3814-2205; Mon–Fri 9am–5pm) houses the municipal council. Enjoy a free 20-minute guided tour of the opulent interior, which features marble floors, impressive stained-glass skylights, and a grand plenary hall. In the middle of the square stands the impressive **D** **Monumento ao Marechal Floriano Peixoto** in honor of the second president of the Republic, Floriano Peixoto. Made in Paris in 1904, the statue includes references to Brazil's indigenous tribes, African heritage, and republican ideals. Toward the end of Avenida Rio Branco stands the largest ornamental fountain in the city, the **E** **Chafariz do Monroe.** Designed in Paris in 1878, this fountain depicts four figures that represent the four continents: Asia, Africa, Europe, and America. If you have an extra 20 minutes, walk into the lovely **F** **Passeio Público,** a leafy, elegant 18th-century park, designed by the baroque sculptor and artist Mestre Valentim.

The Best **in Three Days**

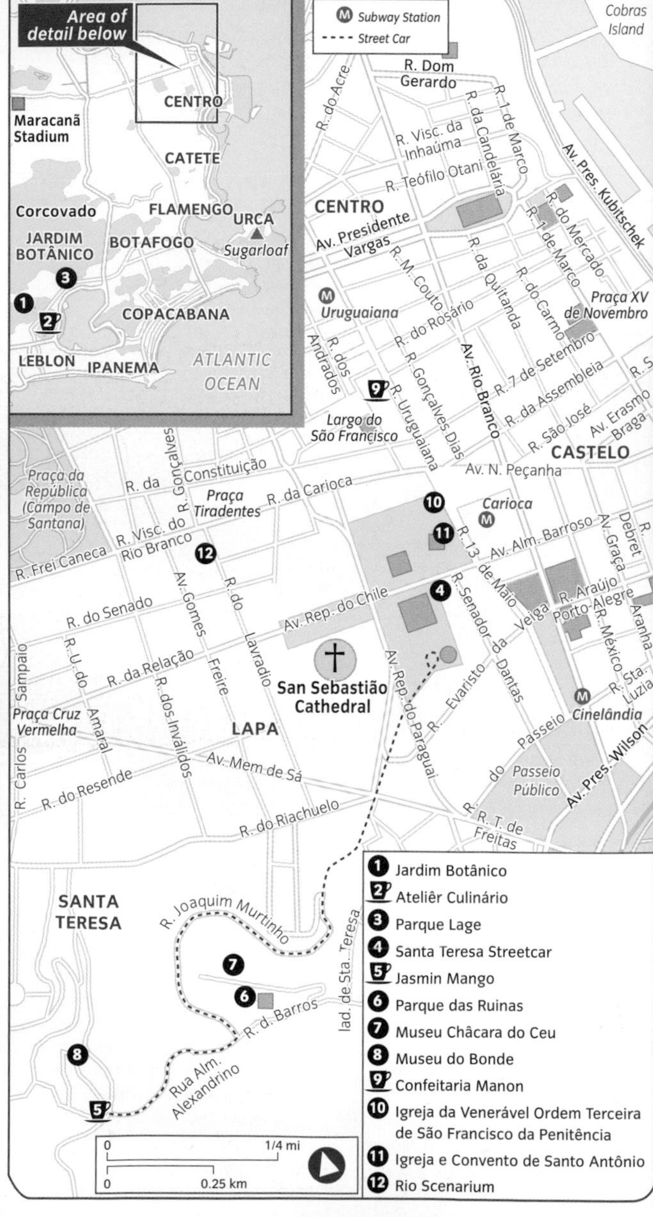

1. Jardim Botânico
2. Ateliêr Culinário
3. Parque Lage
4. Santa Teresa Streetcar
5. Jasmin Mango
6. Parque das Ruinas
7. Museu Châcara do Ceu
8. Museu do Bonde
9. Confeitaria Manon
10. Igreja da Venerável Ordem Terceira de São Francisco da Penitência
11. Igreja e Convento de Santo Antônio
12. Rio Scenarium

On your third day in Rio, you will continue to explore the city's rich history—but don't worry, I throw in plenty of spectacular views and nature. Start the day with a visit to the 200-year-old Botanical Garden and stroll under its majestic Imperial palm trees. Next, board a 100-year-old streetcar and travel across the Lapa Aquaduct to the 19th-century hilltop neighborhood of Santa Teresa, with its beautiful mansions and quaint castles. Conclude the day with a refreshing caipirinha and live samba music in Lapa. **START: Bus 170 to Jardim Botânico.**

1 ★★★ kids Jardim Botânico. Rio's magnificent Botanical Garden is nestled against the lower part of the Parque Nacional da Tijuca and contains more than 8,000 species of flora. The garden was founded in 1808 by Portuguese king D. João IV, who planted the first row of Imperial palm trees that line the main entrance. Make sure you visit the Museum of the Environment, the bromeliad collection, the orchid greenhouse, and flesh-eating plants. There are several beautiful monuments, artwork, fountains, and historic buildings scattered throughout the park (p 58). *2 hr. Rua Jardim Botânico 1008, Jardim Botânico. ☎ 021/3204-2505. www.jbrj.gov.br. Tues–Sun 10am–5pm. Admission R$5. Bus: 170.*

The orchid greenhouse at the Jardim Botânico.

The cafe at the Parque Lage.

2 Atelier Culinário (inside Livrária Ponte de Tábuas). I find it hard to resist this combination bookstore and cafe. Browse the excellent selection of books and sit down to enjoy a coffee with a dessert, snack, or light meal. *Rua Jardim Botânico 585, Jardim Botânico. ☎ 021/2259-8686. $.*

3 ★★ kids Parque Lage. If you (or the kids) have the energy for another walk in the park, consider the lovely Parque Lage. It has less of a landscaped feel to it than the Jardim Botânico and preserves numerous native Mata Atlântica species. Its main attraction is a large mansion built by millionaire Henrique Lage in 1926. This dramatic house with a Roman-style courtyard has been featured in music videos by the Black Eyed Peas and Snoop Dogg. The building houses a school of visual arts, a small exhibit space with student artwork, and Café du Lage. The park also features a playground, a small aquarium, and lovely trails. *1 hr. Rua Jardim Botânico 414, Jardim Botânico. ☎ 021/3257-1800. Daily 9am–5pm. Free admission. Bus: 170.*

4 ★★★ kids Santa Teresa Streetcar. Before Cariocas would flock to the beaches to seek relief from the heat, they sought cooler climes in the hills surrounding the city center. In the 19th and early 20th centuries, many prominent families built their mansions in Santa Teresa. Water was brought down from the Floresta da Tijuca, and a streetcar (which still runs today) transported residents and visitors between downtown and Santa Teresa. Today the neighborhood preserves its picturesque 19th-century charm and is popular among artists and foreigners who love its bohemian feel and small-town atmosphere. The best way to see Santa Teresa is on board the rattling streetcar that winds its way through the hilly streets. After it reaches its final stop on the Largo das Neves, it will retrace the exact same route back to downtown. At only R$.60 each way, it's the cheapest sightseeing tour in town. *45 min.–1 hr. for a return trip. Streetcars run daily from 6:40am–8pm, every 30 min. R$.60 each way. The streetcar station is near the Largo da Carioca Metrô; enter Rua Senador Dantas and take the first right (at the corner of the Banco do Brasil) on Rua Lelio Gama or enter Rua Lelio Gama off Av. Chile.*

The Santa Teresa streetcar.

5 Jasmin Mango. In the heart of Santa Teresa's Largo dos Guimarães is this perfect little neighborhood cafe. From the small courtyard patio, you can keep an eye on what's happening in the square while enjoying a coffee and dessert, a sandwich, quiche, or light meal. *Largo dos Guimarães 143, Santa Teresa. ☎ 021/2242-2605. $.*

6 ★★★ Parque das Ruinas. One of Santa Teresa's most curious attractions is built on the ruins of the mansion of Laurinda Santos Lobo (1878–1946), a rich heiress and feminist who was famous for hosting elegant soirees and literati gatherings in her home. After her death in 1946, the house was abandoned for many years. Almost 50 years later, the city expropriated the dilapidated remains. Instead of restoring the house, they reinforced the ruins with metal stairs and walkways, creating a magnificent viewpoint and contemporary monument. *30 min. Rua Murtinho Nobre 169, Santa Teresa. ☎ 021/2552-1039. Tues–Sun 8am–6pm. Free admission. Bus: 206 or 214.*

7 ★★ Museu Châcara do Ceu. The former residence of wealthy industrialist Raymundo Casto de Maia houses a lovely, small art museum. An avid art collector, Castro de Maia filled his home with exquisite Asian china, rugs, and furniture, as well as

19th- and 20th-century Brazilian and European paintings, prints, maps, and watercolors. *45 min. Rua Murtinho Nobre 93, Santa Teresa. ☎ 021/3970-1126. www.museuscastromaya.com.br. Wed–Sun noon–5pm. Admission R$5, free on Wed. Bus: 206 or 214.*

8 Museu do Bonde (Streetcar Museum). Santa Teresa's streetcar is the only surviving route today, but a century ago streetcars were the main form of public transportation in the city. This small museum next to the streetcar depot features several exhibits with photos and memorabilia that tell the history of streetcars in Rio de Janeiro, from the end of the 19th century until the 1960s. *30 min. Rua Carlos Brant 14, Santa Teresa. ☎ 021/2332-8422. Daily 10am–4pm. Admission R$4. Bus: 206.*

9 Confeitaria Manon. This cute pastry shop with stained glass windows, mosaic tile floors, and antique furniture has been a popular fixture in Rio's downtown for almost 70 years because of its outstanding service of sweets. Grab a table in the tearoom or order a delicious pastry from the counter. *Rua do Ouvidor 187, Centro. ☎ 021/2221-0245. $.*

10 ★★★ Igreja da Venerável Ordem Terceira de São Francisco da Penitência. If you have time to visit only one church in Rio, make it the Igreja da Ordem Terceira de São Francisco (Church of the Third Order of Saint Francis), the most impressive baroque building in the city center. Construction began in 1653 and was only completed a century later, in 1773. Bring your sunglasses; more than 400 kilos (882 lb.) of gold were used to decorate the ornate interior and altar. The carved statues, marble floors, and painted ceiling are truly exquisite. *30 min. Largo da Carioca 5, Centro (the entrance is next to the Convento de Santo Antonio). ☎ 021/2262-0197. Tues–Fri 9am–noon and 1–4pm. Admission R$2. Metrô: Carioca.*

11 ★ Igreja e Convento de Santo Antônio. Immediately beside the Igreja da Ordem Terceira de São Francisco stands an even older colonial construction, the Igreja e Convento de Santo Antônio. Franciscan monks began building this church in 1608. The baroque interior with its main altar dedicated to Saint Francis dates from the end of the 17th century and early 18th century. The vestry is decorated

Parque das Ruinas.

Dancing at Rio Scenarium.

with lovely ceiling paintings and elaborately carved hardwood. The museum of Arte Sacra on site displays a small collection of religious artifacts. 🕘 *20 min. Largo da Carioca 5, Centro.* ☎ *021/2262-0129. Mon–Fri 7:30am–7pm; Sat 7:30–11am; Sun 9–11am. Free admission. Metrô: Carioca.*

⓬ **Rio Scenarium.** Unwind after a day of sightseeing with a caipirinha and some music. The bars and small concert venues in Lapa offer excellent live music, usually samba or *choro,* almost any day of the week. A good bet is Rio Scenarium, where, on weekdays (Tues–Fri), the first show, usually samba, *choro,* or bossa nova, starts around 7:30 or 8pm—perfect for happy hour. 🕘 *1–2 hr. Rua do Lavradio 20, Centro.* ☎ *021/3147-9005. www.rioscenarium.com.br. Cover R$12–R$18. Metrô: Carioca.* ●

Museum Savvy

Rio de Janeiro doesn't offer a museum pass or discount card for its cultural facilities, but fortunately admission prices are very modest, rarely exceeding R$6. Brazilian seniors over the age of 65 and high school or university students are usually entitled to a 50% discount. Foreigners who can prove that they meet these criteria are often granted the same concessions. Even if you aren't entitled to a discount, it is a good idea to bring some form of photo ID (it doesn't have to be a passport) with your name and date of birth, since an ID may be requested upon entering some buildings. Most museums and cultural attractions are open year-round, Tuesday to Sunday, and don't close for lunch.

2 The Best Special-Interest Tours

Rio for Art & Architecture Fans

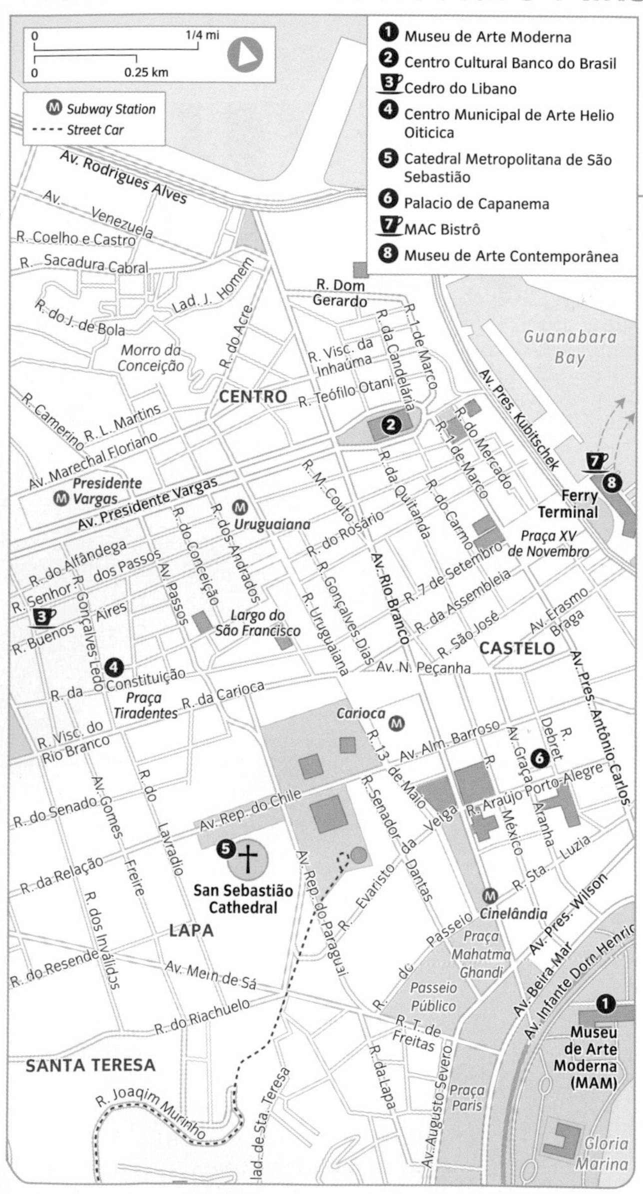

1 Museu de Arte Moderna
2 Centro Cultural Banco do Brasil
3 Cedro do Libano
4 Centro Municipal de Arte Helio Oiticica
5 Catedral Metropolitana de São Sebastião
6 Palacio de Capanema
7 MAC Bistrô
8 Museu de Arte Contemporânea
0 1/4 mi
0 0.25 km
Subway Station
Street Car
Av. Rodrigues Alves
Av. Venezuela
R. Coelho e Castro
R. Sacadura Cabral
Lad. J. Homem
R. do J. de Bola
Morro da Conceição
R. do Acre
R. Dom Gerardo
R. Visc. da Inhaúma
R. da Candelária
R. 1 de Marco
Guanabara Bay
CENTRO
R. Teófilo Otani
R. Camerino
R. L. Martins
Av. Marechal Floriano
Av. Pres. Kubitschek
R. do Mercado
Presidente Vargas
Av. Presidente Vargas
Uruguaiana
R. M. Couto
R. da Quitanda
R. do Carmo
Ferry Terminal
Praça XV de Novembro
R. do Alfândega
R. Senhor dos Passos
R. Buenos Aires
R. Gonçalves Ledo
Av. Passos
R. do Conceição
R. dos Andrados
Largo do São Francisco
R. do Rosário
R. Gonçalves Dias
R. Uruguaiana
Av. Rio Branco
R. 7 de Setembro
R. da Assembleia
R. São José
Av. Erasmo Braga
CASTELO
Av. N. Peçanha
R. da Constituição
Praça Tiradentes
R. da Carioca
Carioca
R. Visc. do Rio Branco
R. 13 de Maio
Av. Alm. Barroso
R. Debret
Av. Pres. Antônio Carlos
Av. Graça Aranha
R. México
R. Araújo Porto Alegre
R. do Senado
Av. Gomes Freire
R. do Lavradio
Av. Rep. do Chile
R. Senador Dantas
R. Evaristo da Veiga
R. Luzia
R. Sta.
R. da Relação
San Sebastião Cathedral
Av. Rep. do Paraguai
Cinelândia
Av. Pres. Wilson
R. dos Inválidos
LAPA
R. do Passeio
Praça Mahatma Ghandi
Av. Beira Mar
Av. Infante Dom Henriq
R. do Resende
Av. Mem de Sá
Passeio Público
R. do Riachuelo
R. T. de Freitas
Museu de Arte Moderna (MAM)
SANTA TERESA
R. da Lapa
Av. Augusto Severo
Praça Paris
R. Joaquim Murinho
lad. de Sta. Teresa
Gloria Marina

Previous page: A Carnaval celebrant.

For an overview of Brazil's contemporary art scene, start with a visit to Rio de Janeiro's premier modern art museum and then check out a few small art galleries for a glimpse at new and upcoming artists. This tour also includes several architectural highlights that have left their mark on the city, including Oscar Niemeyer's work. His best known designs are found in Brasília, but you can certainly get a taste of his work in his hometown. Note that the best time to visit these sights is during business hours, on weekdays. **START: Metrô to Cinelândia.**

1 ★★★ Museu de Arte Moderna. The MAM's permanent collection gives an overview of Brazil's contemporary artists with works by Bruno Giorgo, Di Cavalcanti, Portinari, Helio Oiticica, Lygia Clark, and Lasar Segall. The building is an elegant, modern design by renowned Brazilian architect Affonso Reidy. Burle Marx designed the gardens. The museum also features an outstanding design store and art bookstore. *1 hr. Av. Dom Henrique 85, Centro. ☎ 021/2240-4944. www.mamrio.org.br Adults R$8, seniors and students R$4. Tues–Fri noon–6pm; Sat–Sun noon–7pm. Metrô: Cinelândia. The pedestrian walkway is at the end of Av. Calógeras.*

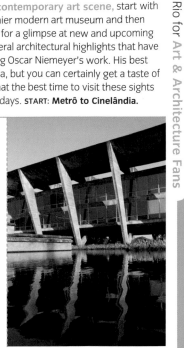

Museu de Arte Moderna.

Galleries Galore

A growing number of Rio's artists have chosen to open their galleries in historic buildings downtown, instead of in the city's posh beach neighborhoods. Check out the below galleries to get a sense of Rio's art scene today:

A Gentil Carioca (Rua Gonçalves Ledo 17; www.agentilcarioca.com.br) represents 18 Brazilian artists and organizes at least eight exhibits a year.

Nearby **Durex Arte Contemporanea** (Praça Tiradentes 85; www.durexart.com) is an owner-artist operated gallery showcasing works that combine several media.

Progretti (Travessa do Comércio 22; www. progettirio.com) was recently founded by a duo of Italian artists living in Rio.

LGC Arte Contemporanea (Rua do Rosario 38; ☎ 021/2263-7353) often hosts photography exhibits around a local theme.

2 ★★★ Centro Cultural Banco do Brasil. This former bank now houses the most comprehensive cultural center in the city. Temporary exhibits showcase national and international contemporary artists, and the program includes music, film, dance, and theater. Film buffs can choose from more than 4,000 titles, including Brazilian contemporary cinema, and reserve a private viewing booth (up to 3 people). ⌚ *At least 1 hr. Rua Primeiro de Março 66, Centro.* ☎ *021/3808-2020. www.bb.com.br. Most events are free. Tues–Sun 10am–8pm. Metrô: Uruguaiana.*

3 Cedro do Libano. This simple restaurant serves outstanding Middle Eastern food. Portions are very generous, so don't get carried away ordering. Check the daily specials or try the lamb kafta, with an order of rice with fried onions and lentils. *Rua Senhor dos Passos 231, Centro.* ☎ *021/2224-0163. $.*

4 ★ Centro Municipal de Arte Helio Oiticica. Unfortunately, this cultural center doesn't display many works by modern artist Helio Oiticica. On the upside, temporary art exhibits showcase a range of national and international artists and projects. ⌚ *30 min. Rua Luis de Camões 68, Centro.* ☎ *021/2232-4213. Free admission. Tues–Fri 11am–6pm; Sat–Sun 11am–5pm. Metrô: Carioca.*

5 Catedral Metrôpolitana de São Sebastião. Inaugurated in 1976, the city's bold and unusual cathedral is inspired by Mayan pyramids. It has a conical concrete structure that creates a soaring, spacious interior. The absence of the usual religious ornaments magnifies the impact of the simple cross "floating" on two cables above a plain altar. Natural light pours in through four

Catedral Metrôpolitana de São Sebastião.

towering stained-glass windows, placed at each of the cardinal points. The Museum of Sacred Art in the basement displays religious artifacts, including wooden and ivory sculptures, paintings, oratories, and silver finery. ***Note:*** If you opt to walk here from the Centro Municipal, do so via the Avenida Chile (starting at the Largo da Carioca), which is the busiest, safest route. ⌚ *30 min. Av. República do Chile 245, Centro.* ☎ *021/2240-2669. www.catedral.com.br. Free admission. Daily 7am–6pm. Museum of Sacred Art: Wed, Sat–Sun 10am–4pm. Metrô: Carioca.*

6 Palacio de Capanema. Architecture fans come from far and wide to worship at Brazil's temple of modern architecture, designed by Lucio Costa, Oscar Niemeyer, Affonso Reidy, and others, assisted by Le Corbusier. Now more than 60 years old, the 16-story concrete structure still has a contemporary feel. Its functionalist straight lines are balanced by slender pilings that lift the building off the ground, creating a spacious plaza, decorated with Portinari tile panels. Visitors may access only the art gallery and

Oscar Niemeyer

The man who put Brazilian modern architecture on the map has created a prolific body of work that includes the U.N. headquarters in New York and Brasília, Brazil's modernist capital. Oscar Niemeyer is best known for his curvaceous, flowing lines that give concrete an unparalleled elegance and lightness. At the age of 102, Niemeyer is still working on several projects. If you only have time to see one Niemeyer building, make it the MAC in Niteroi (see below), with the added bonus of a pleasant ferry ride and fabulous views of Rio de Janeiro. Some other works around the city include the Sambodromo Carnaval parade grounds (p 39) and the CIEP public school buildings (one can be seen at Rua do Catete 77, by the Glória Metrô). Niteroi has also commissioned a series of public buildings for its waterfront, but those have yet to be completed, except for the Caminho Niemeyer, a boulevard to your right as you disembark from the ferry.

theater on the first floor and an exhibit on the history of the building on the second floor. ⏲ *30 min. Rua da Imprensa 16, Centro.* ☎ *021/2220-1490. Mon–Fri 10am–6pm. Free admission. Metrô: Cinelândia.*

7 MAC Bistro. Inside Niemeyer's "flying saucer" is an excellent restaurant, where you can grab a drink or a full meal. Prices are a bit high, but the views soften the blow. *Mirante da Boa Viagem s/n, Niteroi.* ☎ *021/2629-1416. www.bistromac.com.br. $$.*

8 ★★★ Museu de Arte Contemporânea (MAC). Niemeyer's most photogenic building is across the bay in Niteroi. Also known as "the flying saucer," the circular structure rests on a single pillar, overlooking Guanabara Bay. Reflective pools create a variety of perspectives of the water, building, and sky. The small, circular museum space displays local and national contemporary artwork. ⏲ *1 hr. Mirante da Boa Viagem s/n, Niteroi.* ☎ *021/2620-2400. www.macniteroi.com.br. Admission R$4. Tues–Sun 10am–6pm. Ferry from Praça XV to Niteroi. Ferries run Mon–Fri every 15–20 min., Sat–Sun every 30 min. Crossing takes 20 min. and costs R$2.80. From Niteroi ferry terminal, take bus 47B to Boa Viagem.*

Museu de Arte Contemporânea.

Rio's Colonial Treasures

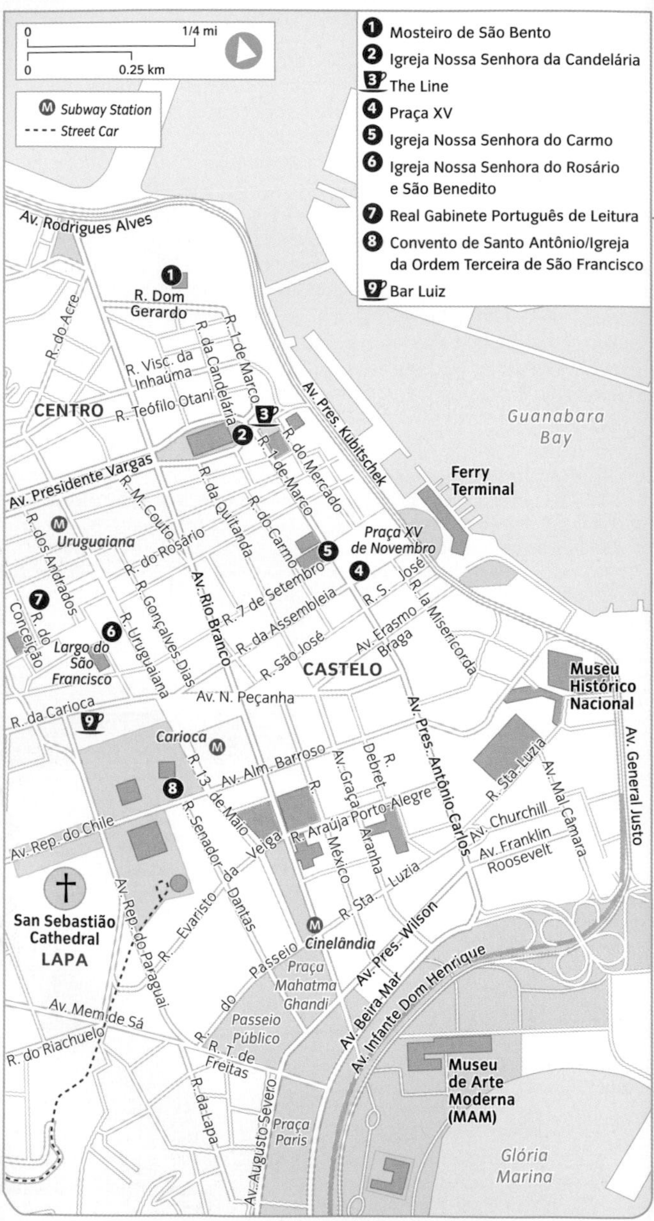
0
1/4 mi
0
0.25 km
Subway Station
Street Car
1 Mosteiro de São Bento
2 Igreja Nossa Senhora da Candelária
3 The Line
4 Praça XV
5 Igreja Nossa Senhora do Carmo
6 Igreja Nossa Senhora do Rosário e São Benedito
7 Real Gabinete Português de Leitura
8 Convento de Santo Antônio/Igreja da Ordem Terceira de São Francisco
9 Bar Luiz
Av. Rodrigues Alves
R. Dom Gerardo
R. do Acre
R. Visc. da Inhaúma
R. da Candelária
R. 1 de Marco
CENTRO
R. Teófilo Otani
Av. Pres. Kubitschek
Guanabara Bay
R. do Mercado
Ferry Terminal
Av. Presidente Vargas
R. M. Couto
R. da Quitanda
R. do Carmo
R. dos Andrados
Uruguaiana
R. do Rosário
Praça XV de Novembro
R. Gonçalves Dias
Av. Rio Branco
R. 7 de Setembro
R. S. José
R. la Misericordia
R. do Conceição
R. Uruguaiana
R. da Assembleia
Av. Erasmo Braga
Largo do São Francisco
R. São José
CASTELO
Museu Histórico Nacional
Av. N. Peçanha
R. da Carioca
Carioca
Av. Pres. Antônio Carlos
Av. General Justo
R. 13 de Maio
Av. Alm. Barroso
Av. Graça Aranha
R. Debret
R. Sta. Luzia
Av. Mal Câmara
R. México
R. Porto Alegre
Av. Churchill
Av. Rep. do Chile
R. Senador Dantas
R. da Veiga
R. Araújo
Av. Franklin Roosevelt
R. Sta. Luzia
R. Evaristo
San Sebastião Cathedral
LAPA
Av. Rep. do Paraguai
Av. Pres. Wilson
Cinelândia
R. do Passeio
Praça Mahatma Ghandi
Av. Beira Mar
Av. Infante Dom Henrique
Av. Mem de Sá
Passeio Público
R. do Riachuelo
R. T. de Freitas
Museu de Arte Moderna (MAM)
R. da Lapa
Av. Augusto Severo
Praça Paris
Glória Marina

Despite its modern appearance, Rio de Janeiro's downtown still preserves some 18th- and 19th-century colonial gems. The most impressive examples of Portuguese baroque and rococo architecture are found in the city's churches and convents. If you want to cut right to the chase, make sure to visit the Igreja da Terceira Ordem de São Francisco da Penitência, Igreja Nossa Senhora do Carmo, and Igreja Nossa Senhora da Lapa dos Mercadores. Bear in mind that the best time to visit this area is weekdays during business hours. START: **Bus 123 or 125 to Praça XV.**

1 ★★ Mosteiro de São Bento. This Benedictine monastery is one of the most important Brazilian baroque constructions and has remained virtually unaltered. Its early 18th-century interior is a masterpiece of baroque woodwork, finished in gold leaf. The main altar is dedicated to Our Lady of Montserrat, flanked by Saint Benedict, the order's patron saint, and his twin sister, Saint Scholastica. The silver lanterns were designed by Mestre Valentim. The convent is still in use today, so most areas, including the cloister and sacristy, are off limits to the public. Sunday mass (10am) is celebrated with Gregorian chanting. ⏱ *30 min. Rua Dom Gerardo 68 (ramp) or Rua Dom Gerardo 40 (elevator), Centro.* ☎ *021/2206-8100. www.osb.org.br. Daily 7am–5pm. Free admission. Metrô: Uruguaiana.*

Igreja Nossa Senhora da Candelaria.

2 ★ Igreja Nossa Senhora da Candelária. Nothing remains of the humble chapel erected in 1609 by a

Gilded woodwork at Mosteiro de São Bento.

grateful Portuguese couple who survived a harrowing sailing. The current church was built in stages, between 1774 and 1865, when the dome was finally added. As a result, it features a colonial facade and a neoclassical interior. Unlike the other churches on this tour, its interior is marble instead of wood, giving it a somber feel. In 1993, Candelaria was the scene of a bloody massacre when eight street children, asleep on the steps, were brutally murdered. ⌚ *15 min. Praça Pio X, Centro.* ☎ *021/2233-2324. Mon–Fri 7:30am–4pm, Sat 8am–noon, Sun 9am–1pm. Free admission. Metrô: Uruguaiana.*

3 The Line. The Casa França Brasil is one of Rio's finest neoclassical constructions, designed by French architect Montigny in 1819. It has served as a stock exchange, customs house, and court, before being reincarnated as a cultural center in 1990. Its excellent bistro, the Line, is a great excuse to check out a free exhibit and grab a bite. The lunch menu includes grilled steak, fish, risottos, pasta, and salads. After 4pm, the kitchen serves an afternoon tea and snack menu. ***Rua Visconde de Itaborai 78, Centro.*** ☎ ***021/2332-5120. $$.***

The Line at the Casa França Brasil.

The ferry station at Praça XV.

4 ★★★ Praça XV. Some of Brazil's most significant historic moments have taken place in this bustling downtown square, such as the arrival of the Portuguese royal family in 1808, the abolition of slavery in 1888, and the proclamation of the Republic on November 15, 1889. Today, Praça XV (pronounced "keen-zay") is an important transit point for tens of thousands of commuters who live across the bay in Niteroi or on Paquetá Island. Its architecture is a hodgepodge of buildings from 4 different centuries. For part of the 19th century, this square was the center of power for Brazil and the entire Portuguese empire. ***Av. Primeira de Março and Rua 7 de Setembro.*** ⌚ ***At least 1 hr. Bus: 123 or 125.*** ***See minitour on the following page.***

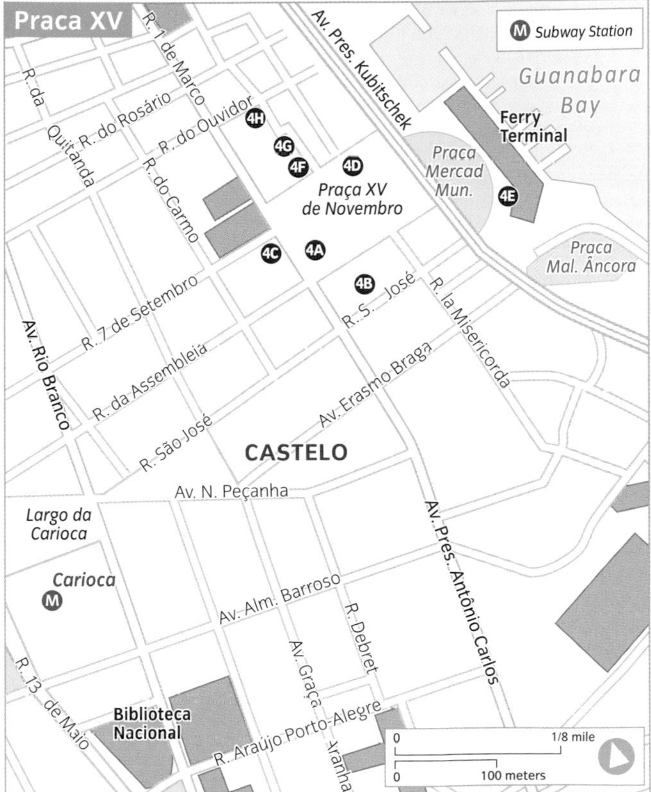

In the center of Praça XV stands the **4A Paço Imperial** (p 14), once the residence of the Portuguese royal family. Next to it stood the city council and jail, where in 1792 Tiradentes, the ringleader of a major uprising against colonial rule, awaited execution. The building was demolished in 1922 and replaced by the new state legislature, named **4B Palácio Tiradentes** in his honor. Founded in 1611, the **4C Convento do Carmo** is the square's oldest construction. In 1808, the Carmelites were forced from the convent to accommodate the queen and her entourage. In the center of the square stands a stone fountain, the **4D Chafariz do Mestre Valentim,** built in 1789 to meet the needs of the growing population. Right on the water stands the elegant late-19th-century ferry building, **4E Estação das Barcas,** with its floating docks. Look for the **4F Arco do Teles,** a stone archway on the north side of the square that leads into the **4G Travessa do Comércio,** a lovely narrow cobblestone alley that preserves the feel of 19th-century Rio. Then take a peek inside the colorful **4H Igreja Nossa Senhora dos Mercadores,** an adorable rococo gem with a unique elliptical shape and two lovely skylights.

5 ★★★ Igreja Nossa Senhora do Carmo da Antiga Sé. The Portuguese crown claimed this as their royal chapel. Two coronations, several royal weddings, and numerous royal baptisms have been celebrated here. Its ornate white-gold interior was recently restored to commemorate the 200th anniversary of the royal family's arrival. A 20-minute sound and light show dramatically renders the church's history (only in Portuguese). *30 min. Rua Sete de Setembro s/n (at Rua Primeiro de Março), Centro. 021/2221-0501. Free admission to church. Sound and light show or guided tours: adults R$8, seniors and children R$4. Mon–Fri 7:30am–4pm, Sat–Sun 10am–2pm. Sound and light show: Tues–Fri 1:30pm, Sat–Sun noon and 1pm. Bus: 123 or 125.*

6 Igreja Nossa Senhora do Rosario e São Benedito. Dedicated to the patron saints of black worshippers, this simple church has played an important role in the Afro-Brazilian community and the abolitionist movement. It was built in 1700, on the edge of the city at that time. Throughout the 18th and 19th centuries, the square was used for African rituals and festivals, the precursors of today's carnival. The small museum of black history here is closed for renovations. *10 min. Rua Uruguaiana 77, Centro. 021/2224-2957. Mon–Fri 7am–5pm; Sat 7am–1pm. Free admission. Metrô: Uruguaiana.*

7 ★★★ Real Gabinete Português de Leitura. Founded in 1837, this library is a fine example of Portuguese late Gothic architecture. Its main reading room is truly magnificent. Under the stained-glass cupola, ornate hardwood shelves packed with thousands of books tower more than 20m (66 ft.) above the jacaranda reading desks in the center of the room. The library houses the largest collection of Portuguese works outside of Portugal. *10 min. Rua Luis de Camões 30, Centro. 021/2221-3138. www.realgabinete.com.br. Free admission. Mon–Fri 9am–6pm. Metrô: Uruguaiana.*

8 ★★★ Convento de Santo Antonio/Igreja da Ordem Terceira de São Francisco. I have saved the best for last: the Igreja da Ordem Terceira de São Francisco. Overlooking Largo da Carioca, the Franciscan religious complex dates from the first half of the 17th century. The convent and Santo Antonio church are undergoing much-needed restoration, so skip these and head inside Igreja to go straight for the gold, literally. The craftsmanship of the church's intricate carvings is truly astounding; more than 400 kilos (882 lb.) of gold were used to cover its altars, pulpits, pillars, ornaments, and statues. Caetano da Costa Coelho's ceiling painting portrays the glorification of Saint Francis. It's Brazil's first illusionistic ceiling, offering a realistic perspective from various angles. Take a minute to climb to the top to contemplate the bustling square and its hodgepodge of modern buildings below. *30 min. Largo da Carioca s/n, Centro. 021/2262-0197. Admission R$2. Tues–Fri 9am–noon and 1–4pm. Metrô: Carioca.*

The Real Gabinete Português de Leitura.

The Igreja da Ordem Terceira de São Francisco.

9 **Bar Luiz.** This 120-year-old bar provides a fitting end to a day in "old Rio." The kitchen specializes in hearty German fare, such as cold cuts, bratwurst, Kassler ribs, sauerkraut, and potato salad, all perfect with a cold beer. *Rua da Carioca 39, Centro. ☎ 021/2262-6900. www.barluiz.com.br. $$.*

Brazil's Colonial Art

Although Brazil's colonial period runs from 1500 until 1822, the most impressive collection of colonial art in Rio de Janeiro dates from the 18th century and consists of beautiful Portuguese baroque and rococo. The finest examples can be found in numerous colonial churches scattered around downtown Rio. The baroque artwork in the first half of the 18th century is ornate and dramatic; not only the altars but also the columns and walls were decorated with ornate wood carvings, finished with a layer of gold leaf, like in the Mosteiro de São Bento (p 29). Toward the end of the 18th century, rococo made its entry—more playful and elegant, less dramatic and intense. One of the loveliest examples is the Igreja Nossa Senhora dos Mercadores (p 31). Brazil's most famous 18th-century artist was Aleijadinho (1738–1815), a sculptor from Minas Gerais who, even crippled by leprosy, created exquisite masterpieces in stone and wood that decorate churches in Ouro Preto and Congonhas, Minas Gerais. Rio had its own master artisan, Valentim da Fonseca e Silva, or Mestre Valentim (1745–1813). Son of a lower Portuguese aristocrat and an African slave, Mestre Valentim's sculptures and carvings decorate at least half a dozen churches in Rio. He also took an interest in urban planning, designing several public water fountains and the layout of the Passeio Publico (p 17), Rio's oldest park.

Rio with Kids

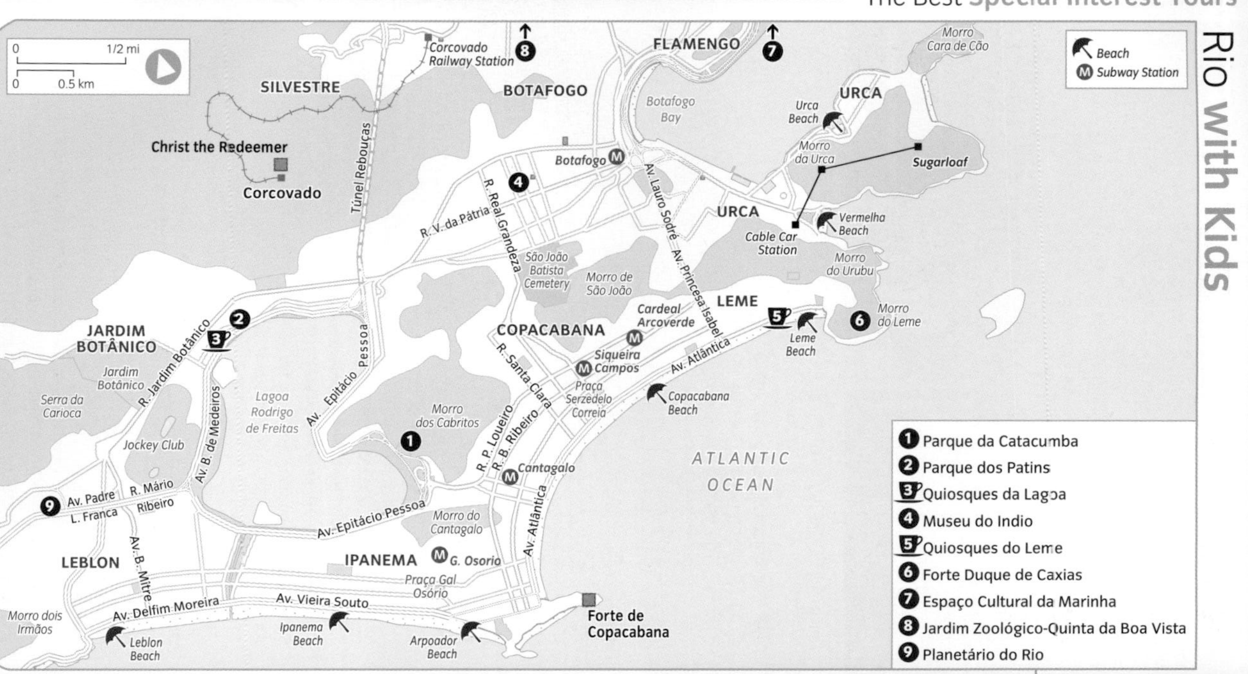

Rio boasts a number of attractions that will amuse even the youngest of travelers. The city's many outdoor attractions, such as its various beaches and parks, allow for plenty of frolicking space, and Rio features a few kid-friendly museums, a planetarium, and a zoo. Most Brazilians are very child-friendly and are happy to accommodate families traveling with children, too.
START: Bus 433 to Parque da Catacumba.

Kids playing at the Parque da Catacumba.

1 ★★★ Parque da Catacumba. A short, fun walk to a lookout that will reward you with fabulous views of the lagoon. The park also offers several adventurous activities, including a climbing wall with rappelling and tree climbing, appropriate for children ages 6 and up. *1–2 hr. Av. Epitácio Pessoa 3000, Lagoa. Tues–Sun 9am–5pm. Admission to the park and lookout is free. For activities, contact ☎ 021/4105-0079. www.lagoaaventuras.com.br. Admission R$15–R$40 per activity. Taxi recommended.*

2 ★★★ Parque dos Patins (Lagoa). The heart-shaped Lagoa is a major leisure area, smack in the middle of the Zona Sul. The 7.5km (4⅔-mile) full loop is very popular with walkers and joggers. This large recreational area on the Jardim Botânico side encompasses several playgrounds, soccer fields, tennis courts, and a roller skating rink. The large amphitheatre often hosts concerts and cultural events. Step onto the large floating deck for an even better view of the lagoon and surroundings. *At least 1 hr. Av. Borges de Medeiros (btw. Rua General Garzon and Rua Mario Ribeiro), Lagoa. Bus: 170.*

3 Quiosques da Lagoa. Next to the Parque dos Patins is a cluster of at least half a dozen casual restaurants with outdoor seating. You'll find a sushi bar, Brazilian cuisine, and Mediterranean food, but my favorite is Arab, which serves up outstanding Middle Eastern cuisine, such as pita and hummus, Moroccan couscous, and grilled lamb kabobs. At night, these restaurants often feature live music. *Parque dos Patins s/n. Arab: Quiosque 7-9. ☎ 021/2540-0747. $$.*

An exhibit at the Museu do Indio.

4 ★★ **Museu do Indio.** This museum introduces visitors to the culture and traditions of Brazil's indigenous people. Exhibits include beautiful photos, everyday utensils, and ceremonial artifacts with plenty of interactive and tactile features. In the museum garden, kids will enjoy exploring the replica of an original *maloca* (Indian hut), an indigenous kitchen and a ceremonial hut. The gift store sells excellent indigenous crafts. ⏲ *1–2 hr. Rua das Palmeiras 55, Botafogo.* ☎ *021/2286-8899. www.museudoindio.org.br. Admission R$3 (Sun free). Tues–Fri 9am–5:30pm; Sat–Sun 1–5pm. Metrô: Botafogo.*

5 **Quiosques do Leme.** What's better than enjoying a snack right on the beach? The new beachside kiosks in Leme offer a variety of beach-friendly snack options, including sandwiches and burgers. *Posto 1, Av. Atlantica s/n, Leme. $.*

6 ★★★ **Forte Duque de Caixias.** Even little kids will have no problem with the short 20-minute walk to the top of this fort. A large cobblestone path winds around the back to the top of the fortification, built between 1776 and 1779 to protect the entrance of Guanabara Bay. Enjoy the spectacular views of Sugarloaf, Copacabana Beach, and Niteroi. Kids should love climbing up and down the installations. ⏲ *At least 1 hr. Praça Almirante Júlio de Noronha s/n, Leme.* ☎ *021/2275-3122. Admission R$4. Sat–Sun 9am–5pm. Bus: 472.*

7 ★★★ **Espaço Cultural da Marinha.** Explore a submarine, a 16th-century replica sailboat, a historic tugboat, and a fairy tale castle, all in one fell swoop. In addition to a maritime museum, the navy's cultural center features several vessels that are open to visitors. From Thursday to Sunday, you can also visit the former customs hall, an enchanting **19th-century palace** on **Ilha Fiscal** (transportation is provided by a navy schooner), or tour the bay onboard a WWI tugboat. ⏲ *At least 2 hr. Av. Alfred Agache, s/n, Centro (near Praça XV).* ☎ *021/2104-5592. www.mar.mil.br/dphdm. Museum/boats: Tues–Sun*

Ilha Fiscal's palace.

The entrance to the Jardim Zoológico.

noon–5pm. Free admission. Boat tour: R$10 adults, R$5 children under 12 and seniors. Thurs–Sun 1:15 and 3:15pm. Ilha Fiscal: Thurs–Sun 12:30, 2, and 3:30pm. R$10 adults, R$5 children under 12 and seniors. Bus: 123.

8 ★★ Jardim Zoológico/Quinta da Boa Vista. Exhibits at Brazil's oldest zoo (founded in 1888) include an interesting variety of Brazilian species, such as jaguars, monkeys, marmosets, birds, and turtles. There is also a petting zoo and aquarium. After visiting the zoo, take a stroll through the beautiful gardens of the Quinta da Boa Vista, the former residence of the Portuguese royal family. To see more animals (although these will be preserved in formaldehyde), also visit the **Museu Nacional** (☎ 021/2562-6924; admission R$3; Tues–Sun 10am–4pm), the natural history museum inside the former palace, which boasts a vast collection of animals, rocks, and archaeological artifacts. 🕘 *At least 2 hr. for zoo, 3–4 hr. for zoo, park, and museum. Quinta da Boa Vista s/n, São Cristóvão. ☎ 021/3878-4200. Admission R$6 adults, R$3 children under 8 and seniors. Tues–Sun 9am–4:30pm. Park daily 5am–6pm. Metrô: São Cristóvão.*

9 ★★ Planetário do Rio. Rio's planetarium is a popular venue for inquiring minds of all ages and a great indoor option for a rainy day. The museum's exhibits include beautiful photographs, models, and replicas, as well as a number of interactive basic science experiments that teach kids about the phases of the moon and the tides. Older kids may also enjoy the displays of astrophysics experiments. On weekends there are several movie sessions on the giant domed screen. The earlier screenings are usually geared toward younger children. Check the website for updated information. Every Wednesday night, the planetarium offers a free sky-watch program. From 6:30 to 7:30pm (an hour later during daylight saving time), scientists will help you observe Rio's night sky through their giant telescopes. 🕘 *At least 2 hr. Rua Vice Governador Rubens Berardo 100, Gávea. ☎ 021/2247-0046. www.planetariodorio.com.br. Films R$16 adults, R$8 seniors and youth under 21; exhibits R$8 adults, R$4 seniors and youth under 21. Movie sessions Sat–Sun and holidays: 3:30, 4:45, and 6pm. Exhibits Tues–Fri 9am–5pm; Sat–Sun and holidays 3–6pm. Sky-watch program Wed 6:30pm (7:30pm during daylight saving time). Bus: 571 or 583.*

Rio's **Carnaval**

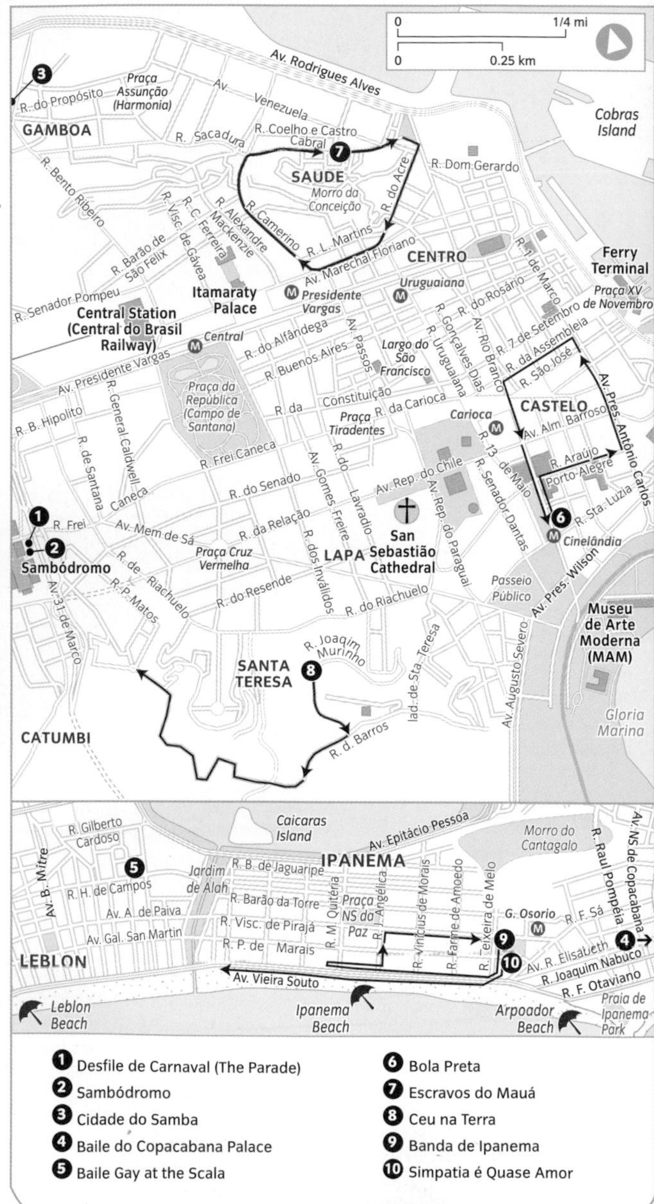

Rio de Janeiro's Carnaval is a colorful feast of elaborate costumes, lavish floats, and frenetic samba rhythms in preparation for Lent, the 40-day period of penitence and fasting before Easter. Although few people still fast, they certainly know how to feast during this 5-day statutory holiday. Preparations for Carnaval start as early as March, when the samba schools choose their theme, write the samba, and begin to design the costumes and floats; see p 161 for info. By July or August, weekly rehearsals get underway for the big night in February or early March. **START: Metrô to Central or Praça XI.**

The Parade grounds during Carnaval.

1 ★★★ kids Desfile de Carnaval (The Parade). The culmination of almost a year's worth of work occurs during Carnaval, when each samba school puts on a 90-minute parade, with as many as 4,000 participants in full costume, including 200 to 300 percussionists and 10 to 12 large floats that represent the central theme of the samba song. It's an amazing spectacle of color and sound. The parade is held in the Sambodromo (see below), a 700m-long (2,297-ft.) venue designed specifically for this event, with room for 70,000 spectators. *For tickets or costumes, contact Blumar. ☎ 021/2142-9300. www.blumar.com.br.*

2 ★★ Sambódromo. Designed by Oscar Niemeyer in 1984, the Sambodromo is ground zero for the Carnaval parade, where the top samba schools try to wow the judges and win the public with their song, costumes, and floats. In the 2 months leading up to Carnaval, the schools are entitled to a technical rehearsal in this venue. The public can attend these rehearsals for free; check the entertainment listing for times and dates (usually Dec and Jan, Sat–Sun evening). Arrive early and try to get a spot in sections 3, 5, 7, or 11; avoid 1 and 13, as you don't get much of an overview of the venue. Expect to pay at least R$500–R$800 for a spot in the bleachers for the big **Grupo Especial parade,** more for a box seat. Tickets also sell out fast, so visitors are usually at the mercy of travel agents or scalpers. An affordable alternative is to attend the **A-league parade** (on Sat night) or the **Winner's Parade** (Sat after Carnaval, when the top five schools come back for a reprise). Tickets to these two events rarely top R$150. You may also buy a costume and actually participate in the parade, though doing so won't allow you access to the bleachers. The rest of the year, the Sambodromo is used as a school and concert venue. *Rua Marques do Sapucai s/n. Metrô: Central (for seats in odd-numbered sections) or Praça XI (for seats in even-numbered sections), Centro.*

3 ★ Cidade do Samba. This year-round venue offers a wonderful introduction to Carnaval. All major samba schools have a space in this building, where they work on costumes, prepare their instruments, and design their floats. A guided tour will give you a greater appreciation of the work that goes into making this event happen. Every Thursday night, a mini-Carnaval parade and show is held. *Rua Rivadavia Correa 60, Gamboa. ☎ 021/2213-2503. Wed, Fri–Mon 9am–5pm; Thurs noon–5pm. R$20 (guided tours at 10am, noon, and 3:30pm). Thurs evening show R$150 (dinner and show). Taxi recommended.*

Carnaval Balls

Once a fixture at Rio's Carnaval, the city's glamorous masked balls have lost their sparkle as revelers prefer to celebrate on the street and enjoy the fun and irreverent blocos. However, two of the city's best balls (*baile* in Portuguese) will probably never go out of style.

4 Baile do Copacabana Palace. The most elegant occasion of the year is the annual Baile do Copacabana Palace, a black-tie event that attracts Rio's well-heeled jet set and international celebrities decked out in fancy costumes. Tickets to this chi-chi affair range from R$300 to R$1,000. *Av. Atlântica 1702, Copacabana. ☎ 021/2548-7070. www.copacabanapalace.com. Metrô: Cardeal Arcoverde.*

5 Baile Gay at the Scala. The Tuesday evening Baile Gay at the Scala is a much more flamboyant and colorful event where guests compete for most outlandish costume. As of press time, the pending closure of the Scala may force the event to move to another venue. *Check with Riotur (☎ 0800/285-0555 or 021/2542-8080) for up-to-date venue information.*

Blocos

Join one of the many free daytime street blocos and jump right into the Carnaval festivities. A bloco is a neighborhood band that parades through the streets, playing songs, followed by throngs of singing and dancing partiers dressed in silly costumes or funny accessories, such as

A percussion group performance.

A Carnaval bloco.

hats or wigs. Blocos usually start parading in the weeks leading up to Carnaval and then go full force during the event itself, with as many as 10 to 15 blocos each day. Practically every neighborhood in the city will have a few. ***Check the schedule at www.rioguiaoficial.com.br and pick one that suits your style.***

❻ **Bola Preta.** Set your alarm so you can get to Cinelândia early on Saturday morning for one of the best blocos in the city. A lot of revelers will don fun and whimsical costumes, including wearing anything with black dots *(bola preta)*. The parade starts in front of the Biblioteca Nacional and goes along Avenida Rio Branco. ***Meeting point (concentração): Cinelândia, Centro (Sat 7am).***

❼ ★ **Escravos do Mauá.** This bloco usually kicks off Carnaval with a parade on Thursday evening. It starts at the Pedra do Sal, next to Largo de São Francisco da Prainha, and leads revelers through the streets around Praça Mauá. ***Meeting point: Largo São Franciscio da Prainha, Centro (Thurs 6pm).***

❽ **Ceu na Terra.** I love this Santa Teresa bloco with its fun, irreverent attitude. It plays the traditional Carnaval tunes from the 1940s and usually parades twice during Carnaval, on Saturday and Sunday. ***Meeting point: Largo do Curvelo, Santa Teresa (Sat and Sun 8am).***

❾ **Banda de Ipanema.** Skip this one if you are claustrophobic; more than a hundred thousand people dressed in outlandish and colorful costumes pack Ipanema's waterfront for this bloco, with a large gay and drag-queen following. ***Meeting point: Rua Gomes Carneiro, Ipanema (Sat and Tues 4pm).***

❿ **Simpatia é Quase Amor.** Flirtatious, young, and hip, this Ipanema bloco is perfect for hooking up with some local cuties and dancing through the streets of Ipanema. ***Meeting point: Praça General Osório, Ipanema (Tues 4pm).***

Dressing the Part

Get in the Carnaval spirit with a costume, a funny wig, glitter make-up, silly hats, or other accessories. The best place to stock up is in the SAARA district downtown (p 71). You don't need to wear a specific costume to join a bloco, but to fit in with your fellow revelers you may want to check out the dozens of shops along Rua Senhor dos Passos that sell inexpensive fun and festive costumes and accessories. To see what a more traditional parade costume with glitter, beads, and feathers looks like, check out the **Casa Turuna** (Rua Senhor dos Passos 122–125; ☎ 021/2221-5708)—this is where the costume designers for the samba schools shop.

The Best of Brazilian Music

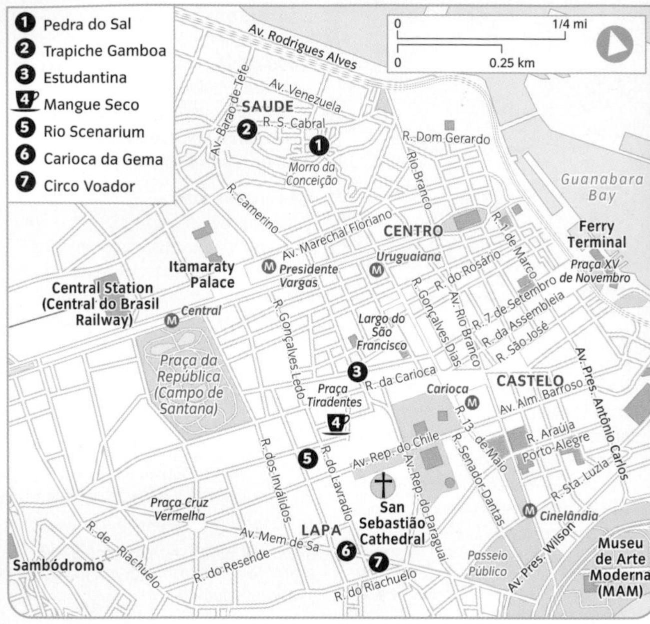

Music fans are in for a real sonic treat with the great variety of Brazilian tunes. First there is samba, Rio's signature rhythm and an expression of Brazil's cultural melting pot. It comes in a range of styles, such as the melancholic *choro,* laid-back and mellow bossa nova, playful and upbeat *samba de roda,* and the frenetic *samba de enredo,* which is performed during carnival. Migrants from the northeast introduced Rio to *forró,* a cheerful two-step, played on an accordion, triangle, and *zabumba* drum. Brazilian funk (a mix between hip-hop and rap) was born in the favelas, but has now gone mainstream and is heard even in Ipanema's chi-chi clubs. The best time to visit the below stops is Tuesday to Saturday; club doors usually open at 7pm, but things don't get hopping until 9 or 10pm. Most bars and clubs stay open until at least 2am. **START: Pedra do Sal (next to Largo São Francisco da Prainha).**

1 ★★★ Pedra do Sal. Samba as we know it today was born in the narrow cobblestone streets around the Pedra do Sal, the former slave market where Rio's first black inhabitants were traded upon arrival from Africa. Later, a large number of black workers from Bahia arrived here by ship and settled in this area, introducing their African-influenced religious traditions, festivals, and music that formed the roots of

A singer at Carioca da Gema (p 130).

modern samba and carnival. Today, the neighborhood remains an important monument to black culture, and samba still rules supreme; a very popular carnival bloco, Escravos do Mauá (Mauá Slaves), takes to the streets every year, and samba often spills out from the bars around Largo São Francisco da Prainha. *1–2 hr. Largo São Francisco da Prainha, Rua Sacadura Cabral s/n, Centro. Taxi recommended.*

2 ★★ Trapiche Gamboa. Housed in a lovely historic warehouse-style brick building, Trapiche Gamboa specializes in *samba de roda,* a traditional form of samba where the musicians sit around a table and play classic samba tunes while the audience dances between the tables. *30 min. Rua Sacadura Cabral 155, Centro. 021/2516-0868. www.trapichegamboa.com.br. Closed Mon. Cover R$12–R$20. Taxi recommended.*

3 ★★★ Estudantina. Founded in 1928, Estudantina is one of the last traditional *gafieira* dance halls in Rio. *Gafieira* is danced by couples to a slower syncopated samba, a very elegant and stylish affair that dominated Rio's salons in the 1930s and 1940s. Over time, Estudantina's large wooden dance floor has been forced to accommodate other music styles, but it's worth attending an evening of *gafieira* to admire stylish couples swirling across the dance floor. *1 hr. Praça Tiradentes 79, Centro. 021/2232-1149. www.estudantinagrill.com.br. Cover R$10–R$15. Metrô: Carioca.*

4 Mangue Seco. Start your evening with live music (Mon–Thurs at 6pm) and traditional northeastern Brazilian cuisine, such as a shrimp pastel or a *casquinha de siri* (crab cake). As a main course, I highly recommend the *moquecas* fish or seafood stew with coconut milk, cilantro, and red palm oil (one order serves two people). *Rua do Lavradio 23, Centro. 021/3852-1947. www.manguesecocachacaria.com.br. $.*

5 ★★★ Rio Scenarium. When Rio Scenarium first opened, it was just a dusty antiques warehouse

A performance at Rio Scenarium.

Lapa Aqueduct after dark.

that rented props for movies and hosted occasional samba music. Over time, the antique props (check out the complete antique pharmacy on the second floor) have become the decor for outstanding Brazilian music. If you only have time for one bar, make it this place. From Tuesday to Sunday, there are two different shows every night, usually a more mellow bossa nova or *choro,* followed by more lively samba, jazz, or *forró.* Unlike most bars, you can usually snag a table here, great for resting your samba-weary feet. ⌚ *1 hr. Rua do Lavrádio 20, Centro.* ☎ *021/3147-9000. www.rioscenarium.com.br. Cover R$12–R$25. Metrô: Carioca.*

❻ ★★★ **Carioca da Gema.** This is another one of my favorite Lapa music venues, where I have never heard a bad performance. Six days a week, at least half a dozen excellent musicians are on stage playing great samba, including on Monday nights, when many bars are closed. ⌚ *1 hr. Rua Mem de Sá 79, Centro.* ☎ *021/2221-0043. www.barcariocadagema.com.br. Cover R$12–R$25. Closed Sun. Bus: 464 or 572.*

❼ ★★ **Circo Voador.** Time to join the circus! This large tentlike music venue underneath the arches of the Lapa Aqueduct offers a great introduction to what is hip and happening in Brazilian music and culture. The lineup may include Brazilian funk, hip-hop, carnival blocos, modern dance, samba, *sertanejo* (Brazilian country music), and golden oldies, such as Paulinho da Viola and Jorge Ben Jor. ⌚ *1 hr. Rua dos Arcos 1, Centro.* ☎ *021/2533-0354. www.circovoador.com.br. Cover varies according to show. Bus: 464 or 572.* ●

Feira Nordestina

You don't have to travel far to experience the vibrant music and culture of northeastern Brazil. The Centro Luiz Gonzaga de Tradições Nordestinas, aka the Feira Nordestina or Northeastern Market (Campo de São Cristóvão s/n, São Cristóvão; ☎ 021/2580-5335; www.feiradesaocristovao.org.br; cover R$2; open Fri–Sun 10am–8pm; taxi recommended), attracts half a million visitors each month. They come to this large year-round fair to shop for handcrafts, such as pottery, lace, hammocks, leather goods, and clothing. There are also dozens of restaurants that specialize in traditional dishes such as *carne de sol* (sun-dried beef), seafood, and *baião de dois* (a bean and rice dish). But above all, people come to listen and dance to the music: *forró, baião, xote, brega,* and other typical northeastern rhythms.

3 The Best Neighborhood Walks

Catete

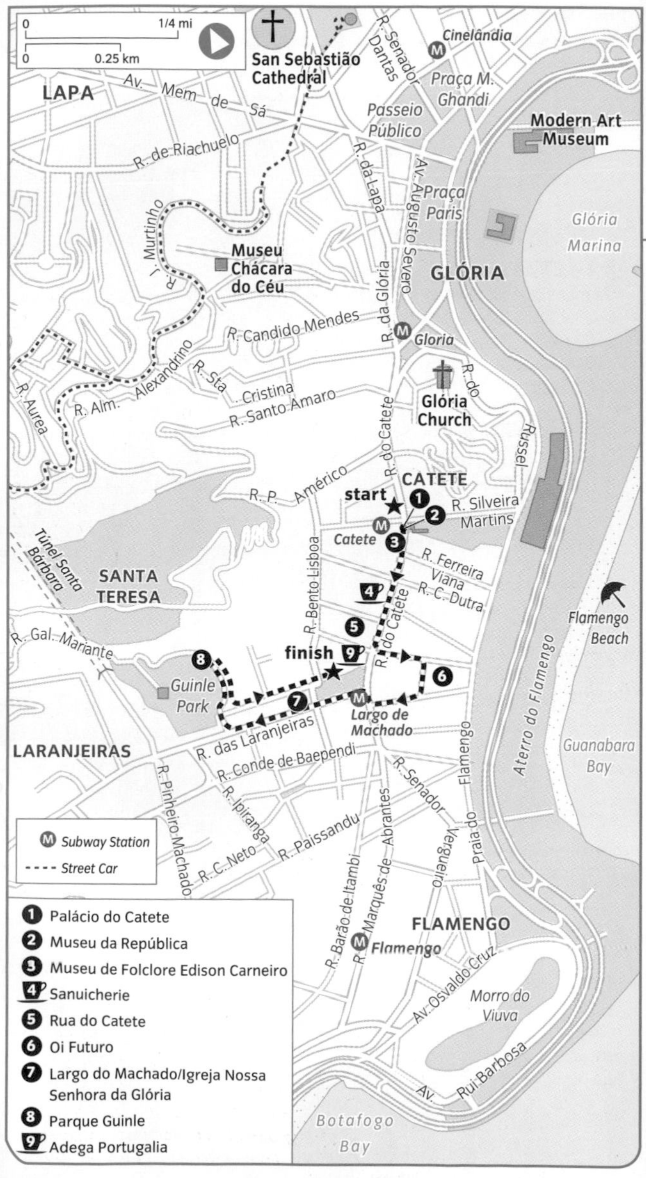
0 1/4 mi
0 0.25 km
San Sebastião Cathedral
Cinelândia
R. Senador Dantas
Praça M. Ghandi
Passeio Público
Modern Art Museum
LAPA
Av. Mem de Sá
R. de Riachuelo
R. da Lapa
Av. Augusto Severo
Praça Paris
Glória Marina
R. J. Murtinho
Museu Chácara do Céu
GLÓRIA
R. da Glória
R. Candido Mendes
Gloria
R. Alm. Alexandrino
R. Sta. Cristina
R. Santo Amaro
Glória Church
R. do Russel
R. Aurea
R. do Catete
CATETE
R. P. Américo
start
R. Silveira Martins
Catete
Túnel Santa Bárbara
SANTA TERESA
R. Ferreira Viana
R. C. Dutra
R. Bento Lisboa
Flamengo Beach
R. Gal. Mariante
finish
Guinle Park
Largo de Machado
Aterro do Flamengo
LARANJEIRAS
R. das Laranjeiras
R. Conde de Baependi
R. Senador Vergueiro
Praia do Flamengo
Guanabara Bay
R. Pinheiro Machado
R. Ipiranga
R. Paissandu
R. C. Neto
R. Barão de Itambi
R. Marquês de Abrantes
Subway Station
Street Car
FLAMENGO
Flamengo
Av. Osvaldo Cruz
Morro do Viuva
Av. Rui Barbosa
Botafogo Bay
1 Palácio do Catete
2 Museu da República
3 Museu de Folclore Edison Carneiro
4 Sanuicherie
5 Rua do Catete
6 Oi Futuro
7 Largo do Machado/Igreja Nossa Senhora da Glória
8 Parque Guinle
9 Adega Portugalia

Previous page: Imperial palm trees at the Jardim Botânico.

This bustling, middle-class neighborhood, wedged between Glória and Flamengo, first developed in the 19th century, when the "nouveau riche" coffee barons spent their fortunes building opulent mansions here. The neighborhood's turning point came in 1889, the year that Brazil became a republic and the president moved into the Palácio do Catete. For the next 60 years, Catete served as the political center of the country. When the capital was transferred to Brasília in 1960, Catete lost its ***raison d'être.*** Thanks to urban renewal projects and the recent real estate boom, however, Cariocas are now rediscovering Catete's attractions. **START: Metrô to Catete.**

1 ★★ kids Palácio do Catete. This mansion was built in 1862 as the private residence of a coffee baron and was later acquired by the federal government; it served as the presidential office and home of 18 presidents, from 1897 until 1960, when the capital was transferred to the brand new city of Brasília. The palace was then converted into a museum (see 2 below). The lovely gardens, off limits to the public until 1960, are now a popular leisure and cultural venue and feature a movie theatre, cafe, bookstore, outdoor exhibits, a craft museum (see 3 below) and children's playground. *1 hr. Rua do Catete 153. 021/3235-2650. Daily 8am–8pm. Free admission.*

2 ★ Museu da República. From 1897 to 1960, the presidential palace was the center of political power. The first two floors of the museum feature the official state rooms, ornately decorated with gleaming hardwood floors, ivory decorations, bronze light fixtures, and chandeliers inlaid with rubies and crystal. The third floor was the former residential area of the palace, including the bedroom where president Getulio Vargas committed suicide in 1954. His bloodstained pajamas and gun are still on display. *45 min. Rua do Catete 153. 021/3235-2650. www.museudarepublica.org.br. Admission R$6, seniors and children under 10 free. Tues–Fri 10am–5pm; Sat–Sun 2–6pm.*

Artwork at the Museu de Folclore.

3 ★ Museu de Folclore Edison Carneiro. This small museum, dedicated to Brazilian arts and crafts, is right next to the Palácio do Catete. The collection features quality handcrafts from all across Brazil, representing various themes, such as religion, festivals, and regional culture. The gift shop stocks an impressive variety of very affordable (I would almost say underpriced) crafts. *30 min. Rua do Catete 179. 021/2285-0441. www.cnfcp.gov.br. Free admission. Tues–Fri 11am–6pm; Sat–Sun 3–5pm.*

Largo do Machado.

4 Sanduicherie. Tucked away inside a small shopping center is this cozy bistro with a short but excellent lunch menu of fish, chicken, or meat dishes, as well as a variety of quiches and salads. Nothing tops R$25, and service is friendly and efficient. ***Rua do Catete 228, loja 116.*** ☎ ***021/2538-9144. $.***

5 ★ Rua do Catete. Join local shoppers for a stroll along the neighborhood's main commercial street, lined with lovely 19th-century walk-ups; the stretch along Rua do Catete from 126 to 196 and Rua do Catete from 179 to 187 has some particularly fine examples. Photography fans may want to duck into the small lane at Rua do Catete 214, where Molduras (Rua do Catete 214, loja 24; ☎ 021/2225-120), sells fabulous black and white photos of old Rio. ***Rua do Catete, btw. Rua Silveira Martins and Largo do Machado.***

Street vendors on the Rua do Catete.

6 ★ Oi Futuro. Behind the 100-year-old facade hides a high-tech modern cultural center. Oi Futuro's forte is digital photo exhibits, video installations, and conversations with artists. There is a cafe with an outdoor patio on the top floor. ***45 min. Rua Dois de Dezembro 63.*** ☎ ***021/3131-3060. www.oifuturo.org.br. Free admission. Tues–Sun 11am–8pm.***

7 Largo do Machado/Igreja Nossa Senhora da Glória. Rua do Catete ends at the Largo do Machado, a bustling 19th-century square, at the junction between Laranjeiras, Flamengo, and Catete. The landscaping was added later, in 1954, by famous Brazilian landscape architect Burle Marx. The square is dominated by the monumental 19th-century Igreja Nossa Senhora da Gloria. The interior is absolutely packed with paintings and statues donated by the city's elite as tokens of their devotion. ⌚ *20 min. Largo do Machado s/n.* ☎ *021/2225-0735. Free admission. Services Mon–Fri 7, 8, and 9am, and 5 and 6pm; Sat 7, 8, and 9am, and 3pm; Sun 7:30, 9, and 10:30am, and 5, 6:30, and 8pm.*

8 kids **Parque Guinle.** It's easy to miss this park; the main entrance is off Rua Gaga Coutinho, 1 block behind the Largo do Machado. An antique iron gate flanked by two granite pillars and sphinxes marks the entrance to the former estate of Eduardo Guinle. The mansion now serves as the official residence of the state governor and is off-limits to the public, but the lush grounds, with a small playground, ponds, and trails, make for a pleasant stroll. The modern apartment complex that encircles the right slope of the park was designed by Lucio Costa in 1944 and gave a sneak preview of his designs for the new capital, Brasília, where he would team up with his former architecture student, Oscar Niemeyer. ⌚ *1 hr. Rua Gago Coutinho 66. Free admission. Daily 8am–8pm.*

9 **Adega Portugalia.** This simple neighborhood restaurant overlooking the Largo do Machado serves up tasty Portuguese food. If you just want a snack, peruse the antipasti on the counter and order some olives, marinated octopus, or spicy potatoes. *Largo do Machado 30.* ☎ *021/2558-2821. $.*

The View from the Top

In 2000, the police set up its Special Operations Unit in the small favela of Tavares Bastos and forced out the ruling drug gangs; the Brazilian movie *Elite Squad (Tropa de Elite)* shows this unit in action. As a result, Tavares Bastos became the first favela where residents and visitors could freely come and go without worrying about turf wars or armed drug gangs.

Lately, the breathtaking views of Sugarloaf and Guanabara Bay have attracted numerous filmmakers (*The Hulk* was shot here) to the favela. Every third Friday of the month, droves of visitors ascend the steep hill to listen to live rock or jazz at *The Maze* (Rua Tavares Bastos 414, casa 66; ☎ 021/2558-5547 or 021/8185-5979; http://jazzrio.info), the Gaudi-esque house of former BBC correspondent Bob Nadkarni. The fascinating space also features an art gallery, and a terrace with breathtaking views. Getting to the Maze is a fun adventure. Board a van or a motorcycle taxi on the corner of Rua Bento Lisboa and Rua Tavares Bastos. At the top of the hill, you enter the favela. Don't bother looking for the house number; just ask for "casa do Bob."

The favela Tavares Bastos.

Santa Teresa

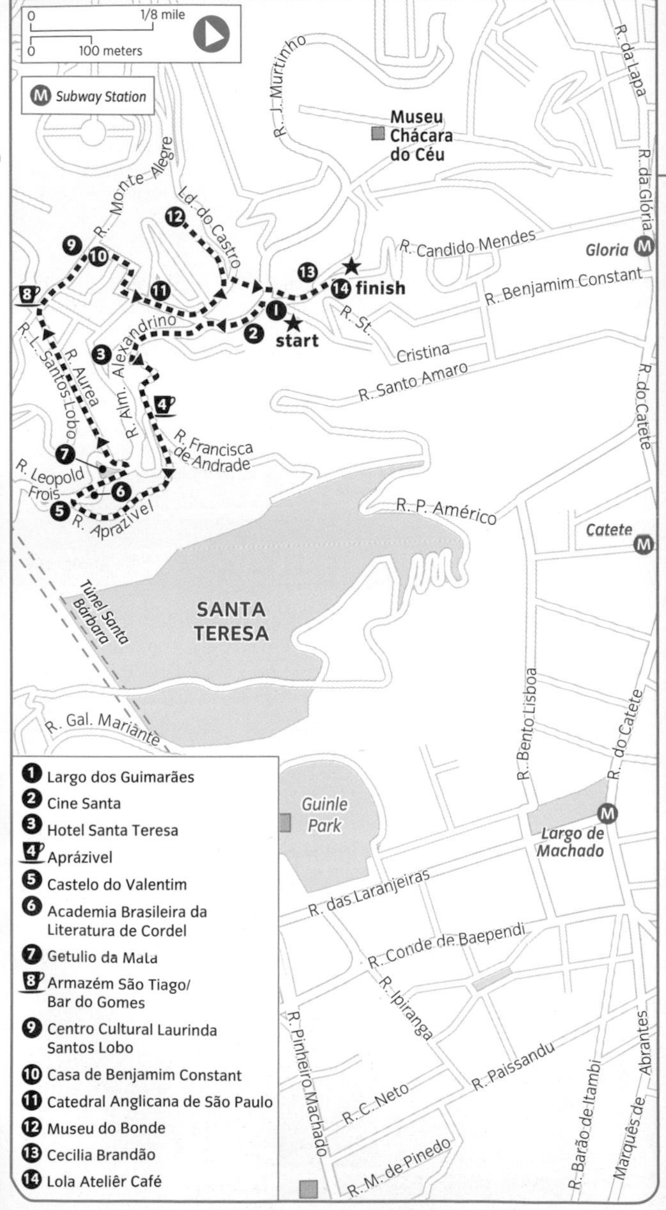
0 1/8 mile
0 100 meters
M Subway Station
R. J. Murtinho
Museu Chácara do Céu
R. da Lapa
R. da Glória
Gloria M
R. Monte Alegre
Ld. do Castro
R. Candido Mendes
R. Benjamim Constant
finish
start
R. St. Cristina
R. Alm. Alexandrino
R. Santo Amaro
R. L. Santos Lobo
R. Aurea
R. Francisca de Andrade
R. Leopold Frois
R. Aprazível
R. P. Américo
R. do Catete
Catete M
Túnel Santa Bárbara
SANTA TERESA
R. Gal. Mariante
R. Bento Lisboa
Guinle Park
Largo de Machado
R. das Laranjeiras
R. Conde de Baependi
R. Ipiranga
R. Pinheiro Machado
R. Paissandu
R. C. Neto
R. M. de Pinedo
R. Barão de Itambi
Marquês de Abrantes
1 Largo dos Guimarães
2 Cine Santa
3 Hotel Santa Teresa
4 Aprázivel
5 Castelo do Valentim
6 Academia Brasileira da Literatura de Cordel
7 Getulio da Mala
8 Armazém São Tiago/ Bar do Gomes
9 Centro Cultural Laurinda Santos Lobo
10 Casa de Benjamim Constant
11 Catedral Anglicana de São Paulo
12 Museu do Bonde
13 Cecilia Brandão
14 Lola Ateliêr Café

It's worth sacrificing a day at the beach to explore this picturesque hilltop neighborhood with its lovely architecture and beautiful views. Santa Teresa also packs in numerous other attractions, including some excellent small museums, funky cafes, artist studios, and wonderful restaurants. Wear comfortable shoes, as you will brave cobblestones, steps, some sloping streets, and streetcar tracks. See p 20 for information on taking the historic streetcar.
START: Streetcar or bus 206 or 214 to Largo dos Guimarães.

1 ★ Largo dos Guimarães. This square is the commercial hub of Santa Teresa, where you will find a few small grocery stores, a movie theater, cafes, and a bookstore. It's the perfect starting place for a walking tour. *Rua Almirante Alexandrino and Rua Paschoal Carlos Magno.*

2 ★ Cine Santa. Despite its small size, this 60-seat movie theater has been recognized in 2008 and 2009 by the Brazilian film board for showing more Brazilian movies than any other theater in the country. The small art gallery at the entrance often showcases work by local artists. *Largo dos Guimarães 136. ☎ 021/2222-0203. www.cinesanta.com.br.*

3 Hotel Santa Teresa. This hotel is a prime example of the neighborhood's recent revitalization. The upscale boutique hotel is housed in an elegant mansion from the 1850s that once belonged to the Chácara dos Guimarães estate. Before reopening in 2008 after a multimillion-dollar overhaul, it was known as the Hotel dos Descasados (the Hotel of the Divorced), where recently separated men and women could rent a room until they had found a place of their own. As a tribute to its history, the hotel's bar has been named the Bar dos Descasados (p 138). *Rua Almirante Alexandrino 660. ☎ 021/2222-2755. Bus: 206 or 214.*

4 ★★ Aprázivel. Rua Aprázivel is one of the best places in the city to enjoy fabulous views of downtown Rio. The restaurant Aprázivel, tucked away on this street, is one of Santa Teresa's more popular restaurants, as famous for its food as its views. *See p 101.*

The patio at Aprázivel.

An architectural detail in Santa Teresa.

❺ ★ **Castelo do Valentim.** At the very end of the Rua Aprazível stands this romantic castle, a combination of medieval and Romanesque styles, built in 1879. It's not open to general visitation, but a few rooms in the castle operate as a bed-and-breakfast and accommodate up to four guests. Contact the Santa Teresa Bed and Breakfast network for information (p 141).

❻ **Academia Brasileira de Literatura de Cordel.** Take a peek inside this small store that promotes the northeastern tradition of *literatura de cordel* (string literature, because it is often displayed on a string). These simple, inexpensive booklets feature folk tales and poems and are illustrated with basic black-and-white woodcut prints. The prints are sold separately as artwork. ***Rua Leopoldo Frões 37.*** ☎ *021/2232-4801. www.ablc.com.br. Free admission. Tues–Sat 11am–5pm.*

❼ ★★ kids **Getulio da Mata.** Most days, you will see artisan Getulio da Mata at work, in his outdoor "studio" under a tree, across from the odd Bavarian-style police station. Da Mata crafts miniature streetcars and other toys from a variety of recycled materials. He is always happy to show you his work and pause for a chat. ***Rua Leopoldo Frões at the corner of Almirante Alexandrino.*** *Tues–Sun 11am–5pm (weather permitting).*

❽ **Armazém São Tiago/Bar do Gomes.** At the intersection of Rua Aurea and Rua Monte Alegre stands this almost 100-year-old traditional Rio "botequim" (pub or cafe) with a lovely marble counter, the perfect pit stop for a drink and snack. ***Rua Aurea 26.*** ☎ *021/2232-0822. $.*

❾ ★ **Centro Cultural Laurinda Santos Lobo.** This opulent yellow

The Santa Teresa streetcar.

Téréze restaurant at Hotel Santa Teresa (p 51).

mansion, built in 1907, is a fine example of Santa Teresa's eclectic architecture. In 1979, it was converted from a residence into a cultural center, named in honor of illustrious Santa Teresa resident Laurinda Santos (p 20). Today it hosts exhibits, plays, concerts, and children's activities. Across the street, on Rua Monte Alegre 313, is another beautiful mansion. Built in 1873, the facade of this private house is covered with pretty glazed tiles. *Rua Monte Alegre 306. ☎ 021/2242-9741. Free admission. Tues–Fri 10am–6pm; Sat–Sun 2–6pm.*

⑩ ★★ **Casa de Benjamim Constant.** A visit to this lovely estate will give you an impression of life in 19th-century Santa Teresa, when wealthy Cariocas built their mansions in the hills to escape the city heat. The former house of politician Benjamim Constant (1837–91) has been beautifully preserved with period furniture and historic artifacts. The spacious grounds are planted with an impressive variety of native plants and trees. ⏲ *1 hr. Rua Monte Alegre 255. ☎ 021/2509-1248. Admission R$2. Wed–Sun 1–5pm.*

⑪ **Catedral Anglicana de São Paulo.** Continue on Rua Pascoal Carlos Magno (follow the streetcar tracks) to return to the Largo dos Guimarães. Along the way you will pass by the Catedral Anglicana de São Paulo. This interesting English gothic construction was built in 1928 and still has an active church community. *Rua Paschoal Carlos Magno 95. ☎ 021/2252-1852. Only open during church services.*

⑫ ★ **Museu do Bonde.** Follow the tracks to the end of Rua Carlos Brant to reach the streetcar depot (note the decorative iron gate at the entrance) and small museum that tells the history of streetcars in Rio de Janeiro through photos, artifacts, replicas, and miniatures. ⏲ *30 min. Rua Carlos Brant 14. ☎ 021/2242-2534. Daily 10am–4pm. Admission R$4.*

⑬ ★ **Cecilia Brandão.** This Brazilian designer's collection of fabulous T-shirts featuring stylish prints is sold in several other stores across the city, but her flagship Santa Teresa shop has the largest selection of styles and items. *Rua Almirante Alexandrino 376. ☎ 021/2232-1389. www.ceciliabrandao.com.br.*

⑭ ★ **Lola Ateliêr Café.** Local resident and artist Lola opened this small cafe and atelier where she displays her colorful creations, turning household items such as coasters, fridge magnets, placemats, and aprons into desirable objects and fabulous souvenirs. *Rua Santa Cristina 181. ☎ 021/2224-7909. Tues–Sun 10:30am–7:30pm.*

Lapa & Glória

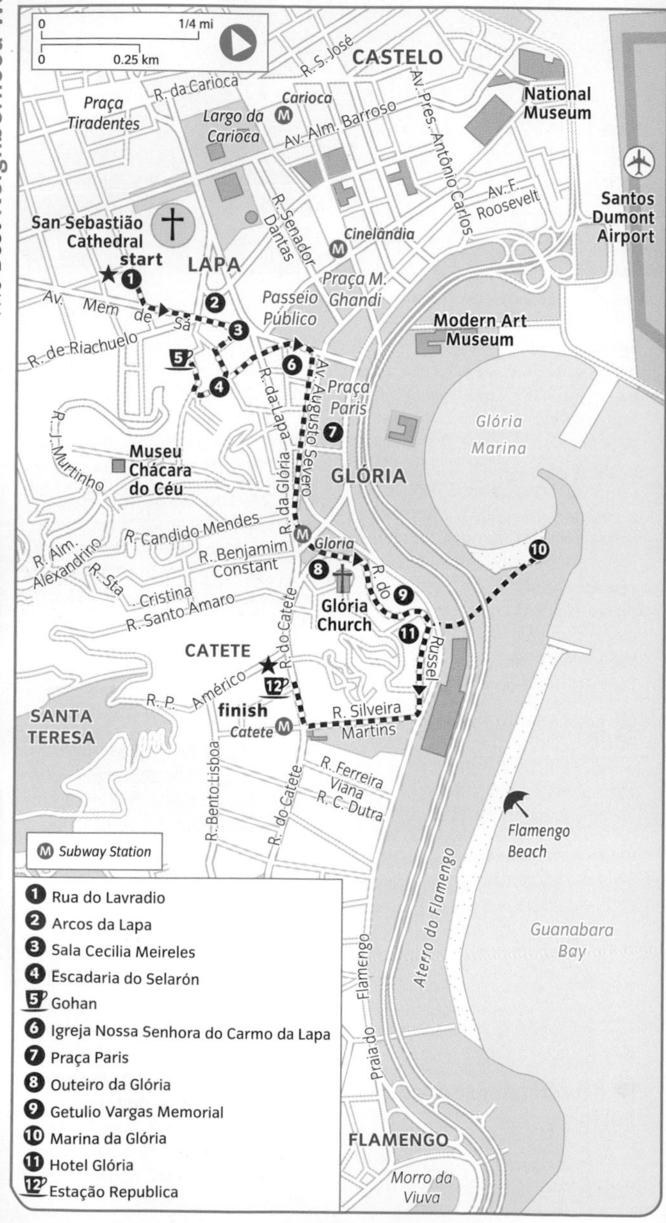
0 1/4 mi
0 0.25 km
CASTELO
R. S. José
R. da Carioca
Praça Tiradentes
Carioca
Largo da Carioca
Av. Alm. Barroso
Av. Pres. Antônio Carlos
National Museum
Santos Dumont Airport
Av. F. Roosevelt
R. Senador Dantas
Cinelândia
San Sebastião Cathedral
start
LAPA
Praça M. Ghandi
Passeio Público
Av. Mem de Sá
R. de Riachuelo
Modern Art Museum
R. da Lapa
Av. Augusto Severo
Praça Paris
Glória Marina
R. J. Murtinho
Museu Chácara do Céu
GLÓRIA
R. da Glória
R. Candido Mendes
R. Benjamim Constant
Gloria
R. Alm. Alexandrino
R. Sta. Cristina
R. Santo Amaro
R. do
Glória Church
Russel
CATETE
R. do Catete
R. P. Américo
finish
Catete
R. Silveira Martins
SANTA TERESA
R. Ferreira Viana
R. C. Dutra
R. Bento Lisboa
R. do Catete
Flamengo Beach
Subway Station
Aterro do Flamengo
Guanabara Bay
Praia do Flamengo
FLAMENGO
Morro da Viuva
1 Rua do Lavradio
2 Arcos da Lapa
3 Sala Cecilia Meireles
4 Escadaria do Selarón
5 Gohan
6 Igreja Nossa Senhora do Carmo da Lapa
7 Praça Paris
8 Outeiro da Glória
9 Getulio Vargas Memorial
10 Marina da Glória
11 Hotel Glória
12 Estação Republica

Although most people visit Lapa for its excellent nightlife, a daytime stroll here reveals some intriguing attractions, including an impressive 18th-century aqueduct, built to supply the city with drinking water, and charming 19th-century buildings. Glória, a neighborhood to the south that was settled in the 18th century, is connected to Lapa via narrow Rua da Lapa, and a walk along this road and through Glória provides more glimpses of old Rio. Today, both neighborhoods are experiencing a real-estate boom, and once run-down areas are being gentrified with new condo and commerce developments. **START: Metrô to Carioca.**

Escadaria do Selarón (p 56).

1 ★★★ Rua do Lavradio. Built in 1771 by the Marques de Lavradio, the Rua do Lavradio is one of the oldest residential streets in downtown Rio. Although most visitors come here for the excellent music and nightlife, it's worth taking a daytime stroll along this street to browse the many antiques and furniture stores along Rio's antiques row. Every first Saturday of the month, the street hosts a large outdoor antiques and craft fair with live music, street theater, and food (10am–5pm).

2 ★★ Arcos da Lapa. It took more than 50 years to build Lapa's landmark monument, the Arches or Aqueduct. Completed in 1750, the aqueduct was designed to bring water from the Carioca River in the Floresta da Tijuca into the city, where the growing population demanded more clean drinking water. The streetcar tracks that run across the aqueduct lead from downtown up to Santa Teresa and were added in 1894. *Rua Riachuelo and Rua da Lapa.*

3 ★ Sala Cecilia Meireles. The Sala Cecilia Meireles was originally inaugurated in 1896 as the prestigious Grande Hotel. Later the building was converted into a movie theater and finally, in 1965, it was transformed into Rio's premier small classic music venue, famous for its excellent acoustics. *Largo da Lapa 47. ☎ 021/2568-8742. www.salaceciliameireles.com.br.*

❹ ★★ **Escadaria do Selarón.** A narrow alley next to the Sala Cecilia Meireles leads to the steps that have been transformed into a work of art by Chilean artist Jorge Selarón. A resident of Santa Teresa, Selarón began decorating the 215 steps with colorful tiles in 1990. ***Note:*** I don't recommend walking all the way up the steps, which lead to the neighborhood of Santa Teresa, as muggings do occur on the quieter backstreets and upper part of the steps. Stick to the main streets and take a bus, streetcar, or taxi to the upper part of Santa Teresa. *Rua Joaquim Silva s/n, on the corner of Rua Teotonio Regadas.*

❺ **Gohan.** This Lapa favorite serves up healthy and generous Japanese stir-fries piled high with fresh veggies, seafood, or meat and brown rice or noodles. Most dishes serve two hungry people. If you are eating alone, ask for a half order. *Rua Joaquim Silva 127. ☎ 021/2232-0479. www.gohanrio.com.br. $.*

❻ ★ **Igreja Nossa Senhora do Carmo da Lapa.** Behind the Carmo da Lapa's unassuming facade hides a lovely 18th-century church that's worth a peek. The church's ornate ceiling and wood carvings have been beautifully restored, and its exquisite altar was sculpted by Mestre Valentim. *Rua da Lapa s/n. ☎ 021/2221-3887. Free admission. Mon–Fri 6:30–11am and 5–7:30pm.*

❼ ★ KIDS **Praça Paris.** At the end of the Rua da Lapa, you'll enter the neighborhood of Glória, where the French-inspired gardens of the Praça Paris offer an elegant refuge from the busy city traffic. When the park was built in 1929, almost 40 years before the large Aterro do Flamengo waterfront park was created, it was the largest green space in this area. The park offers a beautiful view of Outeiro da Gloria (see below). *Rua da Gloria and Av. Beira Mar.*

❽ ★★ **Outeiro da Glória.** I love this small church, which boasts fabulous views from its location on a small hill overlooking the bay. Construction on it began in 1714 and took several decades. Today the church has a unique octagonal shape and a beautiful, sober interior with dark wooden carvings and blue-and-white Portuguese tiles that adorn the sacristy. A large celebration in honor of Our Lady of Glória is held here each August 15. The church can be accessed on foot (or by taxi) via the short but steep Ladeira da Glória, next to the Restaurant Taberna da Glória. There is also an elevator on Praça Luis de Camões 312. The elevator runs Monday to Friday from 7am to 7pm and Saturday to Sunday from 7am to 1pm. *Ladeira da Glória s/n, Glória. ☎ 021/2225-2869. Free admission. Tues–Fri 9am–noon and 1–5pm; Sat–Sun 9am–noon.*

The sacristy tiles at the Outeiro da Glória.

The Marina da Glória.

9 Getulio Vargas Memorial. The bronze bust next to the fountain in Praça Luis de Camões depicts Getulio Vargas, one of Brazil's most controversial presidents. (To learn more about Vargas, see p 47.) An exhibit space underneath the fountain features a movie theater and a permanent exhibit on Vargas, but is currently closed for renovations. The stone statue across from the fountain represents São Sebastião (St. Sebastian), the patron saint of Rio de Janeiro. Every year on January 20, throngs of faithful gather here to leave flowers and light candles. ***Praça Luis de Camões (aka Praça do Russel) s/n. ☎ 021/2557-9444.***

10 Marina da Glória. The centrally located Marina da Glória will be the main Olympic watersports venue in 2016. Major clean-up efforts are underway to reduce pollution of the bay and improve the marina's facilities. The marina is also a popular venue for cultural events, trade fairs, and concerts, and is home to the restaurant Barracuda, which specializes in seafood; it's open Monday to Friday noon to 11pm and Saturday and Sunday noon to 6pm. ***Av. Infante Dom Henrique s/n, Glória. ☎ 021/2225-2200. www.marinadagloria.com.br. Hours vary. In the daytime, cross the pedestrian walkway opposite Praça Luis de Camões. Taxi recommended at night.***

11 Hotel Glória. Just around the corner from the former presidential palace (p 47), the white neoclassical Hotel Glória was for many decades the most glamorous destination in town. However, over the last 20 years this hotel, which was inaugurated in 1922, lost a lot of its old shine and started to look old and tattered. In 2008, the hotel was bought by Brazilian billionaire Eike Batista, who is determined to restore it to its former glory. The hotel is closed for major renovations and will reopen in 2011. ***Rua do Russell 632. www.hotelgloriario.com.br.***

12 Estação Republica. This is one of the best self-service restaurants in Glória, with a large salad buffet, dozens of hot dishes, pasta, stews, seafood, as well as grilled beef and chicken. You pay by weight. ***Rua do Catete 104. ☎ 021/2128-5650. $.***

Jardim Botânico

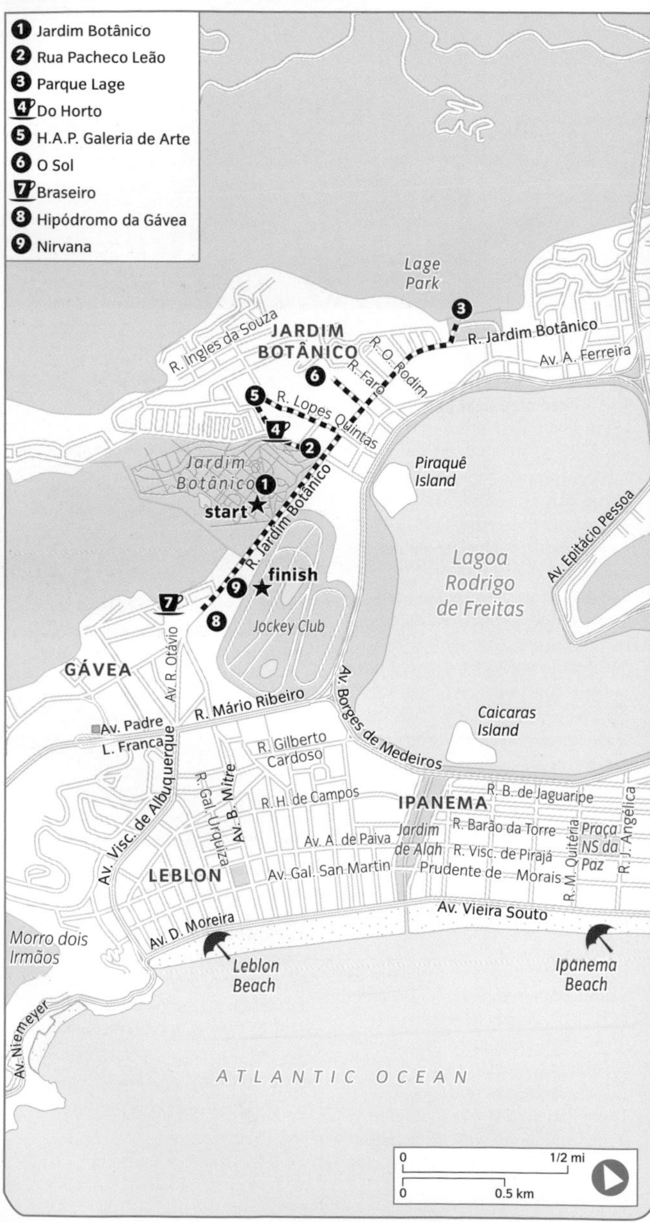

This walking tour will appeal to urban nature lovers. Start by enjoying a stroll in the exquisite 200-year-old Botanical Garden and nearby Parque Lage. Next, explore the streets of the quaint neighborhood of Jardim Botânico, a green oasis nestled at the foot of the Tijuca rainforest, below "the armpit of Christ." A short walk will take you to the lovely Praça Santos Dumont and the city's elegant horse track, as well as a spa where you can work out any kinks you acquired during the day's nature walks. **START: Bus 170 to the main gate of the Jardim Botânico, Rua Jardim Botânico 920.**

The Gate of the School of Fine Arts.

1 ★★★ kids **Jardim Botânico.** Upon his arrival in Rio de Janeiro in 1808, D. João VI expropriated a large swath of land to build a royal gunpowder factory and used a section of this land to create a garden for exotic seedlings brought from India, Macau, and other far-away regions. Today the Jardim Botânico is one of the premier botanical gardens in the world, home to over 5,000 species of trees and 8,000 species of flora that attract a large variety of birds and several monkey species, including playful marmosets. See the box "Jardim Botânico Delights," p 60, for details on the garden's sights. Before you set out, grab a free copy of the excellent English map at the cashier and make sure you stop by the Visitor's Center; it often features lovely photo exhibits of the park. After your visit, you may exit the garden through the **Gate of the School of Fine Arts.** Designed in 1826, this gate marked the entrance to a fine arts school in downtown Rio that was demolished in 1938. This back entrance takes you straight into the heart of the Jardim Botânico neighborhood. ⌚ *2 hr. Rua Jardim Botânico 920. www.jbrj.gov.br. Admission R$5 adults, children under 7 free. Daily 8am–5pm.*

2 ★★ **Rua Pacheco Leão.** This neighborhood's main street hugs the northern side of the park and gives access to a pleasant cul-de-sac with excellent restaurants and nice shops set against the Tijuca rainforest.

Jardim Botânico Delights

The main path of the botanical gardens is framed by a row of majestic Imperial palm trees, leading to the **Chafariz Central,** an elegant cast-iron fountain made in England that once stood in Lapa. The statues represent science, poetry, music, and art. Rio's oldest statues, **Echo and Narcissus,** crafted by colonial sculptor Mestre Valentim at the end of the 18th century, have also been moved here from Lapa, where they originally stood in the **Passeio Publico park** (p 17).

The remains of the gunpowder factory that led to the creation of these gardens can still be seen at **Casa dos Pilões;** this construction housed the mill where the gunpowder components were ground. A small exhibit gives an overview of the process. When the factory was shut down in 1831, this area was incorporated into the botanical garden.

The **bromeliad greenhouse** displays a dazzling array of these spiky flowering plants (somewhat resembling a pineapple), which play an important role in the tropical ecosystem because of their capacity to trap water. The elegant **glass orchid greenhouse** contains more than 500 species of these delicate flowers, the majority hailing from Brazil, but you can also admire some exotic and hybrid examples.

An orchid at the Jardim Botânico greenhouse.

❸ ★ **Parque Lage.** The neighborhood of Jardim Botânico is endowed with more than its fair share of parks. The Parque Lage is almost as impressive as the botanical garden, but with its dense vegetation and swaths of Atlantic rainforest, it has a much more rugged feel. On site are a playground for small children and a lovely cafe that serves lunch and light meals and snacks. *Rua Jardim Botânico 414, Jardim Botânico. ☎ 021/2226-8125. www.cafedulage.com.br. Free admission. Mon–Thurs 9am–10pm; Fri–Sun 9am–5pm.*

❹ **Do Horto.** Colorful and whimsically decorated, this eatery serves outstanding food and cocktails. Order a few appetizers or enjoy a full meal. The most popular lunch dish is the *bobó de camarão,* a bubbly prawn stew with coconut milk and red palm oil, served in a pumpkin shell. *Rua Pacheco Leão 780. ☎ 021/3114-8439. $$.*

5 ★ H.A.P. Galeria de Arte. Founded in 2001, this art gallery showcases the work of a dozen contemporary artists who work in a variety of media. ⌚ *20 min. Rua Abreu Fialho 11, Jardim Botânico. www.hapgaleria.com.br. ☎ 021/3874-2830. Free admission. Daily 8am–6pm.*

6 ★★ O Sol. If you have an interest in Brazilian handcrafts, make sure to visit O Sol. This non-profit organization promotes the work of artisans from all across Brazil, so its collection will give you a wonderful introduction to the country's various regional craft styles. By buying the work, you'll also contribute to the preservation of traditional culture. *Rua Corcovado 213, Jardim Botânico. www.artesanato-sol.com.br. ☎ 021/2294-5099. Mon–Fri 9am–6pm; Sat 9:30am–1pm.*

7 Braseiro. This simple neighborhood restaurant on the lovely Praça Santos Dumont is very popular among residents and students from the nearby elite PUC University. The kitchen specializes in grilled meat. Until 4pm, it serves a R$16 lunch special (steak or chicken with several side dishes); at night people flock here for a cold beer with a serving of grilled sausage, a steak sandwich, or a rotisserie chicken. *Praça Santos Dumont 116. ☎ 021/2239-7494. $.*

8 ★★ Hipódromo da Gávea (Jockey Clube Brasileiro). Brazil's largest horse racetrack is located across the street from the Jardim Botânico. Even if you don't particularly fancy horse races, it's worth taking a peek inside to see the elegant 1920s grandstands, the lovely wooden betting counters, and the crystal chandeliers. The wide-open race field with sweeping views of the Corcovado and surrounding hills is often used for events, concerts, and festivals. *Praça Santos Dumont 31, Gávea. www.jcb.com.br. ☎ 021/3534-9167. Races: Fri 5pm; Sat–Sun 3:45pm; Mon 6:15pm.*

9 ★ Nirvana. Another great reason to wander inside the gates of the Hipódromo is to visit one of the city's best spa facilities, located just to the left of the main entrance. Book a relaxing Thai or shiatsu massage or choose from a number of other therapeutic or relaxing sessions. *Praça Santos Dumont 31, Gávea. www.enirvana.com.br. ☎ 021/2187-0100. Mon–Sat 10am–10pm; Sun 10am–6pm.*

Hipódromo da Gávea.

Ipanema

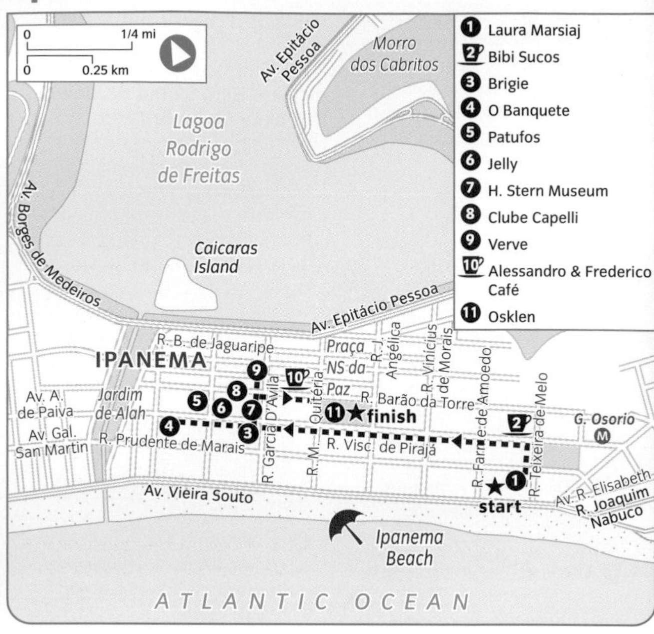

Spend a day in Rio's most upscale neighborhood and you can feel like one of the beautiful girls (or boys) from Ipanema. Within a 6-block radius of the beach, you can shop for a sexy Brazilian bikini or swim trunks, check out the latest shoe fashions, try on some lovely lingerie, admire fabulous gemstones, enjoy a delicious lunch, pamper yourself at a day spa, and peruse the work of contemporary artists. **START: Metrô to General Osório.**

1 ★★★ Laura Marsiaj. Add a dash of culture to your stroll with a visit to this sleek gallery that highlights modern contemporary artists. The main space hosts around seven exhibits per year, usually showcasing Brazilian artists. The annex provides a space for upcoming young artists to display their work. *Rua Teixeira de Melo 31. ☎ 021/2513-2074. www.lauramarsiaj.com.br. Free admission. Tues–Fri 11am–7pm; Sat 11am–4pm.*

2 Bibi Sucos. Boost your energy before a day of shopping with a fresh tropical juice or a vitamin-packed Amazon Açai berry slushy. Remember that Cariocas love their fruit sweet, so ask for "pouco açucar" (little sugar) to preserve the natural juice flavor. My favorites include *maracuja* (passion fruit); *abacaxi com hortelã* (pineapple with mint); the ultra-healthy combo of *laranja, beterreba, e cenoura* (carrot, beet,

Fruit on display at Bibi Sucos.

and orange juice); and the refreshing *melancia* (watermelon). ***Rua Teixeira de Melo 34 (by Av. Visconde de Pirajá). ☎ 021/2522-3949. $.***

❸ ★★★ **Brigie.** In Rio, the bikini is a staple in every woman's wardrobe and Brigie's boutique sells Brazil's most stylish designs by Beach Couture, Vix, Di Bikini, Clube Bossa, and others. Accessorize your look with lovely necklaces, tote bags, or sun hats. ***Rua Visconde de Pirajá 547, 2nd floor. ☎ 021/2512-0775. www.brigie.com.br.***

❹ ★★★ **O Banquete.** Carioca women love unique, one-of-a-kind bijouterie and jewelry. Tucked away inside a small shopping arcade, Banquete sells creative, contemporary jewelry by at least a dozen Brazilian designers; treat yourself or pick up a gift for that special someone. ***Rua Visconde de Pirajá 611, loja 17. ☎ 021/2512-1914. www.obanquete.com.br.***

❺ ★ **Patufos.** Even the little ones can shop for stylish and elegant outfits in Ipanema. Patufos sells a large collection of Brazilian kids' wear, including Toffee, Mini Kids, and Mercatore. ***Rua Anibal de Mendonça 123. ☎ 021/2512-9071.***

❻ ★★ **Jelly.** Kitschy and cute, Jelly's shoe collection is very Ipanema. Here you will find flip-flops, flats, and other interesting styles and designs, all made from high-quality plastic, in a dazzling array of colors. ***Rua Visconde de Pirajá 529. ☎ 021/3813-9328. www.jellyweb.com.br.***

❼ ★★ **H. Stern Museum.** H. Stern marks the most expensive and exclusive stretch of Ipanema, where you'll find names like Louis Vuitton, Cartier, Mont Blanc, and more security guards per square meter than at a J. Lo wedding. But

Jewelry on display at H. Stern.

even if you aren't a big spender, you can tour the H. Stern museum for free and admire the amazing variety of Brazilian gemstones. *30 min. Rua Garcia D'Avila 113. ☎ 021/2106-0000. www.hstern.com.br. Mon–Fri 9am–6pm; Sat 9am–noon (free 20-min. English audio tour anytime).*

8 ★★★ Clube Capelli. It takes work to get that effortless and casual Ipanema look. For a perfect manicure, pedicure, hair style, or the famous Brazilian bikini wax (not painful at all, if done right), there is no better place than Clube Capelli. This stylish salon with English-speaking staff offers a range of excellent services for men and women, including spa treatments, facials, massage sessions, and peelings. Free transportation within the Zona Sul is included in the rates. *Rua Barão da Torre 564. ☎ 021/2511-2588. www.clubcapelli.com.br. Mon–Sat 8am–11pm.*

9 ★ Verve. All lingerie should look and feel this good; Verve's signature style is sensual and elegant, but always with a comfortable fit. Sales staff will take your measurements to recommend the best size. *Rua Garcia D'Avila 149. ☎ 021/3202-2680. www.verve.com.br.*

10 Alessandro & Frederico Café. Join the ladies (and men) who lunch at this popular local restaurant. Everything, from the baked goods to the antipasti, carpaccio, and salads, is deliciously fresh. For a more hearty lunch, there is pasta, grilled steak, and seafood. The outside patio offers prime people-watching. *Rua Garcia D'Avila 134. ☎ 021/2521-0828. www.alessandroefrederico.com.br. $$.*

11 ★★ Osklen. If you are reluctant to adopt the endlessly popular Carioca speedo, check out the stylish swim shorts and Bermudas at Osklen. The corner where this shop is located is somewhat of a fashion mecca, with three excellent men's stores in a row (Richards and Redley are right next door). *Rua Maria Quitéria 85. ☎ 021/2227-2911. www.osklen.com.br.* ●

The Girl from Ipanema Industry

It all started with a song—a mellow bossa nova tune, written by Tom Jobim and Vinicius de Moraes, and immortalized in English by Astrud Gilberto and Stan Getz. That song, "The Girl From Ipanema," was inspired by Heloisa Pinheiro, a real girl from Ipanema, who often walked by Café Veloso on Rua Montenegro, where the two musicians hung out. The street is now called Vinicius de Moraes and the cafe has been renamed **Garota de Ipanema Bar** (Rua Vinicius de Moraes 49). A few doors down you will also find the **Vinicius Piano Bar** (Rua Vinicius de Moraes 39), one of the few places in Rio where you can still hear bossa nova. The "Girl from Ipanema" went on to make a career out of her honorary title, and one of Pinheiro's many endeavors includes a bikini store on Rua Vinicius de Moraes 53, called . . . surprise, surprise, Garota de Ipanema.

4 The Best **Shopping**

Shopping Best Bets

Best **Place to Buy an Engagement Ring**
★★ H. Stern, *Rua Visconde de Pirajá 496 (p 74)*

Best **Hip Women's Clothing**
★★ Farm, *Rua Visconde de Pirajá 365 (p 73)*

Best **Shoe Splurge**
★★ Sarah Chofakian, *Av. Afrânio de Melo Franco 290, loja 305 (p 76)*

Best **Untouristy Beachwear**
★★★ Blue Man, *Rua Visconde de Pirajá 315 (p 70)*

Best **'80s-Inspired Design**
★ Mercado Moderno, *Rua do Lavradio 130 (p 72)*

Best **Brazilian Music**
★★★ Modern Sound, *Rua Barata RIbeiro 502 (p 75)*

Best **Treats for Chocoholics**
★★★ Kopenhagen, *Rua Figueiredo Magalhães 131 (p 74)*

Best **Party Outfits**
★★★ Casa Turuna, *Rua Sr. dos Passos 122 (p 72)*

Best **Footwear Under R$15**
★ Havaianas, *Rua da Alfândega 183 (p 75)*

Best **Trendy Rio Souvenirs**
★★★ Gilson Martins, *Rua Figueiredo Magalhães 304 (p 73)*

Best **Mall for Spotting Celebrities**
★★★ Shopping Leblon, *Av. Afrânio de Melo Franco 290 (p 76)*

Best **Antiques Selection**
★ Shopping Cassino Atlântico, *Av. Atlântica 4240 (p 70)*

Best **Look Good and Do Good Cosmetics**
★ O Boticário, *Rua Santa Clara 70 (p 71)*

Best **Aprés Beachwear**
★★ Salinas, *Rua Visconde de Pirajá 547 (p 71)*

Best **Child's Play**
★★ Artimanha, *Rua Capitão Salomão 14 (p 73)*

Best **Book Browsing**
★★★ Livraria da Travessa, *Rua Visconde de Pirajá 572 (p 72)*

Best **Produce and Free Food Samples**
★★ Glória Sunday Market, *Rua da Glória*

Below: A food stand at Glória Sunday Market. Previous page: Shoes on display at Sarah Chofakian.

Centro & Santa Teresa Shopping

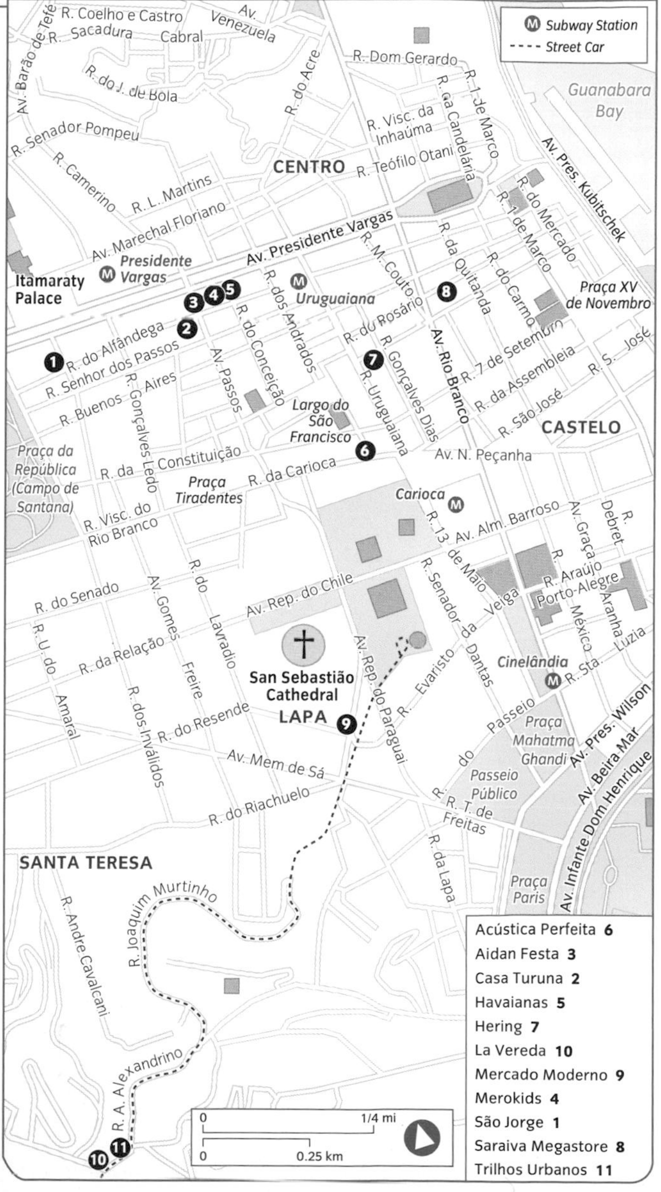

Acústica Perfeita **6**
Aidan Festa **3**
Casa Turuna **2**
Havaianas **5**
Hering **7**
La Vereda **10**
Mercado Moderno **9**
Merokids **4**
São Jorge **1**
Saraiva Megastore **8**
Trilhos Urbanos **11**

Ipanema & Leblon Shopping

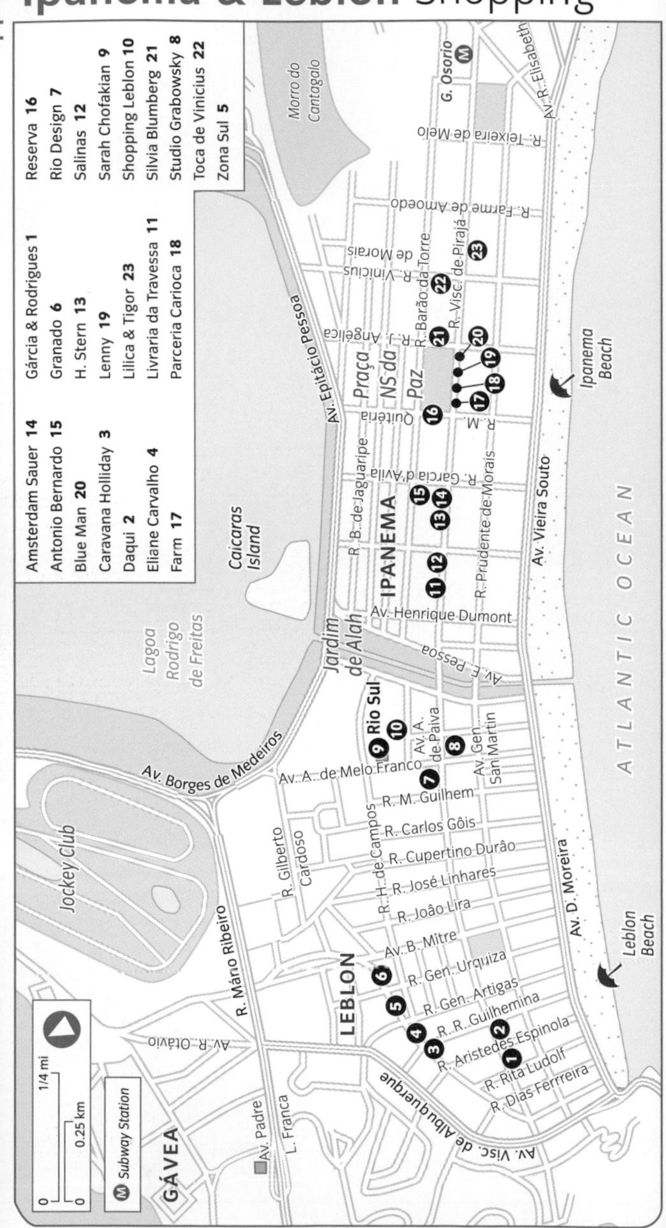

Copacabana Shopping

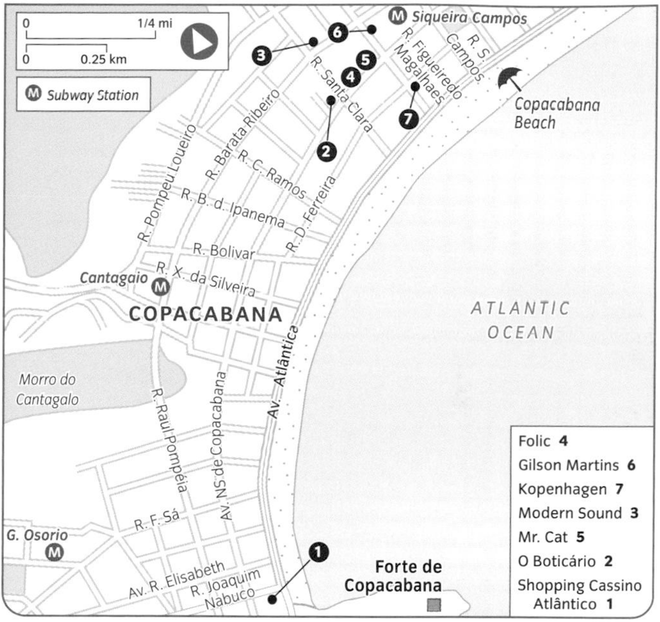

0 1/4 mi
0 0.25 km
Subway Station
Siqueira Campos
R. Figueiredo Magalhaes
R. S. Campos
R. Santa Clara
R. Barata Ribeiro
R. C. Ramos
R. Pompeu Loueiro
R. B. d. Ipanema
R. D. Ferreira
R. Bolivar
R. X. da Silveira
Cantagaio
COPACABANA
Copacabana Beach
ATLANTIC OCEAN
Morro do Cantagalo
R. Raul Pompéia
Av. NS de Copacabana
Av. Atlântica
R. F. Sá
G. Osorio
Av. R. Elisabeth
R. Joaquim Nabuco
Forte de Copacabana

- Folic **4**
- Gilson Martins **6**
- Kopenhagen **7**
- Modern Sound **3**
- Mr. Cat **5**
- O Boticário **2**
- Shopping Cassino Atlântico **1**

Botafogo & Humaitá Shopping

Rio de Janeiro **Shopping A to Z**

Antiques

★ Shopping Cassino Atlântico COPACABANA Not just one shop but a mall with 40 stores and galleries specializing in antiques and art. For more informal browsing, visit the weekly Antiques Fair (every Sat 10am–7pm) with 90 stalls exhibiting glassware, paintings, ceramics, silverware, jewelry, lamps, and more. *Av. Atlântica 4240.* ☎ *021/2523-8709. www.shoppingcassinoatlantico.com.br. AE, MC, V. Bus: 415. Map p 69.*

Arts & Crafts

★★ La Vereda SANTA TERESA La Vereda's impressive collection of rustic furniture, rugs, paintings, hammocks, and smaller items, such as hand-painted dolls, clothing, and jewelry, is perfect for browsing. *Rua Almirante Alexandrino 428.* ☎ *021/2507-0317. www.lavereda.art.br. AE, MC, V. Streetcar: Largo dos Guimarães. Map p 67.*

Parceria Carioca IPANEMA This store sells modern and contemporary arts and crafts from across Brazil that support several NGO projects and local artisans. *Rua Visconde de Pirajá 351, loja 215.* ☎ *021/2267-3222. www.parceriacarioca.com.br. AE, MC, V. Metrô: General Osório. Map p 68.*

★★ Trilhos Urbanos SANTA TERESA In the heart of Santa Teresa, Trilhos Urbanos stocks a wonderful selection of contemporary arts and crafts made by local artists. *Rua Almirante Alexandrino 402.* ☎ *021/2242-3632. AE, MC, V. Streetcar: Largo dos Guimarães. Map p 67.*

Beachwear

★★★ Blue Man IPANEMA My favorite swimwear store, Blue Man stands out for its bold prints and fabulous patterns. You can also mix and match sizes and styles, creating your own combination. *Rua Visconde de Pirajá 315, loja C.* ☎ *021/2247-4905. www.blueman.com.br. AE, MC, V. Bus: 415. Map p 68.*

★★ Lenny IPANEMA São Paulo designer Lenny Niemeyer easily won over Cariocas (and the rest of the world) with her elegant and flattering swimwear designs. *Rua Visconde de Pirajá 351, loja 114.* ☎ *021/2523-3796. www.lenny.com.br. AE, DC, MC, V. Metrô: General Osório. Map p 68.*

★★ Reserva IPANEMA Often forgotten when it comes to beachwear

Bath products for sale at Granado.

Prime Shopping Zones

Rio de Janeiro offers a delightful range of shopping opportunities. In the old downtown, you'll find inexpensive trinkets, souvenirs, clothing, and shoes lining the narrow pedestrian streets of **Rua da Alfândega** and **Rua Senhor dos Passos,** also known as the **SAARA.** Excellent bookstores and high-end retail stores are clustered around **Avenida Rio Branco** between the **Largo da Carioca** and **Avenida Presidente Vargas.** Copacabana is packed with shops and markets that cater specially to tourists. The **Avenida Atlântica** (around Rua Djalma Ulrich) boasts a nightly tourist market, perfect for picking up souvenirs such as Brazilian soccer shirts and inexpensive arts and crafts. The main thoroughfare, **Avenida N.S. de Copacabana,** between **Siqueira Campos** and **Santa Clara,** is lined with affordable clothing and shoe stores. Rio's hip, trendy, and beautiful crowd shops in tony **Ipanema.** The 6- to 8-block radius around **Rua Visconde de Pirajá** (btw. **Rua Maria Quitéria** and **Rua Ánibal de Medonça**) features many exclusive national and international designer stores. Farther west, in **Leblon,** the rich and famous flock to the luxurious mall **Shopping Leblon** (p 76) or shop along **Avenida Ataulfo de Paiva** and **Rua Dias Ferreira.**

Art for sale in tony Ipanema.

design, men will find plenty to choose from at Reserva, which boasts a collection of swimwear and shorts for hip urban men. *Rua Maria Quitéria 77. ☎ 021/2247-5980. www.usereserva.com.br. AE, DC, MC, V. Metrô: General Osório. Map p 68.*

★★ **Salinas** IPANEMA This store's elegant bikinis, one-piece bathing suits, and matching wraps also look fabulous away from the water. *Rua Visconde de Pirajá 547, loja 204. ☎ 021/2274-0644. www.salinas-rio.com.br. AE, MC, V. Bus: 415. Map p 68.*

Beauty Products

★★ **Granado** LEBLON Founded in 1870, Granado has gone from old-fashioned to hip with its lovely retro collection of bath, skin, and hair care products. *Rua General Artigas 470. ☎ 021/3231-6759. www.granado.com.br. AE, MC, V. Bus: 415. Map p 68.*

★ **O Boticário** COPACABANA Brazil's very own version of the Body Shop, O Boticário sells a complete line of affordable beauty and skincare products, made with natural extracts from Brazilian trees or plants. *Rua*

Santa Clara 70. ☎ 021/3208-1902. www.boticario.com.br. AE, MC, V. Metrô: Siqueira Campos. Map p 69.

Books

★★★ Livraria da Travessa IPANEMA One of Rio's best bookstores stocks an excellent selection of Brazilian literature translated into English, guidebooks, stunning coffee-table books on Rio and Brazil, as well as CDs and movies. *Rua Visconde de Piraja 572. ☎ 021/3205-9002. www.travessa.com.br. AE, DC, MC, V. Bus: 415. Map p 68.*

★ Livraria Prefácio BOTAFOGO As a writer, I love this pretty bookstore packed with art, literature, history, and poetry books. It also features a delightful bistro/cafe. *Rua Voluntários da Pátria 39. ☎ 021/2527-5699. www.prefaciolivrarias.com.br. MC, V. Metrô: Botafogo. Map p 69.*

★★ Saraiva Megastore CENTRO Practically a department store, Saraiva stocks dictionaries, language guides, travel guides, foreign magazines, CDs, DVDs, and stationery. *Rua do Ouvidor 98. ☎ 021/2507-9500. www.saraiva.com.br. AE, DC, MC, V. Metrô: Carioca. Map p 67.*

Carnaval & Costumes

Aidan Festa CENTRO Cariocas love getting dolled up for Carnaval, New Year's Eve, soccer games, the June Harvest Festival, you name it! This store has all the right accessories, party favors, decorations, and costumes for any event. *Rua da Alfândega 203. ☎ 021/2252-4781. www.aidanfesta.com.br. MC, V. Metrô: Uruguaiana. Map p 67.*

★★★ Casa Turuna CENTRO Founded almost 100 years ago, this store is *the* place where costume makers of the famous samba schools shop for materials and accessories. *Rua Senhor dos Passos 122. ☎ 021/2509-3908. AE, MC, V. Metrô: Uruguaiana. Map p 67.*

Designer Home Goods & Furnishings

★ Mercado Moderno CENTRO In the heart of old Rio, Mercado Moderno specializes in funky and eclectic vintage furniture and home decorations from the 1950s to the 1980s. *Rua do Lavradio 130. ☎ 021/2508-6083. www.memobrasil.com. MC, V. Bus: 170. Map p 67.*

Studio Grabowsky LEBLON This store's owners travel the world for keepsakes such as picture frames, glassware, throws, pillowcases, or vases. *Av. Ataulfo de Paiva 135, loja 218. ☎ 021/2529-2359. www.studiograbowsky.com.br. AE, MC, V. Bus: 415. Map p 68.*

Fashion & Accessories

C&A BOTAFOGO Top off your vacation wardrobe with affordable casual wear from this large department store. *Rua Voluntários da Pátria 222. ☎ 021/2101-0047. www.cea.com.br. AE, MC, V. Metrô: Botafogo. Map p 69.*

Costume accessories at Casa Turuna.

★★ Caravana Holliday LEBLON This tiny store is packed with hip hand-painted tunics from India, funky T-shirts designed by a tattoo artist, and lovely scarves. *Rua Aristides Espinola 121. ☎ 021/2294-3998. MC, V. Bus: 415. Map p 68.*

The colorful sign for Lilica & Tigor.

Eliane Carvalho LEBLON The lovely collection here includes hats for every occasion and other head/hair accessories such as turbans, scarves, and pins. *Rua Dia Ferreira 242. ☎ 021/2540-5438. AE, MC, V. Bus: 415. Map p 68.*

★★ Farm IPANEMA This hip store gives off a fun Carioca vibe with its collection of colorful women's clothing in gorgeous prints. *Rua Visconde de Pirajá 365. ☎ 021/2522-0023. www.farmrio.com.br. AE, MC, V. Metrô: General Osório. Map p 68.*

★★★ Folic COPACABANA Folic's collection can best be described as Sex and the City meets Banana Republic, with stylish and elegant clothes for confident women over 30. *Av. N.S. de Copacabana 690. ☎ 021/2549-1520. www.folic.com.br. AE, MC, V. Metrô: Siqueira Campos. Map p 69.*

★ Hering CENTRO This is the best known Brazilian brand of basic T-shirts, jeans, shorts, and tank tops made from high-quality cotton. *Rua Uruguaiana 78. ☎ 021/2224-3831. www.hering.com.br. AE, MC, V. Metrô: Carioca. Map p 67.*

★★ kids Lilica & Tigor IPANEMA I don't have kids, but I still can't resist a peek at this adorable and trendy collection for girls and boys, ages 0 to 10. *Rua Visconde de Pirajá 221. ☎ 021/2522-2080. MC, V. Metrô: General Osório. Map p 68.*

★★ Siberian BOTAFOGO Although Siberian sells clothes for men and women, it's the collection of smart, fashionable, and affordable men's wear here that's worth the trek. *Rua Lauro Müller 116 (Riosul Shopping Center). ☎ 021/2543-2881. www.siberian.com.br. AE, MC, V. Metrô: Cardeal Arcoverde, free shuttle bus to Riosul. Map p 69.*

Gifts & Souvenirs

★★ kids Artimanha HUMAITA This little store is packed with creative and educational toys such as old-fashioned stacking blocks, wooden toys, puzzles, and adorable dolls and puppets. *Rua Capitão Salomão 14. www.artimanha.art.br. ☎ 021/2535-4946. MC, V. Bus: 170. Map p 69.*

Daqui LEBLON The two sisters who run Daqui pack their tiny store with great gift ideas such as necklaces, ceramics, purses, clothing, and local artwork. *Av. Ataulfo de Paiva 1174. ☎ 021/2529-8576. www.daquidobrasil.com. AE, DC, MC, V. Bus: 415. Map p 68.*

★★★ Gilson Martins COPACABANA Using images of the Brazilian flag, stylized drawings of Christ the Redeemer, and other Rio icons, Martins has created a fun and colorful line of wallets, purses, bags, and backpacks. *Rua Figueiredo Magalhães 304. ☎ 021/3816-0552. www.gilsonmartins.com.br. AE, MC, V. Metrô: Siqueira Campos. Map p 69.*

Mutações HUMAITA This small eco-design store is crammed with wonderful—and socially responsible—gifts. You'll find embroidered pillowcases, woven baskets, bookmarks, travel cases, purses, placemats, and more, all made with natural or recycled materials. ***Largo dos Leões 81. ☎ 021/2537-9324. MC, V. Bus: 170. Map p 69.***

★ **São Jorge** CENTRO One of Brazil's most popular and beloved saints, dragon-slaying São Jorge (St. George), has his own gift shop that sells T-shirts, mugs, magnets, rosaries, candles, and more. ***Rua da Alfândega 383. ☎ 021/2221-9661. No credit cards. Metrô: Uruguaiana. Map p 67.***

Gourmet Food & Wine

★★ **Cobal de Humaitá** HUMAITA This market hall features several stalls and small stores selling fresh fruit and vegetables, pastries, and deli goods such as cheese, cold cuts, bread, antipasto, and wines. ***Btw. Rua Voluntários da Pátria and Rua São Clemente, across from Rua Capitão Salomão and the Largo dos Leões. Bus: 170. Map p 69.***

★★ **Garcia & Rodrigues** LEBLON A "candy store" for adults, Garcia & Rodrigues is one of the best gourmet stores in Rio, housing a patisserie, bakery, wine cellar, deli, and rotisserie. ***Av. Ataulfo de Paiva 1251. ☎ 021/2512-8188. www.garciaerodrigues.com.br. AE, MC, V. Bus: 415. Map p 68.***

★★★ **Kopenhagen** COPACABANA Chocolate fans will love the tropical flavors, such as the passion fruit or coconut-filled chocolates, at Brazil's premier chocolate store. ***Rua Figueiredo de Magalhães 131. ☎ 021/2257-3186. www.kopenhagen.com.br. AE, MC, V. Metrô: Sigueira Campos. Map p 69.***

Zona Sul LEBLON This grocery store features several excellent deli sections, wines, cheeses, a bakery, and more. Open 24 hours

Wallets by Gilson Martins (p 73).

(Mon–Sat), it's also perfect for last-minute souvenirs such as Brazilian coffee, sweets, or a bottle of *cachaça* (sugar cane brandy). ***Rua Dias Ferreira 290. ☎ 021/2259-4747. www.zonasul.com.br. AE, MC, V. Bus: 415. Map p 68.***

Jewelry

Amsterdam Sauer IPANEMA One of Brazil's best known jewelers, Amsterdam Sauer creates exquisite pieces with Brazilian semi-precious and precious gem stones. ***Rua Visconde de Pirajá 484. ☎ 021/2279-6237. www.amsterdamsauer.com.br. AE, DC, MC, V. Bus: 415. Map p 68.***

★ **Antonio Bernardo** IPANEMA Award-winning designer Antonio Bernardo is known for his contemporary designs featuring clean, simple lines and the use of white, yellow, and red gold. ***Rua Garcia D`Ávila 121. ☎ 021/2512-7204. www.antoniobernardo.com.br. AE, DC, MC, V. Bus: 415. Map p 68.***

★★ **H. Stern** IPANEMA Brazil's other famous jeweler, H. Stern has invested in some beautiful contemporary designs, in addition to its classic gem stone collection. ***Rua Visconde de Pirajá 490. ☎ 021/2274-3447.***

www.hstern.com.br. AE, DC, MC, V. Bus: 415. Map p 68.

★★ Silvia Blumberg IPANEMA Silvia Blumberg's work proves that quality and originality don't have to cost a fortune. In addition to precious metals and stones, she also uses natural materials such as wood or fibers in her pieces. *Rua Visconde de Pirajá 330, loja 214. ☎ 021/2513-4181. www.silviablumberg.com.br. AE, MC, V. Bus: 415. Map p 68.*

Jewelry on display at Silvia Blumberg.

Music

★★ Acústica Perfeita CENTRO The various handheld rhythmic instruments, tambourines, small drums, or even *cavaquinhos* (4-string mandolins) sold here make great gifts for music lovers. *Rua da Carioca 43. ☎ 021/2222-7525. www.acusticaperfeita.com.br. AE, DC, MC, V. Metrô: Carioca. Map p 67.*

★★★ Modern Sound COPACABANA This store boasts one of the best music collections in the city, including imported CDs and vinyl. The in-store Allegro Bistrô regularly hosts free concerts. *Rua Barata Ribeiro 502. ☎ 021/2548-5005. www.modernsound.com.br. AE, DC, MC, V. Metrô: Siqueira Campos. Map p 69.*

Some of the delicious chocolates at Kopenhagen.

★★★ Toca do Vinicius IPANEMA This little shrine to bossa nova and its iconic songwriter Vinicius de Moraes sells CDs, LPs, books, sheet music, songbooks, and souvenirs. *Rua Vinicius de Moraes 129. ☎ 021/2247-5227. AE, DC, MC, V. Metrô: General Osório. Map p 68.*

Shoes

★ Havaianas CENTRO I've never shopped here without buying at least one pair of *Havaiana* flip-flops. You can choose from more than 50 different styles, designs, and colors, for men, women, kids, and babies. *Rua da Alfândega 183. ☎ 021/2507-3107. MC, V. Metrô: Uruguaiana. Map p 67.*

kids Merokids CENTRO A whole store packed with fun footwear for little ones. Shop for cute baby flip-flops, adorable rubber boots, or summer sandals for girls and boys. *Rua da Alfândega 202. ☎ 021/2224-1601. AE, MC, V. Metrô: Uruguaiana. Map p 67.*

★★ Mr. Cat COPACABANA Mr. Cat sells beautiful casual footwear and dress shoes. The elegant and classic collection changes frequently. *Av. N.S. de Copacabana 680. ☎ 021/3208-4704. www.mrcat.com.br. AE, MC, V. Metrô: Siqueira Campos. Map p 69.*

A pair of iconic Havaianas (p 75).

★★ Sarah Chofakian LEBLON These shoes are made to be seen! Brazilian designer Sarah Chofakian creates only 200 models a year. Her small collection is feminine, elegant, and timeless, and a touch retro. *Rua Afrânio de Melo Franco 290, shop 305, 3rd floor (inside Shopping Leblon).* ☎ *021/2512-0026. www.sarahchofakian.com.br. AE, MC, V. Bus: 415. Map p 68.*

Shopping Centers

★ Botafogo Praia Shopping BOTAFOGO This mall is not so big that you'll get lost, and not so small that you'll get bored. The restaurants on the top floor have fabulous views of Sugarloaf and Guanabara Bay. *Praia de Botafogo 400.* ☎ *021/3171-9872. www.botafogopraiashopping.com.br. AE, DC, MC, V. Metrô: Botafogo. Map p 69.*

★★ Rio Design LEBLON Rio Design is mostly filled with women's fashion stores and a few excellent restaurants and cafes. Pick up the latest in Brazilian music at the stand of record label Biscoito Fino (on the ground flood by the escalator). *Av. Ataulfo de Paiva 270.* ☎ *021/3206-9110. AE, DC, MC, V. www.riodesign.com.br. Bus: 415. Map p 68.*

★★★ Riosul BOTAFOGO Rio's oldest mall is centrally located and offers a great mix of inexpensive clothing stores as well as more upscale designers and brand names. *Rua Lauro Müller 116.* ☎ *021/2122-8070. AE, DC, MC, V. www.riosul.com.br. Metrô: Cardeal Arcoverde, then free shuttle bus. Map p 69.*

★★★ Shopping Leblon LEBLON Rio's newest mall offers one of the most upscale shopping experiences in town—great for spotting celebrities and checking the latest fashion trends. *Rua Afrânio de Melo Franco 290.* ☎ *021/3138-8000. www.shoppingleblon.com.br. AE, DC, MC, V. Bus: 415. Map p 68.* ●

Outdoor Markets

Rio boasts several fun street markets for *al fresco* shopping. A popular market for touristy souvenirs (think key chains, bags, and sarongs) is held from Monday to Saturday from 6pm to midnight on the **Avenida Atlântica** in Copacabana (in front of the Rio Othon Hotel). Ipanema hosts a large craft fair on Sundays (9am–6pm), the **Feira Hippie** at Praça General Osório. This market draws both tourists and locals looking for fun gift ideas, colorful crafts, or interesting artwork. You will also find numerous produce and food fairs throughout the city from 6am to 2pm; these are a great opportunity to mingle with locals, snap photos, and sample tropical fruit and snacks. Popular locations include **Praça General Osório** in Ipanema (Tues), **Rua Viveiros de Castro** in Copacabana (Thurs), **Rua Gustavo Sampaio** in Leme (Fri), and **Rua da Glória** in Glória (Sun).

5 The Great Outdoors

Rio's Best **Beaches**

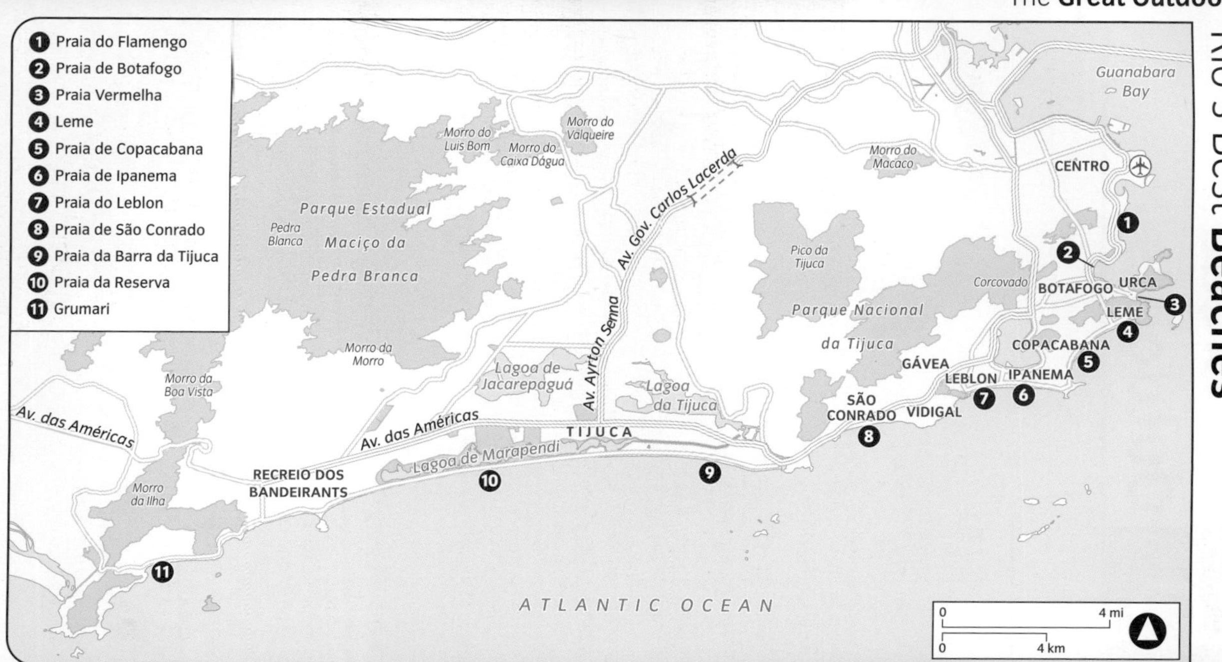

Previous page: Soaring high above Rio de Janeiro.

A visit to Rio wouldn't be complete without experiencing the Carioca beach lifestyle. The city's beaches are much more than just a place to go for a swim or a tan. Day or night, they are an important part of the Rio lifestyle, where people relax, exercise, hang out with friends or family, or gather for major celebrations, such as New Year's or concerts. Make sure you go beyond Copacabana and Ipanema; there are at least a dozen beaches within the city, each with its own vibe and crowd. **START: Metrô to Flamengo.**

❶ ★★★ kids **Praia do Flamengo.** The most popular beach on Guanabara Bay is set in the heart of Parque do Flamengo (p 88), one of the largest green spaces in the city. The beautiful, wide beach boasts fabulous views of Sugarloaf and Niteroi, the city across the bay. Locals flock here to enjoy the excellent sports and recreational facilities, including bike paths, children's playgrounds, beach volleyball, a skateboard park, tennis courts, basketball courts, and soccer fields. The most popular day is Sunday, when the road that parallels the park is closed to traffic. Although the city has embarked on a major clean-up effort, the water in the bay is still polluted and not recommended for swimming. ***Praia do Flamengo, btw. Rua Silveira Martins and Rua Cruz Lima. Metrô: Catete, Largo do Machado, or Flamengo.***

❷ ★ **Praia de Botafogo.** Except for a few people playing soccer, you will rarely see any sunbathers on the white sand of this small bay. There are no facilities, and the water is polluted. What makes it worth a stop is its perfect postcard views of Sugarloaf. ***Praia de Botafogo, btw. Rua Marques de Abrantes and Rua São Clemente. Metrô: Botafogo.***

❸ ★★★ **Praia Vermelha.** This is the first of a string of ocean beaches that line Rio's coast. Tucked away in a cove at the foot of Sugarloaf Mountain, this small strip of beach has almost no waves and is a favorite destination for families with small children. Its slightly red sand gives it the name Praia Vermelha (red beach). ***Praça General Tibúrcio (at the end of Av. Pasteu) in Urca. Bus: 512.***

❹ ★★ **Leme.** Although technically part of Copacabana, the little cul-de-sac between Avenida Princesa Isabel and the Leme Fort is known as Leme and has quite a different feel from its expansive and famous neighbor. You will usually find more locals than tourists here, and it's rarely ever as packed and hectic as Copacabana Beach. The walkway along the rock is a popular fishing spot and offers sweeping views of Copacabana. ***Av. Atlantica, btw. Av. Princesa Isabel and Praça Alm. Julio de Noronha, Leme. Metrô: Cardeal Arcoverde.***

An "Olympic" sand castle on Copacabana Beach.

5 ★★★ kids **Praia de Copacabana.** Rio's most happening beach offers 6.4km (4 miles) of glorious white sand. Its glory days were in the 1930s and 1940s; several elegant Art Deco buildings that line the waterfront attest to this. The signature wavy black-and-white mosaic sidewalk designed by Roberto Burle Marx was added much later, in the 1970s. In the last few decades, Copacabana lost some of its glamour to more upscale neighbors Ipanema and Leblon, but almost any day of the year, locals and tourists still vie for a good spot close to the water here. It's always fun to watch a game of beach soccer or volleyball, or *futevolei,* a combination of the two, where players aren't allowed to touch the ball with their hands. After sunset, the action continues as people come out for a walk or jog along the boulevard, or meet friends for a drink at one of many beachside kiosks. Copacabana is also the city's prime outdoor stage, regularly hosting free events such as concerts and sports tournaments, as well as Rio's largest New Year's celebration—as many as two million people dressed in white pack this sand to ring in the New Year. ***Av. Atlantica, btw. Av. Princesa Isabel and Rua Joaquim Nabuco. Metrô: Cardeal Arcoverde, Siqueira Campos, or Cantagalo.***

6 ★★★ **Praia de Ipanema.** Trendy and hip Cariocas prefer 2km (1¼-mile) Ipanema, the perfect place for beautiful-people-watching. Each "tribe" that comes here to play has its favorite section of sand. The rocks of **Arpoador** are the favorite hangout for surfers. Gay men strut their buff physiques at "Farme," around Rua Farme de Amoedo. *Posto* 9 (lifeguard station 9) is the land of the original Girl from Ipanema, where a hip, alternative crowd gathers. ***Av. Vieira Souto, btw. Rua Teixeira de Melo and Rua Henrique Dumont. Metrô: General Osório.***

7 ★★★ kids **Praia do Leblon.** Once you cross the canal, known as Jardim de Alá (Alah's garden), that connects the lagoon to the sea,

Beach Dos and Don'ts

You don't need to bring much to enjoy a day at the beach. Leave your valuables at your hotel, and just bring a towel, plenty of sunscreen, sunglasses, and some cash to rent a couple of chairs and a sun umbrella, and to buy some mineral water or other refreshments. There are concrete lifeguard stations at regular intervals along the main beaches, from Flamengo to Barra da Tijuca. In addition to first-aid services, these stations (*postos* in Portuguese) offer washrooms and shower facilities. Even if you're a good swimmer, make sure to respect the warning signs; don't underestimate the waves and currents. The waterfront is patrolled by helicopters that carry out fast and effective water rescues, but that is one ride you don't want to take. On Sundays and holidays, the main road along the waterfront (Flamengo, Copacabana, Ipanema, and Leblon) is closed to traffic, giving pedestrians plenty of space to walk, bike, or rollerblade.

Biking along Ipanema Beach.

Ipanema becomes Leblon. Brazilian celebrities who live in this upscale neighborhood are often spotted here. Less hectic than Ipanema, this wide stretch of flat strand is popular with families; a special children's playground (Baixo baby) offers toys and a safe play area for babies and toddlers (near *Posto* 10). ***Av. Delfim Moreira, btw. Rua Afrânio de Melo and Rua Aristides Espínola. Bus: 175.***

8 ★ **Praia de São Conrado.** A narrow strip of beach between Leblon and Barra, São Conrado is best known as the landing pad for hang gliders taking off from the platform at Pedra Bonita (p 85). ***Av. Prefeito Mendes de Morais. Bus: 175.***

9 ★★ **Praia da Barra da Tijuca.** Even on hot summer days, Rio's longest beach (15km/9⅓ miles) can be totally packed. Known as Barra, it draws mainly residents from Rio's newer upscale suburb of Barra da Tijuca. Strong currents and large waves attract surfers but can be treacherous for swimmers. The first stretch, along Avenida do Pepê, is known as Praia do Pepê, a lively meeting point for the young and beautiful. ***Av. Sernambetiba, Barra da Tijica. Bus: 175.***

10 ★★ **Praia da Reserva (Recreio dos Bandeirantes).** To get away from the crowds, continue beyond Barra da Tijuca to Praia da Reserva. This protected nature reserve is popular with surfers and has fluffy white sand and natural dunes. Devoid of any nearby construction, it has a much more secluded feel, but also provides fewer services than the other beaches. ***Av. Sernambetiba, btw. Av. Ayrton Senna and Av. do Contorno. Car recommended.***

11 ★★★ **Grumari.** One of the last beaches in the municipality of Rio is also one of the prettiest; Grumari is entirely inside an environmental protection area and framed by green hills. To avoid crowds, it's best to visit this small beach on weekdays; be careful with the strong undertow here. Just before you reach Grumari, you will see a sign for **Praia do Abricó,** a secluded cove with Rio's only nudist beach, accessible via a short trail. ***Estrada da Guanabara (approx. 40km/25 miles) from Copacabana. Car recommended.***

Surfing by Arpoador, one of the city's best surf spots.

Parque **Nacional da Tijuca**

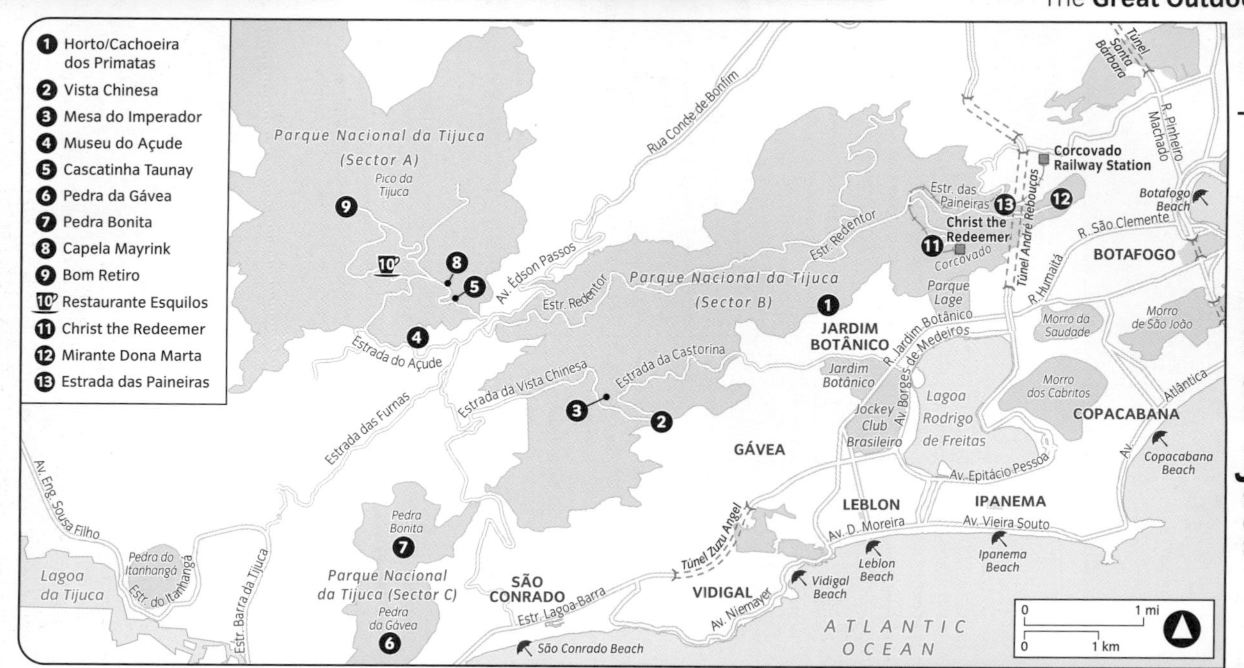
1 Horto/Cachoeira dos Primatas
2 Vista Chinesa
3 Mesa do Imperador
4 Museu do Açude
5 Cascatinha Taunay
6 Pedra da Gávea
7 Pedra Bonita
8 Capela Mayrink
9 Bom Retiro
10 Restaurante Esquilos
11 Christ the Redeemer
12 Mirante Dona Marta
13 Estrada das Paineiras
Parque Nacional da Tijuca (Sector A)
Pico da Tijuca
Parque Nacional da Tijuca (Sector B)
Parque Nacional da Tijuca (Sector C)
Pedra Bonita
Pedra da Gávea
Rua Conde de Bonfim
Av. Édson Passos
Estr. Redentor
Estrada do Açude
Estrada das Furnas
Estrada da Vista Chinesa
Estrada da Castorina
Estr. das Paineiras
Christ the Redeemer
Corcovado
Corcovado Railway Station
Túnel André Rebouças
Túnel Santa Bárbara
R. Pinheiro Machado
Botafogo Beach
R. São Clemente
BOTAFOGO
R. Humaitá
Morro de São João
Morro da Saudade
Morro dos Cabritos
Parque Lage
JARDIM BOTÂNICO
R. Jardim Botânico
Av. Borges de Medeiros
Jardim Botânico
Jockey Club Brasileiro
Lagoa Rodrigo de Freitas
COPACABANA
Av. Atlântica
Copacabana Beach
Av. Epitácio Pessoa
GÁVEA
LEBLON
IPANEMA
Av. Vieira Souto
Av. D. Moreira
Ipanema Beach
Leblon Beach
Vidigal Beach
Túnel Zuzu Angel
VIDIGAL
Av. Niemayer
SÃO CONRADO
Estr. Lagoa-Barra
São Conrado Beach
ATLANTIC OCEAN
Av. Eng. Sousa Filho
Pedra do Itanhangá
Estr. do Itanhangá
Lagoa da Tijuca
Estr. Barra da Tijuca
0
1 mi
0
1 km

The largest urban park in the world, the Parque Nacional da Tijuca boasts 3,500 hectares (86,487 acres) of Atlantic rainforest in the heart of Rio de Janeiro. The park is divided into several regions, including the Floresta da Tijuca, Corcovado, Paineiras, Pedra Bonita, and Pedra da Gávea. Its most visited attraction is the statue of Christ the Redeemer, atop Corcovado Mountain, but the park offers many other attractions, such as museums, restaurants, lookouts, picnic and leisure areas, waterfalls, and nature trails. Unfortunately, trails are not set up for independent hikers; to hike the park, it's best to hire a nature guide. However, a large number of the park's attractions are quite accessible by taxi, car, or a sightseeing tour, because the park is linked to the neighborhoods of Santa Teresa, Jardim Botânico, and Barra da Tijuca by roads. **START: Rua Pacheco Leão, Jardim Botânico.**

1 ★ Horto/Cachoeira dos Primatas. One of the most accessible waterfalls in Rio is in Horto, just beyond Jardim Botânico, on your way into the Parque Nacional da Tijuca. The trail to the waterfalls starts at the end of Rua Sara Vilela. A 30-minute hike takes you to the 20m (66-ft.) Cachoeira dos Primatas, where you can swim in the clear pools and enjoy fabulous views of the Lagoa Rodrigo de Freitas in the Zona Sul. Just be careful on the slippery rocks. *Rua Sara Vilela, Horto. Bus: 409.*

2 ★★★ Vista Chinesa. An exotic pavilion with dragon heads marks the Chinese Lookout (Vista Chinesa) that offers sweeping views of the coastline, Lagoa, and Sugarloaf. The oriental monument is a tribute to the Chinese workers who were initially brought to Brazil in the 19th century to cultivate tea and rice, but were later put to work to construct roads in the park. *Estrada da Vista Chinesa s/n. Taxi recommended.*

3 ★★ Mesa do Imperador. The Emperor's Table, a stone table on a terrace flanked by two palm trees, was a favorite picnic spot of D. Pedro I. At an elevation of 487m (1,598 ft.), it provided a cool refuge from the city heat. *Estrada da Vista Chinesa s/n. Taxi recommended.*

The Vista Chinesa boasts beautiful views of Rio.

The Park's Past & Present

Today's lush Parque Nacional da Tijuca is the result of a major reforestation undertaken 150 years ago to protect the city's source of drinking water and is all that remains of the dense Atlantic rainforest that once surrounded Rio. Deforestation in the area that encompasses the national park first began in the 17th century to clear land for sugarcane plantations, followed by coffee plantations in the 18th and 19th centuries. As the city's population grew, the nearby forest became an important supplier of timber and firewood. However, the intense clear cutting and monoculture resulted in chronic drought.

Parque Nacional da Tijuca.

In 1861, Dom Pedro II issued a decree that expropriated land from coffee barons and created the Tijuca Forest to reverse the staggering environmental damage. Pedro II appointed Major Manoel Gomes Archer to supervise this unprecedented reforestation effort. Using primarily native species, Archer, assistant Thomas Nogueira da Gama, and as few as six slaves, hand planted over 70,000 trees in 12 years, with a more than 80% survival rate. Later, the Baron of Escragnolle continued these efforts, also building roads and leisure areas. Before the end of the 19th century, the area was successfully reforested with over 100,000 trees.

From 1943 to 1946, industrialist and art collector Raymundo Ottoni de Castro Maya hired architect Vladimir Alves de Souza and landscape architect Roberto Burle Marx to further develop the leisure areas in the park, adding more roads, recreational facilities, and restaurants. In 1961, the forest was designated a national park. Today, Tijuca Forest stands as the world's first successful major urban reforestation project and proves man's ability to reclaim severely damaged ecosystems and earth's ability to return barren land to a fertile state.

4 ★★★ Museu do Açude. Starting in 1913, this house served as the residence of Raymundo Castro Maya, a wealthy industrialist and art collector who was charged with restoring and expanding Tijuca

Park facilities. Today his residence houses a lovely museum filled with exquisite art, including 17th- and 18th-century Portuguese tile collections, ceramics, Asian sculptures and artwork, 19th-century European furniture, crystal, and silverware, and modern Brazilian art. ⌚ *45 min. Estrada do Açude 764, Alto da Boa Vista.* ☎ *021/2492-5443. www.museuscastromaya.com.br. Admission R$5 (free on Thurs). Wed–Mon 11am–5pm. Bus: 225.*

Taking a soak in one of Tijuca Park's waterfalls.

5 ★★ kids **Cascatinha Taunay.** This 35m-high (115-ft.) waterfall is named after French painter Nicolas Antoine Taunay, who was one of the first to purchase an estate here, soon followed by other French aristocrats who settled in the area to grow coffee. The former family estate was torn down to make room for the restaurant. Note the lovely map of Tijuca Forest in Portuguese tile and the marble basin; both were added by Castro Maya in 1944. *Estrada da Cascatinha 850, 500m (1,640 ft.) beyond the park gate (enter off Rua Boa Vista).*

6 ★★★ **Pedra da Gávea.** After the Corcovado and Pão de Açucar, this impressive 824m (2,703-ft.) monolith is the most distinctive rock formation visible from many different areas in the city. The 3-hour hike to the top is a strenuous affair, but you will be rewarded with spectacular views of the western and southern regions of Rio and the Floresta da Tijuca. Along the steepest stretch, hikers are roped for additional security.

7 ★★★ **Pedra Bonita.** Most visitors come to this appropriately named rock face (*bonita* means beautiful) to take off on an exhilarating hang gliding flight. But from the parking lot of the ramp, it is just a 30-minute hike to reach the very top of 696m-tall (2,283-ft.) Pedra Bonita,

The view from Pedra Bonita.

which offers spectacular land-based views of the Parque da Tijuca and the southern beach areas.

8 ★★ **Capela Mayrink.** Built in 1850, this cute pink chapel was allowed to remain in the park after the imperial expropriation expelled most of its occupants. In 1943 it underwent a major restoration; the landscaping was done by Burle Marx, and Master Portinari painted three interior panels. In 2001, the original paintings were moved to the Museu de Belas Artes (p 15) and replaced by high-quality photo reproductions. ***Estrada do Imperador s/n.***

9 ★★ kids **Bom Retiro.** At the end of the Estrada Visconde do Bom Retiro, you come to Bom Retiro, a pleasant area with picnic tables and various playgrounds. At 650m high (2,133 ft.), this is the highest point in the park accessible by a paved road; even on hot summer days, the air up here will be cool and pleasant. This is also the starting point of trails to Morro do Archer, Cocanha, Taquara, Bico do Papagaio, and Pico da Tijuca, the highest peak in the park at 1,030m (3,379 ft.). ***Estrada Visc. do Bom Retiro s/n.***

10 **Restaurante Esquilos.** This romantic restaurant in the heart of the rainforest is set on the former estate of D'Escragnolle, the park's second administrator, who continued Archer's reforestation. The kitchen serves up retro classics such as fondue and tournedos, as well as traditional Brazilian dishes, including a hearty *feijoada* lunch on weekends. ***Estrada Barão D'Escragnolle s/n.*** ☎ ***021/2492-2197. www.osesquilos.com.br. $$.***

11 ★★★ **Christ the Redeemer.** In addition to the train from Cosme Velho station, the park's most famous monument, perched atop Corcovado Mountain, can also be accessed via one of the main roads through Tijuca Park. However, private cars are not allowed to drive all the way to the bottom of the viewing platform, but have to park at Paineiras (watch for the signs to Paineiras-Corcovado). From here, a shuttle service transports visitors to the monument. Instead, I highly recommend taking the train (p 13); the ride is truly scenic. ***Estrada do Redentor s/n.***

Christ the Redeemer looming over Rio.

Hiking the Park

The Parque da Tijuca offers fabulous hiking opportunities, but since most trails are poorly marked and hard to access, I recommend hiring a nature guide through **Riohiking** (☎ 021/2552-9204 or 021/9721-0594; www.riohiking.com.br; R$120–R$180 for a day tour). The park's signature hikes are up to **Pedra da Gavea** (see above) and **Pedra Bonita** (see above). Other top hikes include those to **Pico da Tijcua,** the highest point in the Floresta da Tijuca, which looks out over the forest and the northern part of the city; **Pedra do Conde,** which, except for the short, steep final stretch, is a relatively moderate hike that offers fabulous views of the Pico da Tijuca; and **Pico do Papagaio,** a hike to the second highest peak in the Parque da Tijuca, which takes you to an amazing lookout with panoramic views of the northern and southern parts of Rio. Many of the animals who call this park home are most active at dawn or dusk, but keep your eyes peeled for tamarin monkeys; three-toed sloths; anteaters; coatis (a raccoonlike mammal); hummingbirds; parakeets; toucans; various reptiles, such as coral snakes and iguanas; and amphibians like tree frogs.

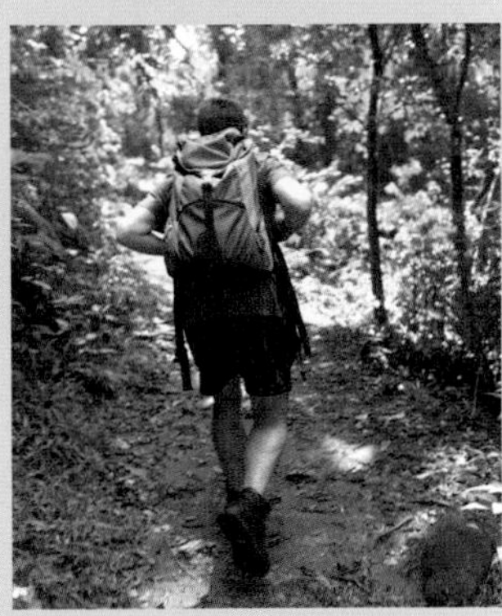

Hiking in Tijuca forest.

12 ★★★ **Mirante Dona Marta.** Although not as high as Corcovado, this lookout offers spectacular views for free. From this vantage point at 400m/1,312 ft. (higher than Sugarloaf Mountain), you can spot Guanabara Bay, Sugarloaf, Botafogo, and the Corcovado. From the nearby helipad you can see all the way to the Lagoa and southern beach neighborhoods. *Estrada do Mirante D. Marta s/n. Taxi recommended.*

13 ★★ **Estrada das Paineiras.** Descending towards Santa Teresa/ Cosme Velho, you reach the Estrada das Paineiras—a drive along this windy mountain road is the perfect way to experience the forest without getting your shoes dirty. This stretch of road boasts fabulous views and several waterfalls where you can take a refreshing (or bone-chilling, depending on your level of cold tolerance) shower. On Sundays, when the main section is closed for traffic, Cariocas flock here to escape the heat and enjoy a leisurely stroll in the forest. *Estrada das Paineiras s/n. Taxi recommended.*

Parque do Flamengo

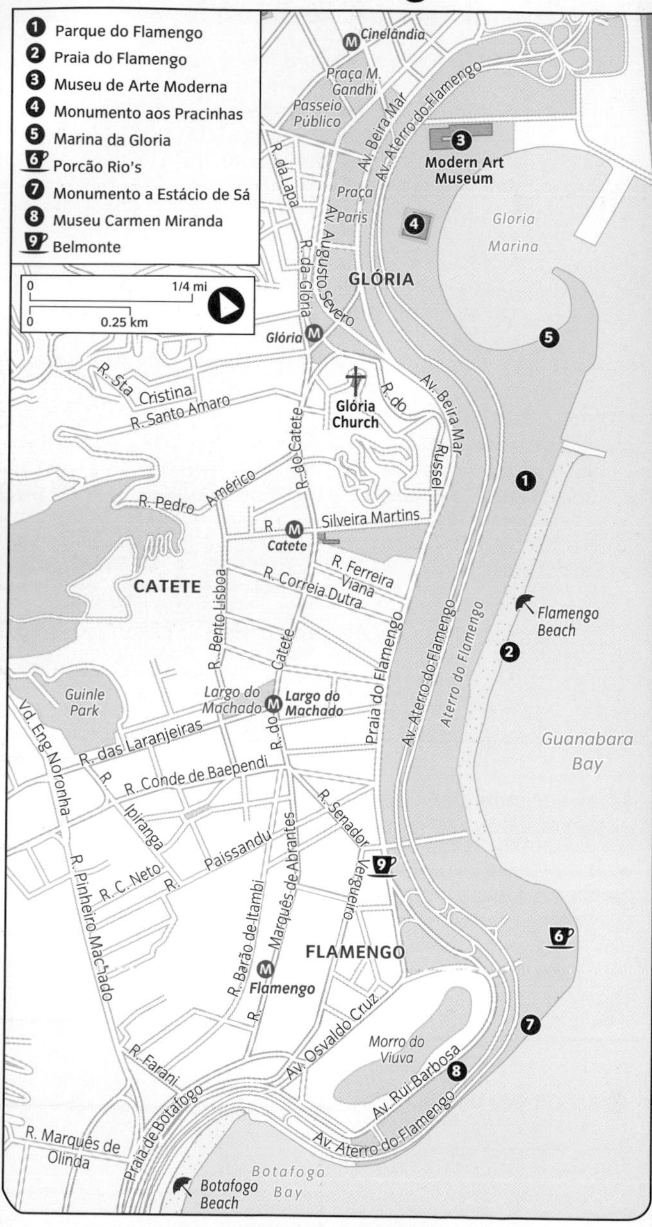
1 Parque do Flamengo
2 Praia do Flamengo
3 Museu de Arte Moderna
4 Monumento aos Pracinhas
5 Marina da Gloria
6 Porcão Rio's
7 Monumento a Estácio de Sá
8 Museu Carmen Miranda
9 Belmonte
0
1/4 mi
0
0.25 km
Cinelândia
Praça M. Gandhi
Passeio Público
Av. Beira Mar
Av. Aterro do Flamengo
R. da Lapa
Modern Art Museum
Praça Paris
Av. Augusto Severo
R. da Glória
Gloria Marina
GLÓRIA
Glória
R. Sta Cristina
R. Santo Amaro
Glória Church
R. do Russel
Av. Beira Mar
R. do Catete
R. Pedro Américo
R. Silveira Martins
Catete
R. Ferreira Viana
R. Correia Dutra
CATETE
R. Bento Lisboa
Praia do Flamengo
Av. Aterro-do-Flamengo
Aterro do Flamengo
Flamengo Beach
Guinle Park
Largo do Machado
Vd. Eng Noronha
R. das Laranjeiras
R. Conde de Baependi
R. Ipiranga
R. Senador Vergueiro
Guanabara Bay
R. Paissandu
R. C. Neto
R. Pinheiro Machado
R. Barão de Itambi
R. Marquês de Abrantes
FLAMENGO
Flamengo
Av. Osvaldo Cruz
Morro do Viuva
Av. Rui Barbosa
R. Farani
Praia de Botafogo
R. Marquês de Olinda
Av. Aterro do Flamengo
Botafogo Bay
Botafogo Beach

Flamengo is best known for its impressive waterfront park, a 7km (4⅓ miles) green belt that runs from Santos Dumont airport to Botafogo Bay. The park can be visited any day of the week, during daylight hours. The stretch between the Museu de Arte Moderna and the Marina da Glória is quite deserted during the week and is best visited on weekends. **START: Overpasses or underpasses to the park can be found at regular intervals. The main beach area runs approximately between Rua Silveira Martins and Rua Barão do Flamengo.**

Kids diving at Flamengo Beach.

1 ★★★ kids **Parque do Flamengo.** Parque do Flamengo, also known as the Aterro do Flamengo, or simply Aterro, is one of the city's most popular waterfront leisure areas. A significant portion of the 7km-long (4⅓-mile) green belt is built on landfill (*aterro* in Portuguese), using rubble from the demolished Santo Antonio hill in downtown Rio. Inaugurated in 1965, the park was designed by Brazil's renowned landscape architect Roberto Burle Marx (see below). You can often spot large flocks of *maitacas* (green parrots); just listen for their unmistakable loud croaky screams. The wide freeway that parallels the Aterro is closed to traffic on Sundays and holidays, giving visitors even more space to walk or bike. Although the park doesn't have a visitor center or main entrance, the heart of the Aterro is Praia de Flamengo's beach with its bike trails, kiosks and fabulous views. The best access is via Rua Dois de Dezembro (Metrô: Largo do Machado) or Rua Silveira Martins (Metrô: Catete). *2–3 hr. Best during daylight hours.*

2 ★★★ kids **Praia do Flamengo.** Flamengo Beach and its adjacent recreation facilities are the most popular part of the park, especially the soccer fields. It's not unusual to see people playing here at midnight. Although the water quality has improved significantly, swimming is not recommended. Pause for a moment when you reach the wooden deck at the south end of the beach—the stream that runs below your feet is the Carioca River flowing into the bay. Walk just around the point for the best views of Sugarloaf. I love coming here an hour or two before sunset to enjoy the golden and pink light the sun casts on the beach's granite stone. ⌚ *At least 1 hr. Best during daylight hours. On Sun the expressway along the park is closed to traffic. Metrô: Flamengo or Glória.*

❸ ★★ **Museu de Arte Moderna.** Rio's premier modern art museum also features a design store, bookstore, cafe, and high-end restaurant. The museum was built well before the park, and its gardens are an opportunity to see how Burle Marx uses plants and stones to "paint" a landscape. When the park was completed, Burle Marx designed a transition garden to integrate the two areas. The best way to appreciate his drawings and design is from the museum's terrace. The overhead view will allow you to notice the subtle colors, relief differences, and patterns created by the grassy lawns and mosaics, framed by slender palm trees. ⌚ *30 min. to visit garden.*

❹ ★ **Monumento aos Pracinhas.** This striking concrete monument was inaugurated in 1960 in memory of the Brazilian soldiers who died in World War II; the burial chamber inside contains 468 marble tombs with the remains of Brazilian soldiers killed in Italy. Alfredo Ceschiatti's granite sculpture pays tribute to the navy, air force, and army who take turns guarding the monument. On September 7, Brazil's Independence Day, this is the stage of an impressive military parade. ⌚ *20 min. Av. Dom Henrique s/n, Centro. ☎ 021/2240-1283. Daily 8am–6pm.*

❺ **Marina da Glória.** Marina da Glória, created in 1977, is the only marina downtown. The large space is a popular venue for concerts, events, and fairs, and boat tours around the bay depart from here (p 57). It will also be the main watersports venue for the 2016 Olympics. ⌚ *30 min. Av. Infante Dom Henrique s/n, Glória. ☎ 021/2555-2200. Open hours vary. Metrô: Glória.*

6 **Porcão Rio's.** If you've worked up an appetite, this is the place to come, one of the best all-you-can-eat barbecue restaurants in town. Its specialty is beef in a variety of cuts and sizes, but the outstanding kitchen also serves chicken and seafood. A large antipasto and salad buffet is included in the price. *Av. Dom Henrique s/n, Flamengo. ☎ 021/3461-9020. www.porcao.com.br. $$$.*

❼ ★ **Monumento a Estácio de Sá.** Just beyond Porcão is a small outdoor exercise area and a popular meeting place for dog

The Burle Marx–designed gardens at MAM.

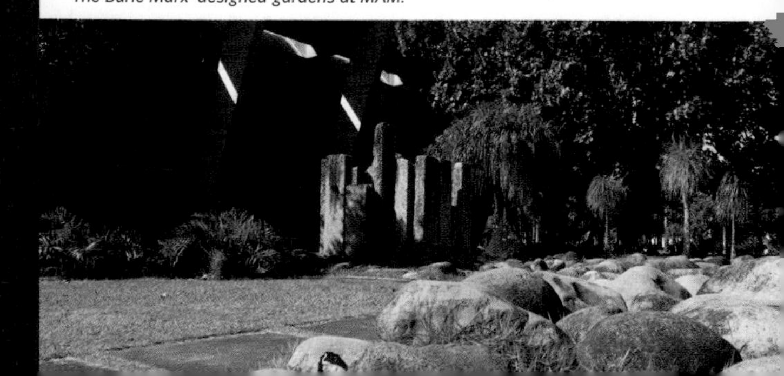

Roberto Burle Marx

It's practically impossible to spend a day in Rio without seeing the work of one of the 20th century's most renowned landscape architects; in addition to Parque do Flamengo, the Santos Dumont Airport plaza, the MAM garden, and the Largo do Machado, Roberto Burle Marx (1909–94) also designed Copacabana's signature wavy black-and-white mosaic sidewalk. A contemporary of Oscar Niemeyer, Burle Marx often collaborated on the architect's projects and created his designs to harmonize the modernist concrete architecture. Used to more traditional European-style gardens, critics disliked his choice of unglamorous, ordinary species, such as grasses or cacti, instead of pretty flowers. They didn't recognize that Burle Marx was a pioneer in sustainable landscaping, designing gardens that were appropriate for the local climate, didn't require excessive watering, insecticides, or maintenance, and would increase people's appreciation for their own environment.

walkers. If you walk a bit farther, you will come to a triangular stone monument. Designed by Lucio Costa, it pays tribute to Estácio de Sá (1520–67), a member of the Portuguese army, who founded São Sebastião do Rio de Janeiro on March 1, 1565. It's only fitting that this monument stands at this privileged location overlooking the entrance of the bay. ⌚ *15 min. 20-min. walk from Flamengo Beach.*

8 ★ Museu Carmen Miranda. It's unfortunate that this museum dedicated to Brazil's first international superstar is such a low-key affair. Plans are to move it to Copacabana, but that may still take a year or two. The collection includes a variety of Carmen's outlandish costumes, tutti-frutti hats, and accessories. Staff members are also happy to play any of the movies or documentaries from their collection. It's a great rainy day option. ⌚ ***45 min. Parque Brigadeiro Gomes (across the street from Av. Rui Barbosa 560), Flamengo. ☎ 021/ 2334-4293. Tues–Fri 10am–5pm; Sat–Sun 1–5pm. Free admission. Bus: 570 or 573.***

9 Belmonte. At this Flamengo institution, waiters come by with a piping hot savory snacks such as empanadas, and *bolinho de bacalhau* (cod fish snacks). ***Praia do Flamengo 300, Flamengo. ☎ 021/ 2252-3449. $.***

A display at the Museu Carmen Miranda.

Rio's Best **Outdoor Sports**

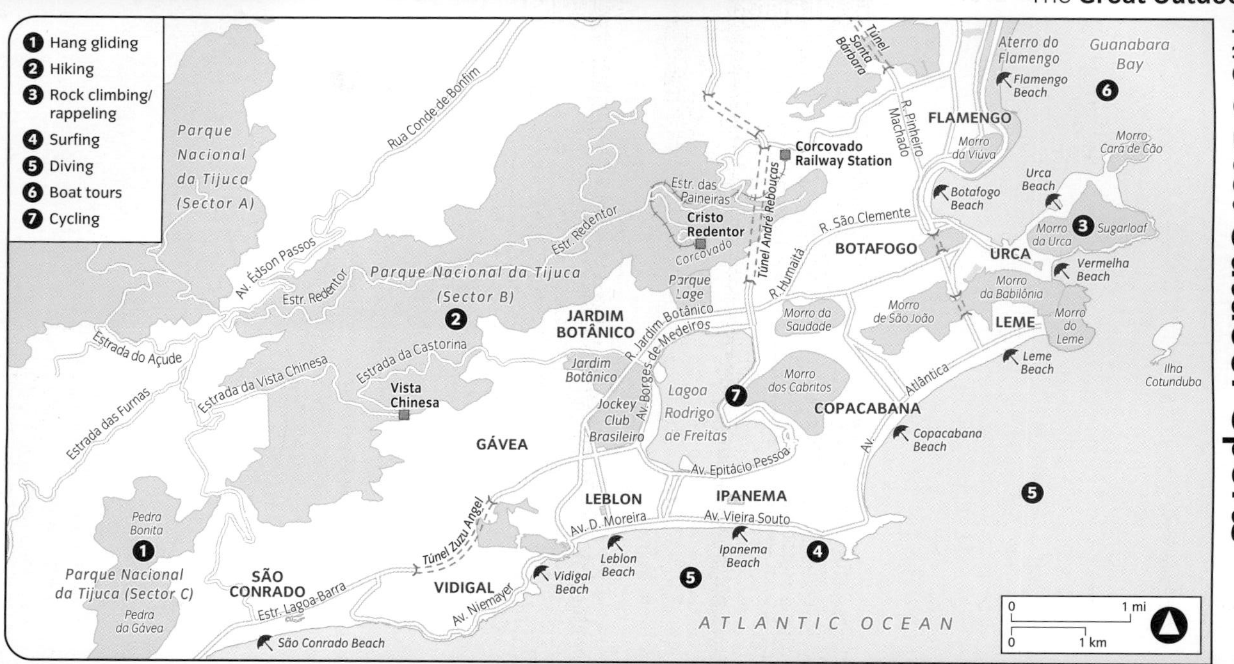
1 Hang gliding
2 Hiking
3 Rock climbing/ rappeling
4 Surfing
5 Diving
6 Boat tours
7 Cycling
Parque Nacional da Tijuca (Sector A)
Parque Nacional da Tijuca (Sector B)
Parque Nacional da Tijuca (Sector C)
Pedra Bonita
Pedra da Gávea
Rua Conde de Bonfim
Av. Édson Passos
Estr. Redentor
Estrada do Açude
Estrada das Furnas
Estrada da Vista Chinesa
Estrada da Castorina
Vista Chinesa
GÁVEA
SÃO CONRADO
Estr. Lagoa-Barra
São Conrado Beach
VIDIGAL
Av. Niemayer
Túnel Zuzu Angel
Vidigal Beach
Leblon Beach
Ipanema Beach
LEBLON
Av. D. Moreira
IPANEMA
Av. Vieira Souto
Av. Epitácio Pessoa
Lagoa Rodrigo de Freitas
Jockey Club Brasileiro
Av. Borges de Medeiros
Jardim Botânico
JARDIM BOTÂNICO
R. Jardim Botânico
Parque Lage
Corcovado
Cristo Redentor
Estr. das Paineiras
Túnel André Rebouças
Corcovado Railway Station
Túnel Santa Bárbara
R. Pinheiro Machado
R. Humaitá
R. São Clemente
BOTAFOGO
Morro da Saudade
Morro dos Cabritos
COPACABANA
Av. Atlântica
Copacabana Beach
Morro de São João
Morro da Babilônia
LEME
Morro do Leme
Leme Beach
FLAMENGO
Morro da Viúva
Botafogo Beach
Aterro do Flamengo
Flamengo Beach
Guanabara Bay
Morro Cara de Cão
Urca Beach
Morro da Urca
Sugarloaf
URCA
Vermelha Beach
Ilha Cotunduba
ATLANTIC OCEAN
0 1 mi
0 1 km

Rio de Janeiro's fabulous ocean setting, framed by mountains and forests, combined with year-round warm weather, lends itself to an array of outdoor activities. Depending on your mood, you can cycle along Copacabana Beach, surf the waves at Arpoador, climb the steep rock face of Sugarloaf Mountain, or soar high above the rainforest.

1 ★★★ Hang gliding. The ultimate thrill for daredevils—strapped into a harness under a tandem hang glider, you and your pilot run down the ramp at Pedra Bonita (520m/1,706 ft.) and within seconds you are soaring high above the Atlantic rainforest for a 15- to 20-minute scenic flight. Paulo Celani is an accredited instructor with almost 25 years of hang-gliding experience under his belt. No experience is required; the weight limit is approximately 100kg (220 lb.). If you are really keen on flying, contact the company as soon as you arrive (or perhaps even a day or two before traveling), so Paulo can contact you when the conditions are optimal (usually on cloudy days or right after a cold front). ☎ *021/2268-0565 or 021/9985-7540. www.justfly.com.br. Tours R$240. Transportation to and from your hotel is included.*

2 ★★★ Hiking. The mountains and hills surrounding the city offer numerous hiking trails that give access to fabulous viewpoints. Even some of Rio's most famous landmarks, the Corcovado and Pão de Açucar, are accessible on foot, with a guide. See p 10 for more info, and contact Riohiking; their guides are knowledgeable and can help you select an appropriate hike. ☎ *021/2552-9204 or 021/9721-0594. www.riohiking.com.br. R$120–R$180.*

Hiking in Tijuca forest.

Climbing Sugarloaf Mountain.

3 ★★★ Rock Climbing/Rappelling. Rio's granite rock faces offer outstanding rock-climbing and rappel opportunities, ranging from beginners to seasoned practitioners. The most popular (and also scenic) destinations are Sugarloaf Mountain and Penhasco dos Dois Irmãos, the twin peaks at the end of Leblon. ☎ *021/2552-9204 or 021/9721-0594. www.riohiking.com.br. R$180.*

Cycling along the bike path in Lagoa.

❹ ★★★ **Surfing.** With plenty of sand and sea, Rio offers great surfing. Conditions vary according to tides, weather, and currents, but the best surf spots are farther out of town, at Recreio, Macumba, and Prainha. Closer in town, São Conrado usually has good conditions for bodyboarding. Beginners and intermediate surfers can catch decent waves at Arpoador and Leblon. The best way to reach the outlying beaches is by Surf Bus (it departs daily from Largo do Machado at 7 and 10am, and 1 and 4pm; allow 1½ hr.). Check the website at www.surfbus.com.br for more details. *Equipment can be rented at Invicta Surf Shop, Francisco Otaviano 67 (inside Galeria River), Arpoador. ☎ 021/2523-0499. For surf lessons, contact Escola Carioca de Surf (☎ 021/7830-6017), or check www.escolacariocadesurf.com.br.*

❺ ★★★ **Diving.** The best diving in Rio is found around Ilha Rasa and the Cagarras Islands off the coast of Ipanema. There are also a number of wrecks around Arpoador. Diver's Quest offers local dive tours for certified divers every weekend, departing from the Glória Marina at 8am. *Diver's Quest: Rua Maria Angélica 171, Jardim Botânico. ☎ 021/2538-0413. www.diversquest.com.br. R$120–R$160 for 2 dives, including gear.*

❻ ★★ kids **Boat tours.** Enjoy a more leisurely outdoor experience with a boat tour of Guanabara Bay. The navy operates regular 1½-hour boat tours around the islands in the bay, onboard a 1910 tugboat (Thurs–Sun). *Espaço Cultural da Marinha, Av. Alfred Agache, s/n, Centro (near Praça XV). ☎ 021/2104-5592. www.mar.mil.br/dphdm. R$10 adults, R$5 children under 12 and seniors. Thurs–Sun 1:15 and 3:15pm.*

❼ ★★★ kids **Cycling.** Although traffic in Rio is unbelievably hectic, if you stick to the city's main bike paths, you can enjoy some great cycling. The entire waterfront, from the Museu de Arte Moderna to Leblon and Barra to Recreio, is paralleled by a paved, flat bike path. On Sundays, the main road along Flamengo, Copacabana, and Ipanema beaches is closed to motor vehicles, giving cyclists even more space. Another great route is the 7.5km (4⅔-mile) loop around the Lagoa. *Bike rental is available at Bike e Lazer, Rua Visconde de Pirajá 135, Ipanema. ☎ 021/2267-7778. R$60 per day or R$15 per hr.* ●

6 The Best Dining

Dining Best Bets

Best **Traditional Brazilian *Feijoada***
★★ Casa da Feijoada $$ *Rua Prudente de Moraes 10 (p 103)*

Best **Brazilian Comfort Food**
★ Aurora $ *Rua Capitão Salomão 43 (p 101)*

Best **Beachfront Dining**
★★ Arab $$ *Av. Atlântica 1936 (p 101)*

Best **Deli**
★ Talho Capixaba $ *Rua Ataulfo Paiva 1022 (p 109)*

Best **Affordable Seafood**
★ Berbigão $ *Rua do Catete 150 (p 103)*

Best **Desserts**
★ Eça $$$$ *Av. Rio Branco 128 (p 105)*

Best **Pizza**
★ Capricciossa $$$ *Rua Maria Angelica 37 (p 103)*

Best **Gourmet Dining**
★★★ Olympe $$$$ *Rua Custódio Serrão 62 (p 108)*

Best **Restaurant for Foodies**
★★★ Le Pré-Catelan $$$$ *Av. Atlântica 4240 (p 107)*

Best **Affordable Fine Dining**
★★★ Roberta Sudbrack $$$ *Rec 79–89 (p 109)*

Best **Service**
★★★ Térèze $$$ *Rua Almirante Alexandrino 660 (p 109)*

Most **Romantic Dining**
★★★ Aprazível $$$ *Rua Aprazível 62 (p 101)*

Best **Healthy Lunch**
★★★ Celeiro $$ *Rua Dias Ferreira 199 (p 104)*

Best **Sushi**
★★★ Sushi Leblon *$$$ Rua Dias Ferreira 252 (p 109)*

Most **Interesting Japanese Menu**
★★★ Mok Sakebar *$$$ Rua Dias Ferreira 78 (p 107)*

Best **Hip Tapas Joint**
★★★ Oui Oui *$$ Rua Conde de Irajá 85 (p 108)*

Best **A La Carte Steak**
★★★ Esplanada Grill $$$$ *Rua Barão da Torre 600 (p 106)*

Best **Stuff-Yourself-Silly Steak Restaurant**
★ Churrascaria Palace $$ *Rua Rodolfo Dantas 16 (p 104)*

One of the superb dishes at Le Pré-Catelan.

Centro & Santa Teresa Dining

Albamar **6**
Aprazível **12**
Bar do Arnaudo **9**
Beco do Carmo **1**
Bar do Mineiro **10**
Berbigão **15**
Cais do Oriente **5**
Cria da Terra **3**
Confeitaria Colombo **2**
Eça **4**
Espirito Santa **8**
Intihuasi **14**
Mangue Seco Cachaçaria **7**
O Bom Galeto **13**
Térèze **11**

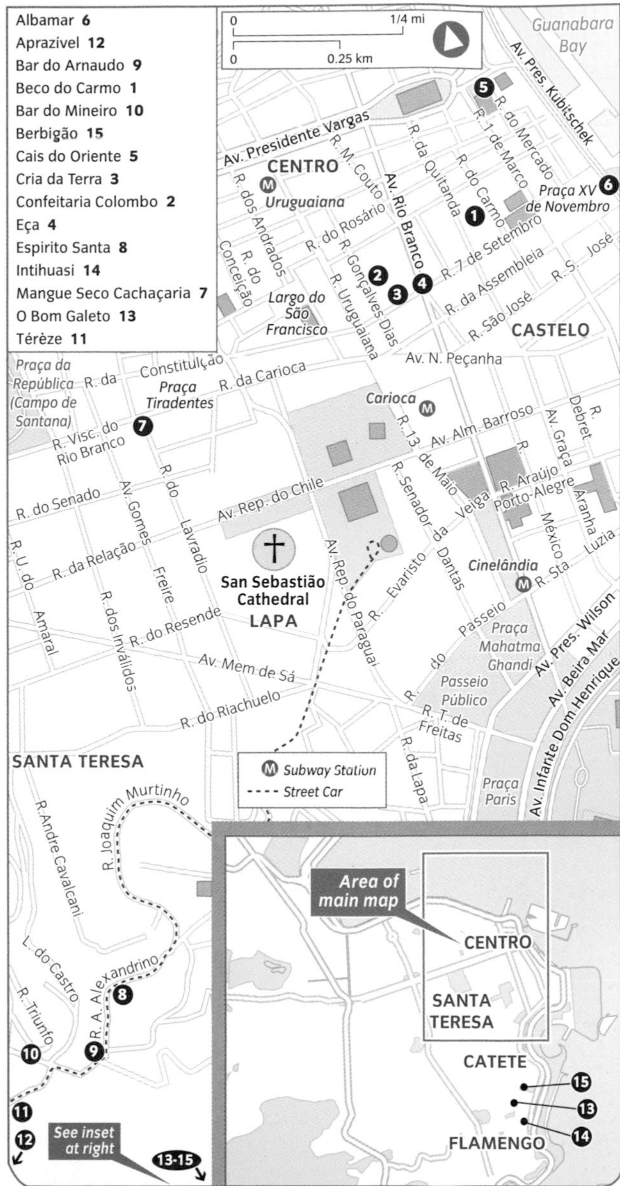

Previous page: Getting ready to dig in at Olympe.

Botafogo & Humaitá Dining

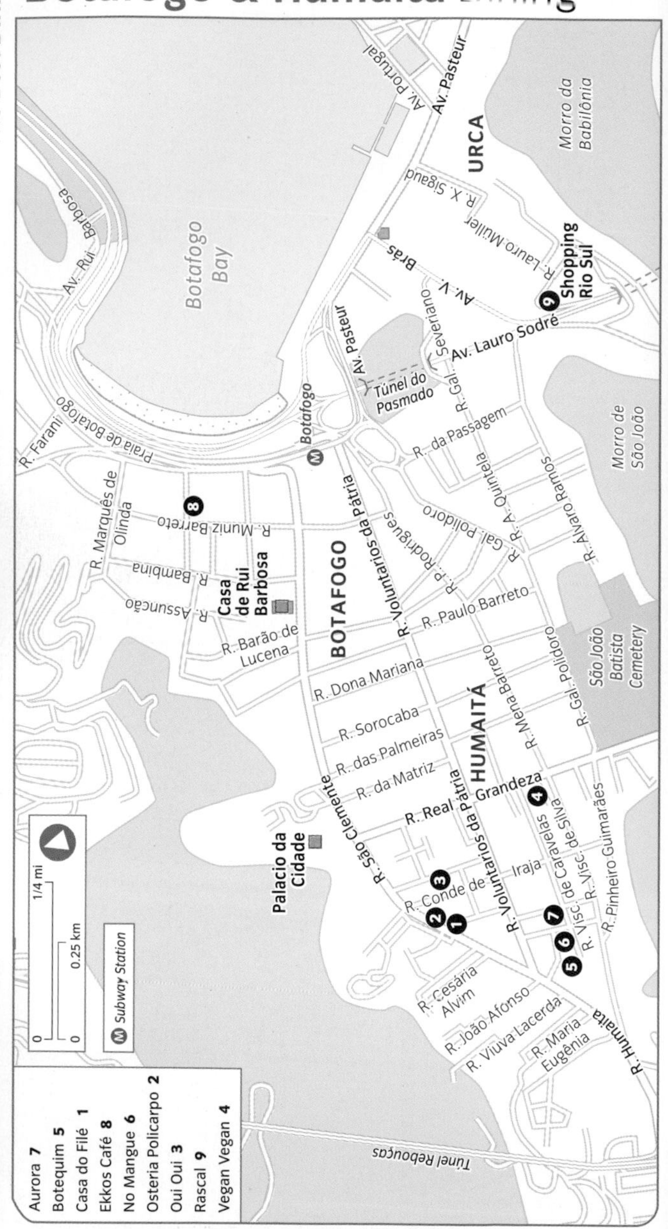
Aurora 7
Botequim 5
Casa do Filé 1
Ekkos Café 8
No Mangue 6
Osteria Policarpo 2
Oui Oui 3
Rascal 9
Vegan Vegan 4
0 1/4 mi
0 0.25 km
Subway Station
Botafogo Bay
BOTAFOGO
HUMAITÁ
URCA
Morro da Babilônia
Morro de São João
São João Batista Cemetery
Shopping Rio Sul
Casa de Rui Barbosa
Palacio da Cidade
Túnel do Pasmado
Túnel Rebouças
Botafogo
Av. Pasteur
Av. Portugal
Av. Rui Barbosa
Praia de Botafogo
R. Farani
R. Marquês de Olinda
R. Muniz Barreto
R. Bambina
R. Assunção
R. Barão de Lucena
R. Dona Mariana
R. Sorocaba
R. das Palmeiras
R. da Matriz
R. Real Grandeza
R. São Clemente
R. Voluntarios da Pátria
R. Conde de Irajá
R. Cesária Alvim
R. João Afonso
R. Viuva Lacerda
R. Maria Eugênia
R. Humaitá
R. Visc. de Caravelas
R. Visc. de Silva
R. Pinheiro Guimarães
R. Gal. Polidoro
R. Mena Barreto
R. Paulo Barreto
R. P. Rodrigues
R. A. Quintela
R. Alvaro Ramos
R. da Passagem
R. Gal. Severiano
Av. Lauro Sodré
Av. V. Brás
R. Lauro Müller
R. X. Sigaud

Beaches Dining

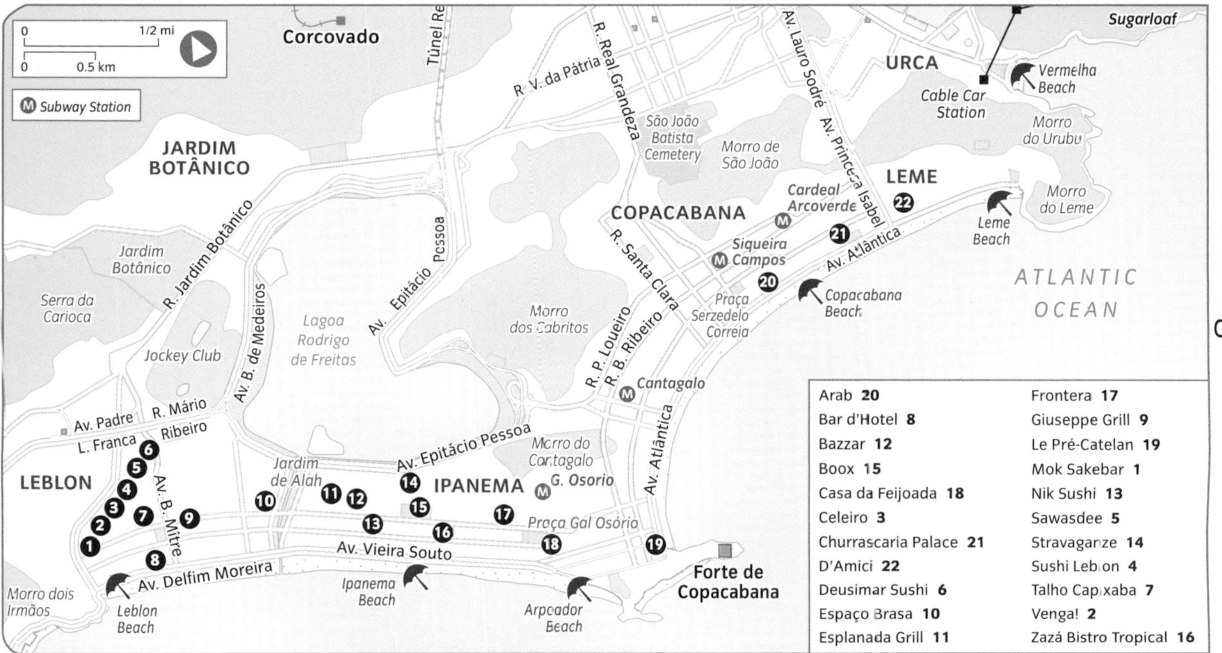

Jardim Botânico & Lagoa Dining

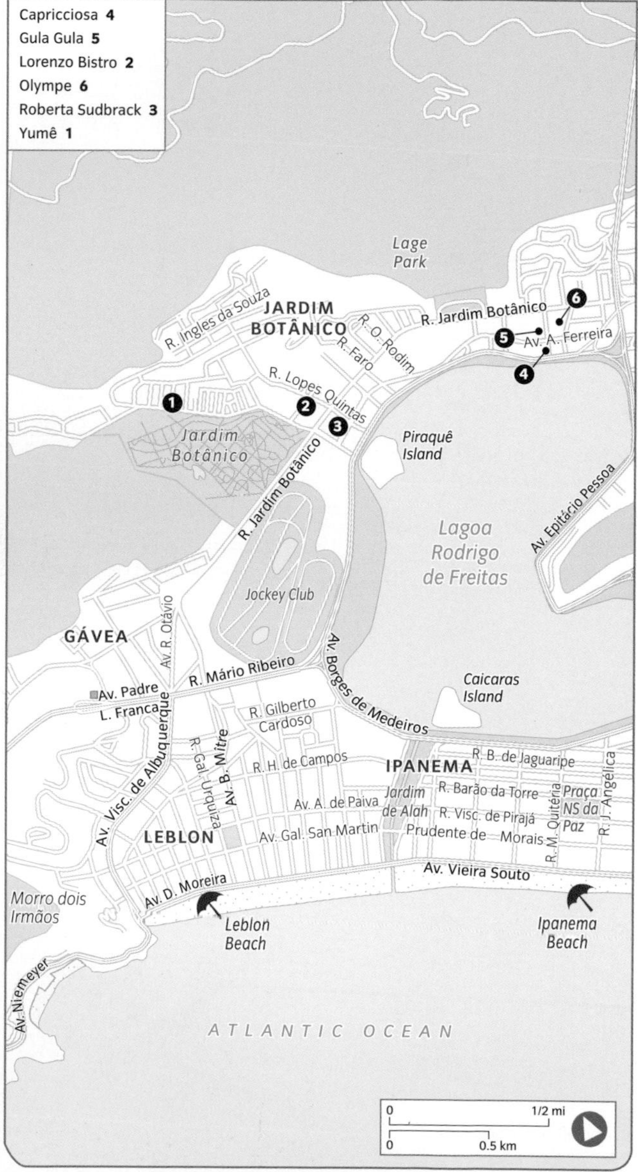

Rio de Janeiro Restaurants A to Z

Dining Hours Tip

Cariocas usually have lunch between noon and 3pm and dinner after 9pm. Many restaurants don't close between lunch and dinner, especially on weekends, when people may enjoy a late lunch after going to the beach.

★ **Albamar** CENTRO *SEAFOOD* Half the fun of this restaurant is the building itself, a round birdhouse tower overlooking Guanabara Bay. The revamped kitchen dishes out delicious seafood; the large fish platters and stew serve two people. ***Praça Marechal Ancora 186. ☎ 021/2240-8378. www.albamar.com.br. Entrees R$35–R$55. AE, DC, MC, V. Lunch daily. Bus: 472. Map p 97.***

★★★ **Aprazível** SANTA TERESA *BRAZILIAN* One of Santa Teresa's most romantic restaurants serves modern Brazilian cuisine, such as grilled fish with coconut rice and baked plantains or succulent duck with wild rice. Views are fabulous any time of the day, but at night the garden is beautifully illuminated. ***Rua Aprazível 62. ☎ 021/2508-9174. www.aprazivel.com.br. Entrees R$42–R$58. AE, DC, MC, V. Lunch Tues–Sun; dinner Tues–Sat. Bus: 206 or 214. Map p 97.***

★★ **Arab** COPACABANA *MIDDLE EASTERN* A fabulous covered sidewalk patio and excellent Middle Eastern food—a perfect combination, rain or shine. For a fast lunch, the buffet offers over a dozen delicious hot dishes, salads, grilled lamb, and freshly baked pita. The a la carte menu features tasty *mezze* (appetizer plates), great for sharing. ***Av. Atlântica 1936. ☎ 021/2235-6698. www.restaurantearab.com.br. Entrees R$22–R$48. AE, DC, MC, V. Lunch Tues–Sun; dinner daily. Metrô: Cardeal Arcoverde. Map p 99.***

★ **Aurora** BOTAFOGO *BRAZILIAN* A neighborhood favorite, Aurora serves generous portions of traditional Brazilian food at very affordable prices. The *picanha* (premium beef steak) with french fries is always popular. On Friday and Saturday, people line up for the black bean *feijoada* (one serving feeds two people!). ***Rua Capitão Salomão 43. ☎ 021/2539-4756. Entrees R$21–R$36. AE, DC, MC, V. Lunch and dinner Mon–Sat; Sun dinner until 9pm. Bus: 463. Map p 98.***

★ **Bar D'Hotel** LEBLON *CONTEMPORARY BRAZILIAN* Join Rio's beautiful crowd for fun Brazilian fusion creations in a hip retro dining room overlooking Leblon Beach. ***Av. Delfim Moreira 696. ☎ 021/2172-1100. www.hoteismarina.com.br.***

A modern Brazilian dish at Aprázivel.

A mezze platter at Arab (p 101).

Entrees R$42–R$69. AE, DC, MC, V. Lunch and dinner daily. Bus: 571. Map p 99.

Bar do Arnaudo SANTA TERESA *BRAZILIAN* This simple eatery specializes in rustic dishes from the northeast, such as *carne de sol* (sun-dried beef) with cassava, *queijo coalho* (grilled cheese), or beans. Save some room for the oh-so-sweet but tasty homemade desserts made with banana, pumpkin, or coconut. *Rua Almirante Alexandrino 316. ☎ 021/2210-0817. Entrees R$18–R$32. MC, V. Lunch Sat–Mon; dinner Tues–Fri. Bus: 206 or 214. Map p 97.*

One of the fusion dishes on offer at Bar D'Hotel (p 101).

★ **Bar do Mineiro** SANTA TERESA *BRAZILIAN* If you don't like crowds, avoid the weekend lunchtime rush, when people line up for an order of delicious *pastel* (turnover) filled with black beans, chicken or sun-dried beef, or any of the other hearty dishes to come out of the tiny kitchen. *Rua Paschoal Carlos Magno 99. ☎ 021/2221-9227. Entrees R$22–R$38. AE, DC, MC, V. Lunch and dinner Tues–Sun. Bus: 206 or 214. Map p 97.*

★ **Bazzar** IPANEMA *CONTEMPORARY BRAZILIAN* This bright restaurant (with a great patio overlooking the street) serves up excellent Brazilian cuisine, prepared with fresh ingredients and delicious sauces and spice blends. You'll also find an outstanding wine list with some unusual selections, including Japanese wine. *Rua Barão da Torre 538. ☎ 021/3202-2884. www.bazzar.com.br. Entrees R$46–R$61. AE, DC, MC, V. Lunch and dinner daily. Metrô: General Osório. Map p 99.*

Beco do Carmo CENTRO *SEAFOOD* A fabulous destination for seafood in the heart of downtown. If you find the a la carte entrees too pricey, check out the daily lunch specials (R$40), which include a bread basket, main course, dessert, and soft drink. *Rua do Carmo 55, 2nd floor.* ☎ *021/2508-9400. Entrees R$40–R$85. AE, DC, MC, V. Lunch Mon–Fri. Metrô: Carioca. Map p 97.*

★ **Berbigão** CATETE *SEAFOOD* This simple neighborhood restaurant specializes in affordable seafood. The large menu includes grilled fish, a variety of shrimp dishes, *moquecas*, and pasta with seafood. Most dishes serve two people. In the evening you can grab a table on the sidewalk overlooking the Palácio do Catete. *Rua do Catete 150.* ☎ *021/2205-7245. Entrees R$32–R$48 (for two). AE, MC, V. Lunch and dinner daily. Metrô: Catete. Map p 97.*

★★ **Boox** IPANEMA *CONTEMPORARY BRAZILIAN* Fresh and creative dishes served until 2am are the big draw at this hip dining room. *Rua Barão da Torre 368.* ☎ *021/2522-3730. www.boox.com.br. Entrees R$34–R$48. AE, DC, MC, V. Dinner Mon–Sat. Bus: 571. Map p 99.*

Botequim HUMAITA *BRAZILIAN* The competent cooks at this neighborhood fave dish out top-notch Brazilian cuisine, served in a lovely heritage building in the heart of Humaitá. I highly recommend the *bobó de camurão* (shrimp stew with coconut milk). *Rua Visconde de Caravelas 184.* ☎ *021/2286-3391. www.botequimrestaurante.com.br. Entrees R$28–R$54. AE, DC, MC, V. Lunch and dinner daily. Bus: 170. Map p 98.*

★★ **Cais do Oriente** CENTRO *CONTEMPORARY BRAZILIAN* Housed in a 19th-century walk-up building, the Cais do Oriente is one of the most beautiful restaurants downtown. Enjoy tasty fusion dishes amidst a rustic tropical decor, in an elegant refuge from the hustle and bustle of Centro. *Rua Visconde de Itaborai 8.* ☎ *021/2203-0178. www.caisdooriente.com.br. Entrees R$38–R$58. AE, DC, MC, V. Lunch Sun and Mon; dinner Tues–Sat. Metrô: Uruguaiana. Map p 97.*

Diners enjoying the pizzas at Capricciosa.

★ **Capricciosa** JARDIM BOTÂNICO *PIZZA* I find them a little overpriced, but fans swear that Capricciosa's thin-crust wood-oven baked pizzas, loaded with fresh ingredients, are worth every centavo. *Rua Maria Angelica 37.* ☎ *021/2527-2656. www.capricciosa.com.br. Entrees R$38–R$62. AE, DC, MC. Dinner daily. Bus: 571 or 573. Map p 100.*

★★ **Casa da Feijoada** IPANEMA *BRAZILIAN* Most Brazilian restaurants serve traditional black bean stew on Fridays or Saturdays, but here you can indulge every day of the week; the *feijoada* is served with all the trimmings, including a variety of high-grade meats and sausages. *Rua Prudente de Moraes 10.* ☎ *021/2247-2776. www.cozinhatipica.com.br. Entrees R$55 (all you can eat, includes a drink and dessert). AE, DC, MC, V. Lunch and dinner daily. Metrô: General Osório. Map p 99.*

★ **Casa do Filé** HUMAITA *STEAK* The secret to Casa do File's succulent, juicy steaks is that they're seared at a high temperature. My favorite is the Filé Oswaldo Aranha, topped with a vampire-repelling amount of crunchy fried garlic, a side of rice, french fries, and tangy onion and green-pepper vinaigrette. *Largo dos Leões 11. ☎ 021/2246-4901. Entrees R$41–R$60. AE, DC, MC, V. Lunch Tues–Sun; dinner Tues–Sat. Bus: 170. Map p 98.*

★★★ **Celeiro** LEBLON *BRAZILIAN* Celeiro is proof that healthy, organic food doesn't have to be boring. Take your choice from the large buffet and try the delicious salads, chicken, fish, grilled vegetables, and grains. *Rua Dias Ferreira 199. ☎ 021/2274-7843. www.celeiroculinaria.com.br. Entrees R$32–R$50. DC, MC, V. Lunch Mon–Sat. Bus: 571. Map p 99.*

★ **Churrascaria Palace** COPACABANA *BRAZILIAN* Work up an appetite before sitting down to an all-you-can-eat feast of prime beef, lamb, pork, chicken, and seafood. An excellent salad buffet and side dishes are also included. *Rua Rodolfo Dantas 16. ☎ 021/2541-5898. www.churrascariapalace.com.br. Entrees R$49 all you can eat (dessert and drinks not included). AE, DC, MC, V. Lunch and dinner daily. Metrô: Cardeal Arcoverde. Map p 99.*

★★★ **Confeitaria Colombo** CENTRO *BRAZILIAN* This lovely 19th-century salon is a feast for the eyes. Enjoy a delicious lunchtime buffet with excellent meat, pasta, and fish dishes. Or stop in for a coffee and dessert. *Rua Goncalves Dias 32. ☎ 021/2505-1500. www.confeitariacolombo.com.br. Entrees R$32–R$59. AE, DC, MC, V. Lunch Mon–Sat. Metrô: Carioca. Map p 97.*

Cria da Terra CENTRO *BRAZILIAN* Cria da Terra serves a delicious spread of raw organic dishes, salads, and hot vegetarian and non-vegetarian options. *Rua Sete de Setembro 48 (inside the Shopping Vertical). ☎ 021/2242-9009. www.criadaterra.com.br. Entrees R$20–R$34. AE, DC, MC, V. Lunch Mon–Fri. Metrô: Carioca. Map p 97.*

★★ **D'Amici** LEME *ITALIAN* This elegant bistro is Rio's best kept secret, serving traditional Italian cuisine that ranges from hearty lamb or veal stews to fresh seafood and savory pasta. The innovative wine list includes several interesting

A feijoada *spread at Casa da Feijoada (p 103).*

The beautiful dining room of Confeitaria Colombo.

German and Austrian whites that perfectly complement the rich and aromatic dishes. *Rua Antonio Vieira 18. ☎ 021/2541-4477. www.damici ristorante.com.br. R$37–R$59. AE, DC, MC, V. Lunch and dinner daily. Bus: 591. Map p 99.*

★ **Deusimar Sushi** LEBLON *JAPANESE* For fresh, tasty, and affordable sushi and sashimi, check out Deusimar, tucked away at the end of a dead-end street. Bahian sushi chef Deusimar specializes in tuna, salmon, and prawn combos, all perfectly prepared and served in generous portions. *Rua General Urquiza 188. ☎ 021/2512-6827. Entrees R$32–R$48. AE, DC, MC, V. Lunch & dinner, Sat–Sun, dinner only Mon–Fri. Bus: 571. Map p 99.*

★ **Eça** CENTRO *CONTEMPORARY BRAZILIAN* Splurge on affordable haute cuisine at this elegant lunch restaurant inside the H. Stern building. Eça's chef offers several daily specials, served with fresh vegetables or a leek risotto. Chocoholics will love the Belgian chocolate creations of the pastry chef. *Av. Rio Branco 128. ☎ 021/2401-2399. Entrees R$34–R$52. AE, DC, MC, V. Lunch Mon–Fri. Metrô: Carioca. Map p 97.*

★ **Ekko's Cafe** BOTAFOGO *KILO* Just behind the Botafogo Praia shopping center is this excellent healthy restaurant that serves a large buffet with fresh Japanese dishes, 20 different salads, and other hot dishes. *Rua Vicente de Souza 25. ☎ 021/2527-0388. www. ekkos.com.br. Entrees R$18–R$30. DC, MC, V. Lunch daily. Metrô: Botafogo. Map p 98.*

Espaço Brasa Leblon LEBLON *STEAK* This all-you-can-eat steak restaurant offers an excellent value, serving high-end beef, lamb, and pork, as well as a decent seafood spread with oysters, sashimi, sushi, and grilled fish. *Av. Afrânio de Melo Franco 131. ☎ 021/2111-5700. www.espacobrasa.com.br. Entrees R$54–R$64 (all you can eat). AE, DC, MC, V. Lunch and dinner daily. Bus: 571. Map p 99.*

★★ **Espirito Santa** SANTA TERESA *BRAZILIAN* Chef Natacha Fink provides a great introduction to the exotic flavors of the Amazon. Reserve a table on the cozy patio and try the grilled *namorado* fish with cashew rice or grilled beef with fresh hearts of palm. *Rua Almirante Alexandrino 264. ☎ 021/2508-7095. www.espiritosanta.com.br. Entrees*

Weight Watching

The proliferation of *quilo* (kilo) restaurants in Rio allows busy Cariocas to enjoy a traditional hot lunch on the fly. It's also a great way to try a variety of dishes. Just grab your plate and help yourself to a buffet with a selection of salads, vegetables, pasta, rice, and beans. Often there is a grill with freshly prepared steak, chicken, and fish. Since the food is priced per kilo (ranging from R$19–R$49, depending on the quality and variety), your plate is weighed and you are billed accordingly. Desserts are also by weight, so go ahead and have that sliver of coconut pudding or chocolate cake.

R$32–R$41. AE, DC, MC, V. Lunch Mon and Wed; dinner Thurs–Sun. Bus: 206 or 214. Map p 97.

★★★ **Esplanada Grill** IPANEMA *STEAK* You have to be a real meat lover to pay R$80 for a steak, but it's worth it. Cuts are succulent, tender, and grilled to absolute perfection. ***Rua Barão da Torre 600. ☎ 021/2512-2970. Entrees R$65–R$95. AE, DC, MC, V. Lunch and dinner daily. Bus: 571. Map p 99.***

★ **Frontera** IPANEMA *KILO* For a fast and delicious lunch or dinner, try this outstanding kilo restaurant. The Dutch chef even includes some of his Indonesian favorites among the usual spread of salads, pasta, grilled meat, and seafood. ***Rua Visconde de Pirajá 128. ☎ 021/3289-2350. www.frontera.com.br. Entrees R$25–R$35. AE, DC, MC, V. Lunch and dinner daily. Metrô: General Osório. Map p 99.***

An upscale steak meal at Esplanada Grill.

★★★ **Giuseppe Grill** LEBLON *STEAK* This a la carte steak restaurant serves excellent grilled cuts of beef (pick your favorite and add any side dishes of your choice). Non-carnivores will be happy to know that the seafood selection is equally outstanding. ***Av. Bartolomeu Mitre 370. ☎ 021/2249-3055. Entrees R$45–R$68. AE, DC, MC, V. Lunch and dinner daily. Bus: 571. Map p 99.***

★★ **Gula Gula** JARDIM BOTÂNICO *BRAZILIAN* For a Brazilian version of light cuisine, try Gula Gula. Its specialties are salads and grilled chicken, beef, or fish, served with fresh vegetables, rice, or roasted potatoes. ***Rua Alexandra Ferreira 220. ☎ 021/2537-8906. www.gulagula.com.br. Entrees R$17–R$33. AE, DC, MC, V. Lunch and dinner daily. Bus: 583. Map p 100.***

★ **Intihuasi** FLAMENGO *PERUVIAN* Treat your taste buds to some Peruvian flavors. Start with a pisco sour cocktail and *ceviche* (raw fish marinated in lime juice). Main courses include seafood and pork, prepared with traditional ingredients such as corn, quinoa, and peppers. ***Rua Barão do Flamengo 35. ☎ 021/2225-7653. www.intihuasi.art.br. Entrees R$29–R$43. AE, DC, MC, V. Lunch Tues–Sun; dinner Tues–Sat. Metrô: Largo do Machado. Map p 97.***

★★★ **Le Pré Catelan** COPACABANA *FRENCH FUSION* Hands-down the best restaurant in Rio. Chef Roland Villard combines his French haute cuisine skills with his passion for Brazilian ingredients, creating some of the most inventive and delicious dishes I have ever had the pleasure of trying. ***Av. Atlântica 4240, 1st floor (inside Sofitel Hotel). ☎ 021/2525-1160. ww2.leprecatelan.com.br. Entrees R$65–R$110. AE, DC, MC, V. Dinner daily. Metrô: Cantagalo. Map p 99.***

★ **Lorenzo Bistro** JARDIM BOTANICO *CONTINENTAL* This cute bistro serves a combination of Italian and French "staples," such as a classic onion soup, polenta with a truffle oil, pumpkin ravioli, or grilled lamb cutlets. Peruse the wine list for affordable Chilean or Argentinean reds to complement your meal. ***Rua Visconde de Carandai 2. ☎ 021/2294-7830. www.lorenzobistro.com.br. Entrees R$38–R$62. AE, MC, V. Lunch Sun; dinner Mon–Sat. Bus: 170. Map p 100.***

★★★ **Mangue Seco Cachaçaria** CENTRO *BRAZILIAN* This lovely downtown restaurant across from the Rio Scenarium offers excellent Brazilian seafood dishes, steak cuts, and appetizers. Most dishes serve two people. ***Rua do Lavradio 23. ☎ 021/3852-1947. www.manguesecocachacaria.com.br. Entrees R$23–R$38. AE, DC, MC, V. Lunch and dinner Mon–Sat. Metrô: Carioca. Map p 97.***

★★★ **Mok Sakebar** LEBLON *JAPANESE* This is not your average Japanese restaurant. In addition to the daily, fresh sushi creations, French chef Pierre Landry is on hand to serve up fabulous fusion dishes such as cured salmon with basil oil or grilled duck with a spicy crust. The sommelier (or "sakelier") will help you pick out a wine or sake to enhance your dining experience. ***Rua Dias Ferreira 78. ☎ 021/2512-6526. www.moksushi.com.br. Entrees R$42–R$58. AE, V. Lunch and dinner daily. Bus: 571. Map p 99.***

Sushi chefs at work at Mok Sakebar.

Small plates at Oui Oui.

★★ **Nik Sushi** IPANEMA *JAPANESE* To pig out on decent Japanese fare, check out the all-you-can-eat lunch or dinner here. For approximately R$50, you can eat as much sashimi, sushi, and an array of hot dishes, including yakisoba, skewers, and tempura, as you like. ***Rua Garcia D'Avila 83. ☎ 021/2512-6446. www.niksushi.com.br. Entrees R$48–R$58. AE, DC, MC, V. Lunch and dinner Tues–Sun. Bus: 574. Map p 99.***

★ **No Mangue** HUMAITA *SEAFOOD* Except for a few token meat dishes, this simple restaurant is all about seafood. Try the grilled trout filet, spicy *moqueca* seafood stews with coconut milk, sautéed prawns, stir-fried octopus with garlic, or pasta with seafood. ***Rua Visconde de Caravelas 180. ☎ 021/2225-4028. www.nomangue.com.br. Entrees R$42–R$60. AE, DC, MC, V. Lunch Tues–Sat; dinner Mon. Bus: 170. Map p 98.***

★★ **O Bom Galeto** CATETE *BRAZILIAN* This popular neighborhood restaurant specializes in tender, charcoal-grilled chicken, served regular or spicy. Order a couple of side dishes, such as a salad, rice, fries, or black beans, for a delicious and affordable meal. ***Rua do Catete 282. ☎ 021/2557-6378. www.obomgaleto.com.br. Entrees R$15–R$28. No credit cards. Lunch and dinner daily. Metrô: Largo do Machado. Map p 97.***

★★★ **Olympe** JARDIM BOTÂNICO *FRENCH* Charismatic French chef and longtime Rio resident Claude Troisgro has become the darling of Carioca foodies with his creative, elegant dishes that highlight fresh Brazilian ingredients. ***Rua Custodio Serrão 62. ☎ 021/2539-4542. www.claudetroisgros.com.br. Entrees R$45–R$96. AE, DC, MC, V. Lunch Fri; dinner Mon–Sat. Bus: 571. Map p 100.***

★ **Osteria Policarpo** HUMAITA *ITALIAN* Just around the corner from the Cobal market is this local Italian restaurant. Start off with the fabulous antipasti platter of grilled vegetables, cheeses, and olives (serving two to three people), followed by a fresh pasta dish. ***Largo dos Leões 35. ☎ 021/2579-0051. www.osteriapolicarpo.com.br. Entrees R$28–R$36. AE, DC, MC, V. Lunch Tues–Sun; dinner Tues–Sat. Bus: 571. Map p 98.***

★★★ **Oui Oui** HUMAITA *CONTEMPORARY BRAZILIAN* Say yes to tasty tapas, fun cocktails, excellent wine, and a hip crowd. Oui Oui's small dishes include plenty of vegetarian options, as well as some fish and meat selections. ***Rua Conde de Iraja 85. ☎ 021/2527-3539. Entrees R$18–R$26. AE, DC, MC, V. Dinner Tues–Sun. Bus: 170. Map p 98.***

★★ **Rascal** BOTAFOGO *MEDITERRANEAN* Normally I wouldn't recommend a mall restaurant, but I'll make an exception for Rascal. It has the most delicious vegetable and salad buffet I have ever tasted in Rio, as well as pasta and other hot dishes. *Rua Lauro Muller 116, Rio Sul Mall, Ground floor. ☎ 021/3873-0339. www.rascal.com.br. Entrees R$47–R$56. AE, DC, MC, V. Lunch and dinner daily. Bus: 123. Map p 98.*

★★★ **Roberta Sudbrack** JARDIM BOTÂNICO *BRAZILIAN* Top chef Roberta Sudbrack wows guests with her sophisticated preparation of typical Brazilian ingredients, such as okra, bananas, or sweet potatoes. Every Tuesday she serves a small tasting menu (appetizer, entree, and dessert) for only R$49; it's perfect for more modest holiday budgets. *Av. Lineu de Paula Machado 916. ☎ 021/3874-0139. www.robertasudbrack.com.br. Entrees R$49–R$89. MC only. Lunch Fri; dinner Tues–Sat. Bus: 571. Map p 100.*

★★★ **Sawasdee** LEBLON *THAI* Thai cuisine is slowly gaining popularity in Brazil as Cariocas learn to appreciate its spicy, tangy flavors. Sawasdee serves an excellent selection of Thai favorites, slightly adjusted to please the Brazilian palate. *Rua Dias Ferreira 571. ☎ 021/2511-0057. www.sawasdee.com.br. Entrees R$43–R$68. DC, MC, V. Lunch and dinner daily. Bus: 571. Map p 99.*

★ **Stravaganze** IPANEMA *PIZZA* Even if you are a more traditional pizza person, try at least one of the more extravagant toppings here, such as the grilled figs and goat cheese or gorgonzola and pears. You'll be pleasantly surprised. *Rua Maria Quiteria 132. ☎ 021/2523-2391. www.stravaganze.com.br. Entrees R$42–R$56. AE, DC, MC, V. Dinner daily. Bus: 573. Map p 99.*

★★★ **Sushi Leblon** LEBLON *JAPANESE* The best sushi bar in town, Sushi Leblon goes way beyond standard Japanese fare. Their sashimi selection alone includes at least 8 to 10 different kinds of fresh fish every day. The menu can be overwhelming; it's better to just sit at the bar and point at whatever catches your fancy. *Rua Dias Ferreira 256. ☎ 021/2512-7830. Entrees R$38–R$62. AE, MC, V. Lunch and dinner daily. Bus: 571. Map p 99.*

★ **Talho Capixaba** LEBLON *DELI* Browse the counters for delicious baked goods, cold cuts and cheeses to go, or nab a highly coveted spot on the sidewalk for some fabulous people-watching. *Rua Ataulfo de Paiva 1022. ☎ 021/2512-8760. www.talhocapixaba.com.br. R$10–R$18. DC, MC, V. Daily 7am–10pm. Bus: 571. Map p 99.*

★★★ **Térèze** SANTA TERESA *CONTEMPORARY BRAZILIAN* Térèze's trendy and modern interior provides the perfect setting for French chef Damien Montecer's elegant contemporary dishes. The presentation and attention to detail are incredible and service is attentive and friendly. *Rua Almirante Alexandrino 660. ☎ 021/2221-1406. www.santateresahotel.com.br. Entrees R$52–R$68. AE, DC, MC, V. Lunch Mon–Sun; dinner Mon–Sat. Bus: 206 or 214. Map p 97.*

Preparing the sushi at Sushi Leblon.

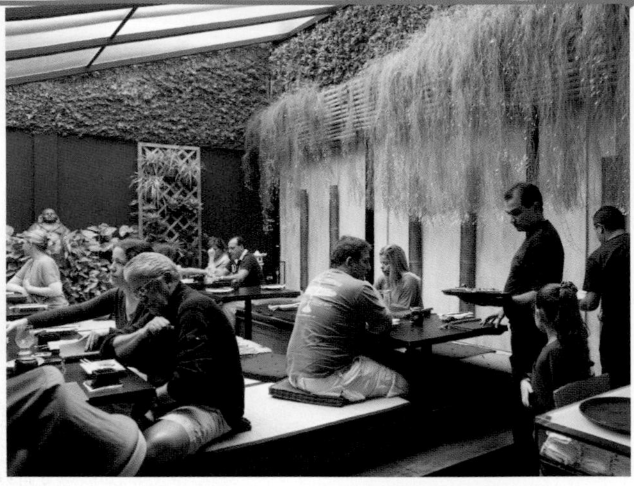

The peaceful garden at Yumê.

★ **Vegan Vegan** BOTAFOGO *VEGAN* This is one of the few true vegan restaurants in Rio. Choose from a la carte dishes or, for R$17, fill up your plate with a soup or salad and a main course. *Rua Voluntários da Pátria 402. ☎ 021/2286-7078. www.veganvegan.com.br. Entrees R$17–R$28. DC, MC, V. Lunch Mon–Sat. Metrô: Botafogo. Map p 98.*

★★ **Venga!** LEBLON *TAPAS* Rio's first tapas restaurant specializes in original Spanish bites that include plenty of seafood, meat, and vegetarian selections. From noon to 4pm, the kitchen serves up lunch specials, including a delicious *paella* for two. At night, attractive Cariocas flock to this hip lounge to sip sangria or bubbly *cava*. *Rua Dias Ferreira 113. ☎ 021/2512-9826. www.venga.com.br. Tapas R$14–R$28. AE, MC, V. Dinner daily; lunch Tues–Sun. Bus: 571. Map p 99.*

★★ **Yumê** JARDIM BOTÂNICO *JAPANESE* I first visited Yume for its lovely winter garden patio, but it's the food that keeps me coming back. In addition to the usual Japanese fare, there are more exotic dishes, like grilled squid stuffed with shiitake or breaded oysters with tamarind sauce. *Rua Pacheco Leão 758. ☎ 021/3205-7321. Entrees R$38–R$62. AE, DC, MC, V. Lunch Fri–Sun; dinner daily. Bus: 571. Map p 100.*

★★★ **Zazá Bistro Tropical** IPANEMA *ASIAN FUSION* One of Rio's first fusion restaurants, Zazá still draws a crowd with its delicious spicy dishes inspired by Asian flavors and its funky, playful decor. *Rua Joana Angelica 40. ☎ 021/2247-9101. www.zazabistro.com.br. Entrees R$40–R$56. DC, MC. Dinner Mon–Sat. Metrô: General Osório. Map p 99.* ●

7 The Best Nightlife

Nightlife Best Bets

The patio at Bar dos Descasados.

Best Cork-Popping Bar

★★ Champanheria Ovelha Negra *Rua Bambina 120 (p 116)*

Best Patio Bar

★★★ Bar dos Descasados *Rua Almirante Alexandrino 660 (p 120)*

Best Bar for Channeling Your Inner Gloria Gaynor

★ Buraco da Lacraia *Rua André Cavalcanti 58 (p 119)*

Best Lapa Live Music Venue

★★★ Circo Voador *Rua dos Arcos 1 (p 121)*

Best Swanky Hotel Bar

★★★ Bar do Copa *Av. Atlântica 1702 (p 120)*

Best Bar for Spotting Celebrities

★ Baretto-Londra *Av. Vieira Souto (inside Hotel Fasano) (p 120)*

Best Après Beach Bar

★★★ Bar da Praia *Rua João Lira 5 (inside Marina Palace Hotel) (p 120)*

Most Quintessential Carioca Botequim

★★ Bip Bip *Rua Almirante Gonçalves 50 (p 118)*

Best Pop-Art Gay Bar

★★★ TV Bar *Av. N.S. de Copacabana 1417 (inside Shopping Cassino Atlântica) (p 120)*

Best Cocktails

★★★ Meza Bar *Rua Capitão Salomão 69 (p 117)*

Best Cachaça Drink Menu

★ Academia da Cachaça *Rua Conde Bernadotte 26 (p 115)*

Previous page: Drinks at Trapiche Gamboa.

Centro & Santa Teresa Nightlife

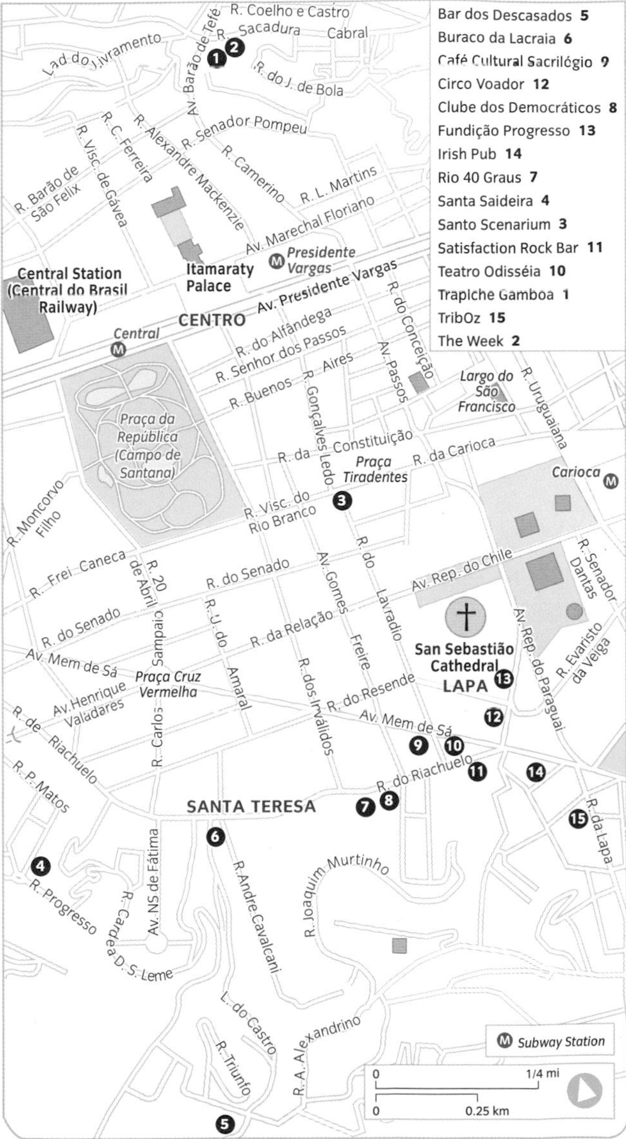
Bar dos Descasados 5
Buraco da Lacraia 6
Café Cultural Sacrilógio 9
Circo Voador 12
Clube dos Democráticos 8
Fundição Progresso 13
Irish Pub 14
Rio 40 Graus 7
Santa Saideira 4
Santo Scenarium 3
Satisfaction Rock Bar 11
Teatro Odisséia 10
Trapiche Gamboa 1
TribOz 15
The Week 2
Central Station (Central do Brasil Railway)
Itamaraty Palace
Presidente Vargas
CENTRO
Central
Praça da República (Campo de Santana)
Largo do São Francisco
Praça Tiradentes
Carioca
San Sebastião Cathedral
LAPA
Praça Cruz Vermelha
SANTA TERESA
R. Coelho e Castro
R. Sacadura Cabral
Lad do Livramento
R. do J. de Bola
Av. Barão de Tefé
R. Senador Pompeu
R. Camerino
R. L. Martins
R. Alexandre Mackenzie
R. C. Ferreira
R. Visc. de Gávea
R. Barão de São Felix
Av. Marechal Floriano
Av. Presidente Vargas
R. do Alfândega
R. Senhor dos Passos
R. Buenos Aires
R. do Conceição
Av. Passos
R. Uruguaiana
R. Gonçalves Ledo
R. da Constituição
R. da Carioca
R. Visc. do Rio Branco
R. Moncorvo Filho
R. Frei Caneca
R. 20 de Abril
R. do Senado
Av. Gomes Freire
R. do Lavradio
Av. Rep. do Chile
R. Senador Dantas
R. J. do Amaral
R. da Relação
Av. Mem de Sá
R. Sampaio
Av. Rep. do Paraguai
R. Evaristo da Veiga
Av. Henrique Valadares
R. Carlos
R. dos Inválidos
R. do Resende
R. de Riachuelo
R. do Riachuelo
R. P. Matos
R. da Lapa
R. Progresso
Av. NS de Fátima
R. Andre Cavalcani
R. Joaquim Murtinho
R. Cardea D. S. Leme
L. do Castro
R. Triunfo
R. A. Alexandrino
Subway Station
0 1/4 mi
0 0.25 km

Beaches Nightlife

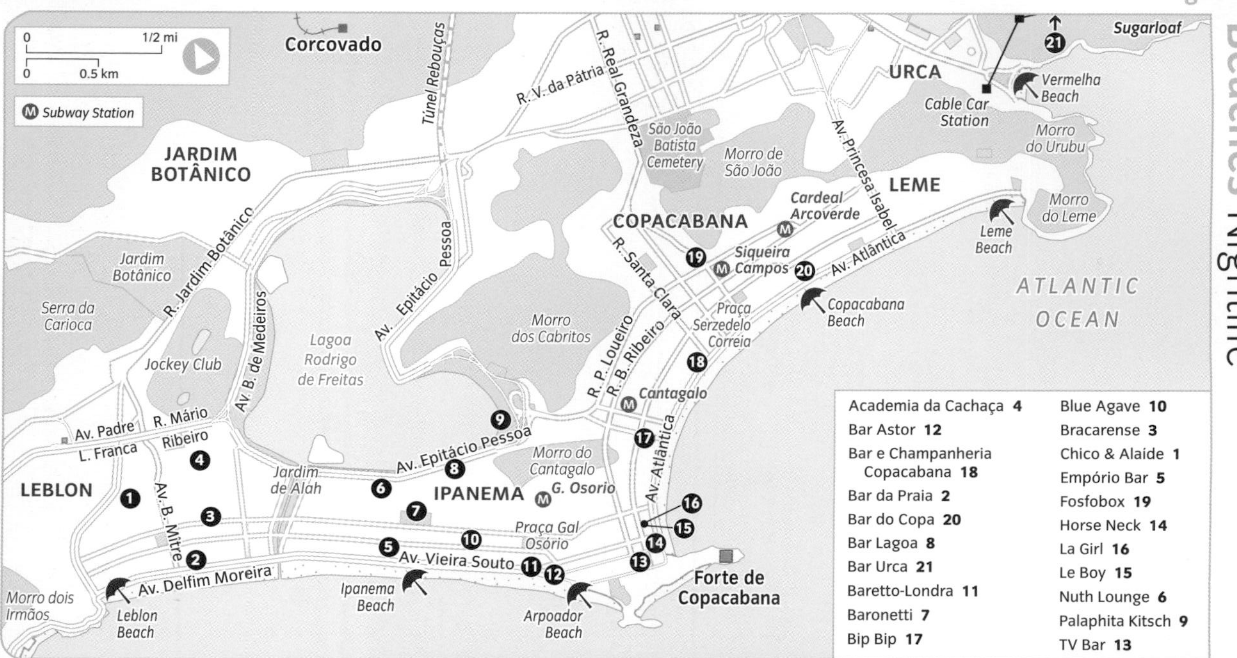

Botafogo & Humaitá Nightlife

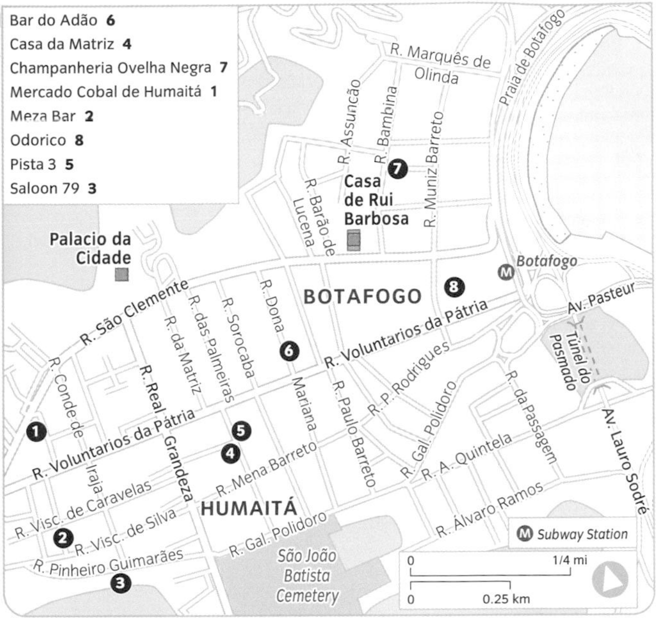

Bar do Adão **6**
Casa da Matriz **4**
Champanheria Ovelha Negra **7**
Mercado Cobal de Humaitá **1**
Meza Bar **2**
Odorico **8**
Pista 3 **5**
Saloon 79 **3**

R. Marquês de Olinda
Praia de Botafogo
R. Assunção
R. Bambina
R. Muniz Barreto
R. Barão de Lucena
Casa de Rui Barbosa
Palacio da Cidade
Botafogo
BOTAFOGO
Av. Pasteur
R. São Clemente
R. das Palmeiras
R. Sorocaba
R. Dona Mariana
R. da Matriz
R. Real Grandeza
R. Conde de Irajá
R. Voluntarios da Pátria
R. P. Rodrigues
R. Paulo Barreto
R. Gal. Polidoro
R. da Passagem
Túnel do Pasmado
Av. Lauro Sodré
R. A. Quintela
R. Mena Barreto
R. Visc. de Caravelas
R. Visc. de Silva
HUMAITÁ
R. Álvaro Ramos
R. Pinheiro Guimarães
São João Batista Cemetery
Subway Station
0 1/4 mi
0 0.25 km

Rio de Janeiro Nightlife A to Z

Nightlife Tip

Cariocas are night owls; dance clubs usually don't even open until 10pm and only get hopping by midnight or so. In most upscale bars, you receive a swipe card upon entry to record all your orders, paying only when you leave.

Bars

★ Academia da Cachaça

LEBLON This bustling cafe specializes in Brazil's signature firewater, *cachaça,* a hard liquor made from sugarcane. The comprehensive English-language menu lists over 100 varieties from all over Brazil that go well with the tasty pub food. Try the *caldinho de feijão,* a delicious and savory black bean soup. ***Rua Conde***

A few of the cachaças available at Academia da Cachaça.

Bernadotte 26. ☎ 021/2529-2680. www.academiadacachaca.com.br. Taxi recommended. Map p 114.

★ **Bar Astor** IPANEMA This brand new version of a traditional Rio bar is one of the few places in Ipanema where you can enjoy a drink overlooking the beach. *Av. Vieira Souto 110. ☎ 021/2523-0085. www.barastor.com.br. Metrô: General Osorio. Map p 114.*

★★ **Bar e Champanheria Copacabana** COPACABANA Find a spot on this lovely beach-side patio on Copacabana's signature black-and-white mosaic sidewalk and raise a champagne toast to Yemanjá, the goddess of the sea. *Av. Atlântica s/n, btw. Rua Constante Ramos and Santa Clara (near Posto 4). ☎ 021/9943-2822. Metrô: Siqueira Campos. Map p 114.*

★ **Bar do Adão** BOTAFOGO Savory *pasteis* (turnovers) have been cast in the leading role at Bar do Adão. The menu here includes more than 60 different varieties of these piping hot snacks, stuffed with chicken, beef, brie, gorgonzola, shiitake, prawns, palm hearts, and more. *Rua Dona Mariana 81. ☎ 021/2535-4572. www.bardoadao.com.br. Metrô: Botafogo. Map p 115.*

Bluo Agave IPANEMA In the heart of bossa nova central stands this little Tex-Mex bar run by two Americans. The food is somewhat forgettable, but the tequila menu and drinks are outstanding. *Rua Vinicius de Moraes 68. ☎ 021/3592-9271. Metrô: General Osorio. Map p 114.*

★★ **Champanheria Ovelha Negra** BOTAFOGO An attractive 30-plus crowd gathers at this sophisticated pick-up bar over a glass of chilled, sparkling *cava, prosecco,* or champagne, all perfect drinks on a sultry Rio night. *Rua Bambina 120. ☎ 021/2226-1064. www.champanhariaovelhanegra.com.br. Metrô: Botafogo. Map p 115.*

Empório Bar IPANEMA Not every place in Ipanema plays just samba or house. For old-fashioned rock 'n' roll, check out this fun, casual bar. Count the number of motorcycles parked outside to guess the size of the crowd inside. *Rua Maria Quiteria Bambina 37. ☎ 021/3813-2526. Metrô: General Osorio. Map p 114.*

★★ **Irish Pub** LAPA This fun pub in Lapa features an excellent selection of beer that goes beyond the obligatory Guinness and includes New Castle, Old Speckled Hen, Abbot Ale, and Wexford. It's popular

Pouring a pint of Guinness at the Irish Pub.

Botequins

The botequim or boteco is Rio's quintessential traditional pub; also known as "pé sujo" (dirty feet), these are simple, casual neighborhood bars that serve cold draft beer and typical finger food, such as *pasteis de carne* (deep-fried turnovers with ground beef) and *bolinho de bacalhau* (a codfish snack). This is also where locals stop in for a drink and discuss the state of their soccer teams, samba schools, or politics (possibly in that order of priority).

with visiting gringos. ***Rua Evaristo da Veiga 147.*** ☎ ***021/2221-7236. www.lapairishpub.com.br. Bus: 433 or 464. Map p 113.***

★★ **Mercardo Cobal de Humaitá** HUMAITA This produce and food market hall also houses a dozen bars and casual restaurants that draw a crowd until the early hours of the morning. My favorite is Galeto Mania, which serves cold beer and delicious grilled sausages and chicken. ***Rua Voluntários da Patria 446, Humaitá.*** ☎ ***021/2527-0616. www.galetomania.com.br. 11:30–1am (later on weekends). Bus: 170. Map p 115.***

★★★ **Meza Bar** HUMAITA I love this little bar with its unpretentious and hip vibe, fun sidewalk patio, and creative drink menu. Try a mango-tini, apple mojito, or *bordello* (sake, lychee, peach liquor, and fresh basil). ***Rua Capitão Salomão 69.*** ☎ ***021/3239-1951. www.mezabar.com.br. Bus: 572. Map p 115.***

★ **Odorico** BOTAFOGO Located in the heart of Botafogo's "cinema" row, this upscale version of a typical Rio botequim is a popular destination before or after a movie. It serves excellent drinks (try the passionfruit caipirinha) and delicious, although meat-heavy, snacks, such as grilled sausage or tender beef slices. ***Rua Voluntarios da Patria 31.*** ☎ ***021/2266-3773. Metrô: Botafogo. Map p 115.***

★★★ **Palaphita Kitch** LAGOA Nothing beats spending a hot tropical night on the romantic deck of this Polynesian-style bar on the Lagoa shore. ***Av. Epitácio Pessoa s/n (Parque do Cantagalo).*** ☎ ***021/2229-0837. www.palaphitakitch.com.br. Taxi recommended. Map p 114.***

Botequins

★★ **Bar Lagoa** LAGOA Even after 80 years, locals will still line up for a table at this neighborhood favorite, famous for its perfect draft beer, tasty German food, and notoriously surly waiters. ***Av. Epitácio Pessoa***

Mixing colorful drinks at Meza Bar.

1674. ☎ 021/2523 1135. www.bar lagoa.com.br. Bus: 415. Map p 114.

★★ **Bar Urca** URCA Skip the sit-down restaurant here unless you want a full meal. Instead, grab a "seat" on the seawall across the street, overlooking Guanabara Bay, and order a cold beer; the view is absolutely priceless. *Rua Candido Gaffree 205. ☎ 021/2295-8744. www.barurca.com.br. Bus: 511. Map p 114.*

★★ **Bip Bip** COPACABANA This tiny hole-in-the-wall is best known for its excellent samba (Mon and Thurs), *choro* (Tues), and bossa nova (Wed) and often attracts well-known local musicians. To keep the neighbors happy, the music only goes until 11pm or so. *Rua Almirante Gonçalves 50. ☎ 021/2267-9696. Metrô: Cantagalo. Map p 114.*

★★ **Bracarense** LEBLON One of the city's most famous botequins, Bracarense was elected best bar in Brazil by *The New York Times* and draws a steady stream of tourists and locals who spill out onto the sidewalk, cold beers in hand. *Rua José Linhares 85, Leblon. ☎ 021/2294-3549. www.bracarense.com.br. Bus: 571. Map p 114.*

Bracarense's lively sidewalk patio.

★ **Chico & Alaíde** LEBLON Friends and former staff members of the famous botequim Bracarense set up their own shop here. Alaíde serves up delicious savory snacks like her *Bolinho da Alaide,* while Chico plies the crowds with cold beer. *Rua Dias Ferreira 679.*

Bars with a View

With almost year-round warm weather, it's no surprise that Cariocas like to be outside, even at night. The revamped sidewalk kiosks in Copacabana feature lovely wooden decks overlooking the ocean; enjoy a chilled glass of bubbly at **Champanheria Copacabana** or a draft beer at the **Boteco da Orla,** both near *Posto* 4, between Rua Figueiredo Magalhães and Rua Constante Ramos. The **Lagoa Rodrigo de Freitas** provides another photogenic outdoor venue. Next to the **Parque dos Patins,** you'll find at least half a dozen outdoor restaurants and bars (btw. Rua General Garzon and Rua Mario Ribeiro).

One of the most popular outdoor gatherings takes place every Friday and Saturday against the scenic backdrop of the **Lapa Aqueduct,** when locals and tourists pack the Rua da Lapa, Rua Joaquim Silva, and the square in front of the CIrco Voador to chat, drink, and flirt. Street vendors keep the crowds plied with drinks and snacks.

☎ 021/2512-0028. *www.chicoe alaide.com.br. Bus: 471. Map p 114.*

★★ **Santa Saideira** SANTA TERESA Away from the bustle of the Largo dos Guimarães, this cute neighborhood bar on the lovely Largo das Neves (where the streetcar turns around) is one of Santa's best kept secrets. Live music is played occasionally. *Rua do Progresso 5.* ☎ *021/3233-0122. www.santasaideira.com.br. Taxi recommended. Map p 113.*

Dance Clubs

★★ **Baronetti** IPANEMA Baronetti is a typical swanky Ipanema nightclub with an elegant, sophisticated interior, hip DJs, burly bouncers, and lineups of beautiful people (although the really hot or famous ones don't need to wait). *Rua Barão da Torre 354.* ☎ *021/2247-9100. www.baronetti.com.br. Cover R$40–R$75. Bus: 570. Map p 114.*

★★ **Casa da Matriz** BOTAFOGO A young, more alternative crowd flocks here to listen to rock, pop, funk, jazz, indie, and soul. One of the most popular events is the Friday night Brazooka party—it's all Brazilian music, all the time. *Rua Henrique de Novaes 107.* ☎ *021/2226-9692. www.beta.matrizonline.com.br. Cover R$15–R$25. Bus: 463. Map p 115.*

Behind the DJ booth at Baronetti.

★★★ **Fosfobox** COPACABANA Gay-friendly Fosfobox regularly hosts celebrity DJs that keep the crowds hopping with alternative pop, indie, and electronic tunes. *Rua Siqueira Campos 143.* ☎ *021/2548-7498. www.fosfobox.com.br. Cover R$30. Metrô: Siqueira Campos. Map p 114.*

★ **Nuth Lounge** LAGOA This classy dance club opens only from Thursday to Sunday and is popular with visiting gringos and well-heeled Ipanema and Leblon residents. *Av. Epitácio Pessoa 1244.* ☎ *021/3575-6850. www.nuth.com.br. R$20–R$40. Bus: 415. Map p 114.*

★ **Pista 3** BOTAFOGO Pista 3 offers plenty of pop, indie, and alternative tunes, attracting a more diverse crowd than the usual chi-chi clubs in Ipanema. *Rua São João Batista 14.* ☎ *021/2266-1014. http://beta.matrizonline.com.br. Cover R$25. Bus: 463. Map p 115.*

Gay & Lesbian Bars & Clubs

★ **Buraco da Lacraia** LAPA So cheesy that it's hip, cult bar Buraco da Lacraia packs them in with kitschy karaoke, live shows, and music. *Rua André Cavalcanti 58.* ☎ *021/2242-0446. www.buraco dalacraia.com. Cover R$15. Bus: 464 or 572. Map p 113.*

★ **La Girl** COPACABANA La Girl is the city's most glamorous bar for women who like women. It hosts special events several nights a week. Check the website for programming. *Rua Raul Pompeia 102.* ☎ *021/2247-8342. www.lagirl.com.br. Cover R$15. Metrô: Cantagalo. Map p 114.*

★★ Le Boy COPACABANA Rio's most flamboyant gay bar offers a variety of entertainment, including strippers, go-go boys, shows, and different DJs and theme nights. *Rua Raul Pompeia 102. ☎ 021/2513-4993. www.leboy.com.br. Cover R$10–R$25. Metrô: Cantagalo. Map p 114.*

★★★ TV Bar COPACABANA A fun eye-popping decor with fabulous colors , funky futuristic furniture, and great music attracts a diverse gay crowd. Open Thursday to Sunday only. *Av. N.S. de Copacabana 1417, Shopping Cassino Atlantico. ☎ 021/2267-1663. www.bartvbar.com.br. Cover R$15–R$30. Metrô: Cantagalo. Map p 114.*

★★ The Week GAMBOA Behind the lovely 19th-century facade hides an über-hip mega dance club that draws up to 1,000 people a night on the weekends. *Rua Sacadura Cabral 154. ☎ 021/2253-1020. www.theweek.com.br. Cover R$30–R$45. Taxi recommended. Map p 113.*

Hotel Lounges

★★★ Bar da Praia LEBLON This Leblon hot spot in the Marina Palace Hotel is a popular après-beach happy-hour destination. Listen to smooth tunes on the veranda while drinking a delightful cocktail. *Rua João Lira 5. ☎ 021/2540-5212. www.hotelmarina.com.br. Bus: 511 or 571. Map p 114.*

★★★ Bar do Copa COPACABANA The queen of the chi-chi hotel lounges makes everybody feel like a celebrity with its swanky, sophisticated decor and fabulous music and drinks. *Av. Atlântica 1702. ☎ 021/2548-7070. www.bardocopa.com.br. Thurs–Sat. Cover R$50. Metrô: Cardeal Arcoverde. Map p 114.*

★★★ Bar dos Descasados SANTA TERESA This elegant and romantic bar in Santa Teresa has the best patio in the city and zero attitude. No bouncers, no door politics, no lineups, just great drinks, delicious food, and fabulous views. *Rua Almirante Alexandrino 660. ☎ 021/2222-2755. http://santa-teresa-hotel.com. Bus: 206. Map p 113.*

★ Baretto-Londra IPANEMA Dress to impress if you want to stand a chance to get into the Fasano's super cool bar. The celebrity

The packed dance floor at the Week.

Mixing drinks at the Horse Neck lounge.

spotting potential is very high. ***Av. Vieira Souto 80. ☎ 021/3202-4000. www.hotelfasano.com.br. Cover R$30. Metrô: General Osorio. Map p 114.***

★★ **Horse Neck** COPACABANA The Sofitel's hip and funky watering hole has the added bonuses of a spacious deck overlooking the ocean and live music during happy hour. ***Av. Atlântica 4240. ☎ 021/ 2525-1232. Cover R$20. Metrô: Cantagalo. Map p 114.***

Live Brazilian Music

★★★ **Café Cultural Sacrilégio** LAPA This small live-music venue in a renovated historic Lapa building offers excellent samba 5 nights a week. The music starts at 9pm; come early if you want to grab a table. ***Rua Mem de Sá 81, Lapa. ☎ 021/3470-1461. www.sacrilegio.com.br. Cover R$15–R$25. Bus: 433 or 464. Map p 113.***

★★★ **Circo Voador** LAPA The Circo Voador serves as a wonderful gauge of what is hip and happening in Brazilian music. This lovely outdoor venue underneath the Lapa Aqueduct is perfect for a hot summer night. ***Rua dos Arcos 1. ☎ 021/2533-0354. www.circovoador.com.br. Bus: 433 or 464. Map p 113.***

★★★ **Clube dos Democráticos** LAPA One of Lapa's oldest venues, founded in 1867, Clube dos Democráticos still knows how to fill its spacious dance floor with bands that play *forró* (the upbeat two-step rhythm from the northeast) and samba. ***Rua do Riachuelo 91. ☎ 021/2252-4611. Wed–Sat. Cover R$10–R$25. Bus: 433 or 464. Map p 113.***

★★★ **Fundição Progresso** LAPA Lapa's largest concert venue draws big Brazilian and international artists. Located inside a former foundry, it adds a certain post-apocalyptic *je ne sais quois* to your evening. Acoustics leave a bit to be desired, and shows are mainly standing-room only. ***Rua dos Arcos 24. ☎ 021/2220-5070. www.fundicaoprogresso.com.br. Cover varies. Bus: 433 or 464. Map p 113.***

★★ **Rio 40 Graus** LAPA This endeavor is owned by Rio's most famous dance instructor, Carlinhos de Jesus, who provides a great stage for live music and of course plenty of room to dance. Check the website for upcoming shows. *Rua Riachuelo 97. ☎ 021/3970-1338. www.lapa40graus.com.br. Cover R$15–R$30. Bus: 433 or 464. Map p 113.*

★★ Teatro Odisséia LAPA At Teatro Odisséia, the lineup goes beyond samba to include Brazilian pop and rock. Behind the heritage building's facade hides a large concert space that can accommodate up to 700 people. *Rua Mem de Sá 66. ☎ 021/2224-6367. www.teatroodisseia.com.br. Cover R$20–R$30. Bus: 433 or 464. Map p 113.*

★★ Trapiche Gamboa GAMBOA Come here to listen to traditional *samba de roda,* the more mellow *choro,* and even *jongo,* an African rhythm seen as the precursor of modern samba. The club attracts a 30- and 40-something crowd that appreciates good music. *Rua Sacadura Cabral 155. ☎ 021/2516-0868. www.trapichegamboa.com.br. Cover R$15–R$25. Taxi recommended. Map p 113.*

Live Alternative Music

★★ Saloon 79 HUMAITA This small venue packs quite a punch with its alternative rock and indie shows. In between sets, you can pass time playing pool upstairs or perusing the extensive beer menu. *Rua Pinheiro Guimarães 79. ☎ 021/3239-0735. www.saloon79.com.br. Bus: 572 or 584. Map p 115.*

★★ Santo Scenarium CENTRO Right next to Rio Scenarium, this smaller cousin features mellower jazz and instrumental Brazilian music from Thursday to Sunday. *Rua do Lavradio 36. ☎ 021/3147-9007. www.santoscenarium.blogspot.com. Metrô: Carioca. Map p 113.*

★★★ Satisfaction Rock Bar LAPA With a name like this, it should be no surprise that this bar is sheer rock, both on the turntable and on stage. *Rua do Riachuelo 18. ☎ 021/3970-1845. Bus: 433 or 464. Map p 113.*

★ TribOz GLÓRIA In the mood for a great place to hear Brazilian and international jazz artists play fusion jazz, bossa nova, and other smooth tunes? Check out TribOz, on the edge of Lapa. *Rua Conde de Lages 19. ☎ 021/2210-0366. www.triboz-rio.com. Metrô: Glória. Map p 113.*

A band performing at Trapiche Gamboa.

8 The Best Arts & Entertainment

Arts & Entertainment Best Bets

Most **Elegant Theater Venue**
★★★ Theatro Municipal *Praça Floriano s/n (p 127)*

Best **Small-Venue Shows**
★★★ Allegro Bistrô Musical *Rua Barata Ribeiro 502 (p 129)*

Best **Acoustics**
★★ Sala Cecilia Meireles *Largo da Lapa 47 (p 127)*

Best **Bossa Nova Bar**
★ Vinicius Show Bar *Rua Vinicius de Moraes 39 (p 129)*

Best **Brazilian Music**
★★★ Teatro Rival Petrobras *Rua Alvaro Alvim 33 (p 129)*

Best **Film-Festival Theater**
★★★ Odeon *Praça Floriano 7 (p 127)*

Best **Foreign Flicks**
★★★ Unibanco Arteplex *Praia de Botafogo 316 (p 128)*

Best **Brazilian Soccer**
★ Maracanã Stadium *Rua Professor Eurico Rabelo s/n (p 130)*

Most **Comprehensive Cultural Programming**
★★★ Centro Cultural Banco do Brasil *Rua Primeiro de Março 66 (p 128)*

Best **Expensive Concert Splurge**
★ Vivo Rio *Av. Infante Dom Henrique 85 (p 130)*

Best **High-Tech Performing Arts Venue**
★★★ Oi Futuro *Rua Visconde de Pirajá 54 (p 128)*

Best **Cultural Center**
★★★ Centro Cultural da Justiça Federal *Av. Rio Branco 241 (p 128)*

Best **New Samba Venue**
★★ Mas será o Benedito? *Rua Gomes Freire 599 (p 130)*

The Odeon theater in Cinelândia. Previous page: The ornate lobby of the Theatro Municipal.

Centro & Lapa A&E

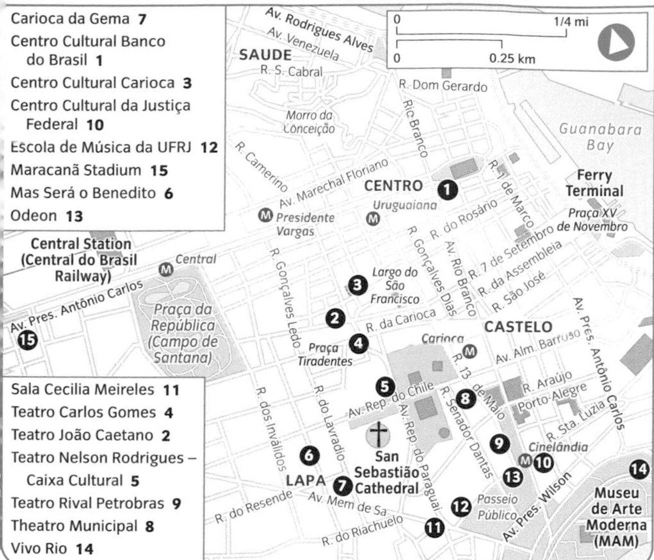

Carioca da Gema **7**
Centro Cultural Banco do Brasil **1**
Centro Cultural Carioca **3**
Centro Cultural da Justiça Federal **10**
Escola de Música da UFRJ **12**
Maracanã Stadium **15**
Mas Será o Benedito **6**
Odeon **13**
Sala Cecilia Meireles **11**
Teatro Carlos Gomes **4**
Teatro João Caetano **2**
Teatro Nelson Rodrigues – Caixa Cultural **5**
Teatro Rival Petrobras **9**
Theatro Municipal **8**
Vivo Rio **14**

Beaches & Jardim Botânico A&E

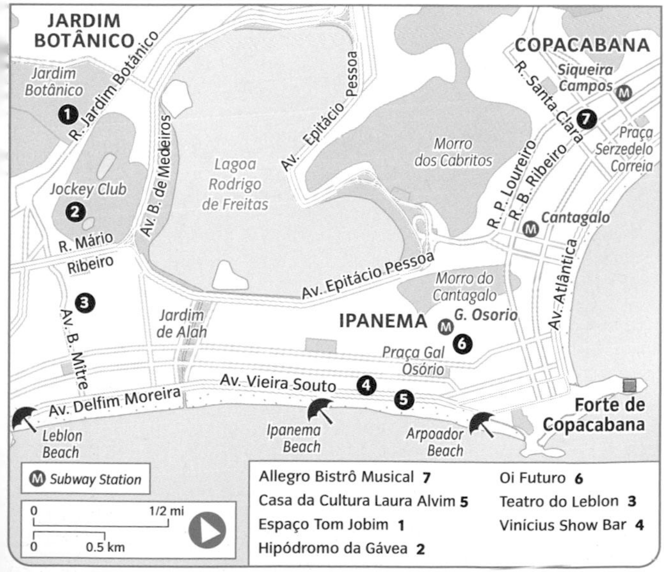

JARDIM BOTÂNICO
COPACABANA
Jardim Botânico
R. Jardim Botânico
Av. Epitácio Pessoa
R. Santa Clara
Siqueira Campos
Praça Serzedelo Correia
Av. B. de Medeiros
Lagoa Rodrigo de Freitas
Morro dos Cabritos
R. P. Loureiro
R. B. Ribeiro
Jockey Club
R. Mário Ribeiro
Cantagalo
Av. Atlântica
Morro do Cantagalo
Av. B. Mitre
Jardim de Alah
IPANEMA
G. Osorio
Praça Gal Osório
Av. Vieira Souto
Av. Delfim Moreira
Forte de Copacabana
Leblon Beach
Ipanema Beach
Arpoador Beach
Subway Station
0 1/2 mi
0 0.5 km

Allegro Bistrô Musical **7**
Casa da Cultura Laura Alvim **5**
Espaço Tom Jobim **1**
Hipódromo da Gávea **2**
Oi Futuro **6**
Teatro do Leblon **3**
Vinícius Show Bar **4**

Botafogo & Humaitá A&E

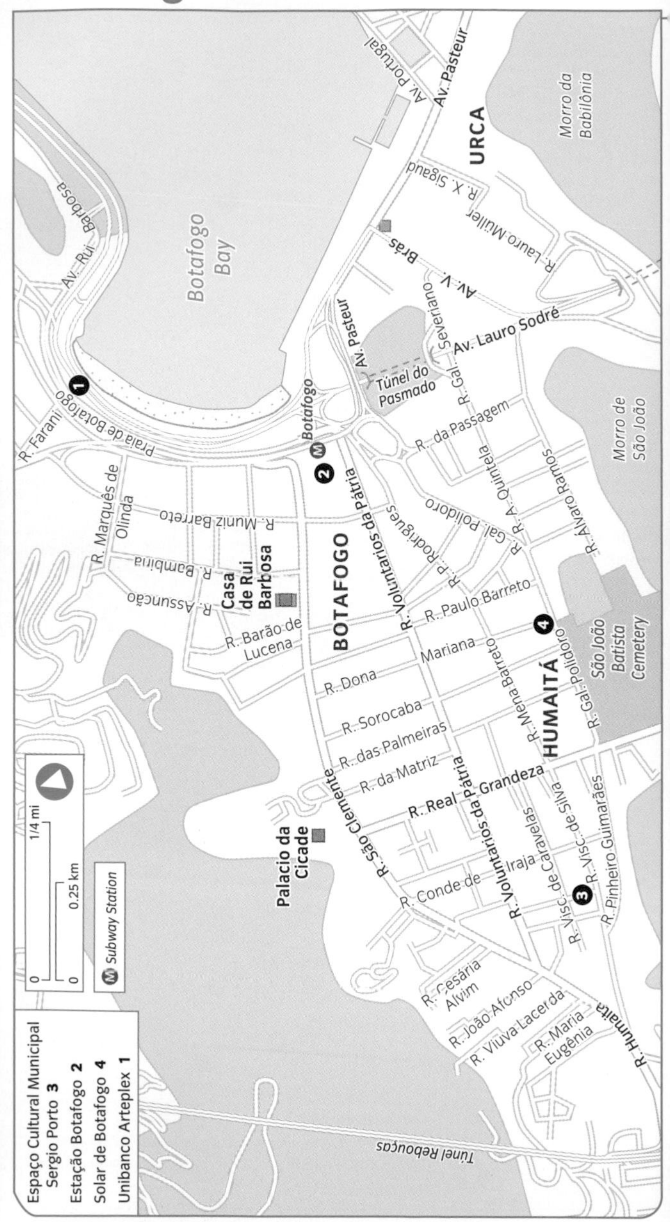
Espaço Cultural Municipal Sergio Porto 3
Estação Botafogo 2
Solar de Botafogo 4
Unibanco Arteplex 1
Subway Station
0 1/4 mi
0 0.25 km
Botafogo Bay
URCA
BOTAFOGO
HUMAITÁ
Morro da Babilônia
Morro de São João
São João Batista Cemetery
Casa de Rui Barbosa
Palacio da Cicade
Túnel do Pasmado
Túnel Rebouças
Botafogo
Av. Pasteur
Av. Portugal
Av. Rui Barbosa
Praia de Botafogo
R. Farani
Av. Lauro Sodré
Av. V. Brás
R. X. Sigaud
R. Lauro Müller
R. Gal. Severiano
R. da Passagem
R. A. Quintela
R. Álvaro Ramos
R. Gal. Polidoro
R. Marquês de Olinda
R. Muniz Barreto
R. Bambina
R. Assunção
R. Barão de Lucena
R. Voluntarios da Pátria
R. Rodrigues
R. Paulo Barreto
R. Dona Mariana
R. Sorocaba
R. das Palmeiras
R. da Matriz
R. Real Grandeza
R. São Clemente
R. Mena Barreto
R. Conde de Iraja
R. Visc. de Caravelas
R. Visc. de Silva
R. Pinheiro Guimarães
R. Cesária Alvim
R. João Afonso
R. Viuva Lacerda
R. Maria Eugênia
R. Humaitá

Rio de Janeiro A&E A to Z

Arts & Entertainment Tip

Detailed weekly entertainment listings can be found in the Friday edition of *O Globo* newspaper or the weekly edition of *Veja* magazine (published on Sat). An excellent Internet resource for classical music listings is www.vivamusica.com.br.

Classical Music

Escola de Música da UFRJ CENTRO You'll listen to upcoming big artists at any of the events performed by students from the Federal University's School of Music. The programming includes classical music and opera staged in a lovely building on the edge of Lapa. *Rua do Passeio 98.* ☎ *021/2262-8742. www.musica.ufrj.br. Tickets free–R$20. Metrô: Cinelândia. Map p 125.*

★★ **Sala Cecilia Meireles** CENTRO This lovely, small venue in Lapa offers some of the best acoustics in town and hosts both classical and contemporary music. Now that the Theatro Municipal has been restored, however, the Sala Cecilia Meireles may close next for renovations. Check the current schedule. *Largo da Lapa 47.* ☎ *021/2233-2324. www.salaceciliameireles.com.br. Ticket prices vary. Metrô: Cinelândia. Map p 125.*

★★★ **Theatro Municipal** CENTRO After 2 years of renovations, this 100-year-old theater has recently been re-inaugurated as Rio's premier arts venue for ballet, classical music, opera, and recitals. The magnificent building alone makes it worth a visit. *Praça Floriano s/n.* ☎ *021/2332-9462. www.theatromunicipal.rj.gov.br. Ticket prices vary. Metrô: Cinelândia. Map p 125.*

Dance

★★ **Deborah Colker** GLÓRIA Rio's best contemporary dance ensemble is so successful that unfortunately (for those in Rio) it spends a lot of time performing abroad. However, if you are a dance fan, it's worth checking the website for any upcoming performances—some may even be in your hometown. *Various venues.* ☎ *021/2221-4632. www.ciadeborahcolker.com.br. Ticket prices vary.*

Film

★ **Estação Botafogo** BOTAFOGO This pleasant, modern movie theater shows a mix of blockbusters and art films (with Portuguese subtitles). The heavily air-conditioned rooms make for a cool refuge on hot summer days. *Rua Voluntários da Pátria 35.* ☎ *021/2266-9952. www.grupoestacao.com.br. Tickets R$16. Metrô: Botafogo. Map p 126.*

★★★ **Odeon** CENTRO This elegant 1930s theater features a lovely, old-fashioned screening room with red-velvet curtains and comfy chairs. It's a popular venue for festivals, such as Anima Mundi

An exterior detail of the Theatro Municipal.

The lobby and dome of the Centro Cultural Banco do Brasil.

(showcasing animated films), the Rio International Film Festival, and the Short Film Festival. ***Praça Floriano 7.*** ☎ ***021/2240-1093. www.grupo estacao.com.br. Tickets R$10. Metrô: Cinelândia. Map p 125.***

★★★ **Unibanco Arteplex** BOTAFOGO One of Rio's best movie theaters for art and foreign films also features an excellent cafe and bookstore packed with art books. ***Praia de Botafogo 316.*** ☎ ***021/2559-8750. www.unibancocinemas.com.br. Tickets R$12–R$18. Metrô: Botafogo. Map p 126.***

Performing Arts

★ **Casa de Cultura Laura Alvim** IPANEMA This large mansion along Ipanema's waterfront houses a theater, a tiny cinema, and an exhibit space. ***Av. Vieira Souto 176.*** ☎ ***21/2247-6946. www.casade laura.com.br. Ticket prices vary. Metrô: General Osório. Map p 125.***

★★★ kids **Centro Cultural Banco do Brasil** CENTRO One of the most comprehensive cultural centers in Rio, the Centro Cultural Banco do Brasil hosts theater, music, dance, and film. On Sundays there are often activities for children; it's a good rainy-day venue. ***Rua Primeiro de Março 66.*** ☎ ***021/3808-2020. www.bb.com.br. Many events are free. Metrô: Uruguaiana. Map p 125.***

★★★ **Centro Cultural da Justiça Federal** CENTRO Another excellent cultural facility (and gorgeous building from 1910 to boot), this former courthouse offers a theater and shows films, and hosts a weekly program of Brazilian music. ***Av. Rio Branco 241.*** ☎ ***021/3261-2550. www.ccjf.trf2.gov.br. Ticket prices vary. Many events are free. Metrô: Cinelândia. Map p 125.***

★ **Espaço Cultural Municipal Sergio Porto** HUMAITA This theater is best known as a venue for upcoming and avant-garde artists. Programming includes dance, music, theater, and visual art performances. ***Rua Visconde Silva s/n.*** ☎ ***021/2535-3846. http://entre sergioporto.wordpress.com. Ticket prices vary. Bus: 170. Map p 126.***

Espaço Tom Jobim JARDIM BOTÂNICO Just inside the gate of the Botanical Garden, this venue hosts theater, classical music, jazz, and samba performances. ***Rua Jardim Botânico 1008.*** ☎ ***021/3874-1808. www.jbrj.gov.br. Ticket prices vary. Bus: 170. Map p 125.***

★★★ **Oi Futuro** IPANEMA Enjoy high-tech contemporary performing arts at this new Ipanema venue, which is trying to appeal to young

An exhibit at the Centro Cultural da Justiça.

A performance at the Teatro Rival Petrobas.

people with hip exhibits and performances by up-and-coming Brazilian artists. *Rua Visconde de Pirajá 54. ☎ 021/3201-3010. www.oifuturo.org.br. Most events are free. Metrô: General Osório. Map p 125.*

Teatro Carlos Gomes CENTRO For 120 years, Cariocas have been coming to the Teatro Carlos Gomes for entertainment. The Art Deco building on the Praça Tiradentes dates from 1932 and stages plays and concerts. *Praça Tiradentes 19. ☎ 021/2224-3602. Ticket prices vary. Metrô: Carioca. Map p 125.*

Teatro do Leblon LEBLON One of Rio de Janeiro's most important theaters, Teatro do Leblon hosts major Brazilian plays with well-known actors, comedy acts, and poetry readings. *Rua Conde de Bernadotte 26. ☎ 021/2529-7700. www.teatros.art.br. Tickets R$30–R$50. Taxi recommended. Map p 125.*

Teatro João Caetano CENTRO Founded in 1813, the Teatro João Caetano still draws a crowd with regular Brazilian music and theater performances. *Praça Tiradentes s/n. ☎ 021/2332-9166. Tickets R$20–R$50. Metrô: Carioca. Map p 125.*

★ Teatro Nelson Rodrigues-Caixa Cultural CENTRO This theater across the street from the modern cathedral offers a diverse and affordable cultural agenda of dance, classical music, and theater. *Av. República do Chile 230, Centro. ☎ 021/2262-8152. Tickets R$10–R$40. Metrô: Carioca. Taxi recommended on weekends. Map p 125.*

Live Music

★★★ Allegro Bistrô Musical COPACABANA Rio's best music store also hosts regular small concerts and CD premieres. The events are always free, but space is limited (and highly in demand), so reserve early. Check the website for upcoming concerts. *Rua Barata Ribeiro 502. ☎ 021/2548-5005. www.modernsound.com.br. Free admission. Metrô: Siqueira Campos. Map p 125.*

★ Solar de Botafogo BOTAFOGO This lovely and elegant early-20th-century mansion offers a diverse program of Brazilian film, theater, and music at affordable prices. *Rua General Polidoro 180. ☎ 021/2543-5411. www.solardebotafogo.com.br. Tickets R$20–R$40. Metrô: Botafogo. Map p 126.*

★★★ Teatro Rival Petrobras CENTRO An excellent lineup of Brazilian artists and affordable ticket prices are the major draws at this mid-sized downtown theater. *Rua Alvaro Alvim 33. ☎ 021/2240-4469. www.rivalpetrobras.com.br. Tickets R$20–R$50. Metrô: Cinelândia. Map p 125.*

★ Vinicius Show Bar IPANEMA Although bossa nova may be inextricably associated with sensual Brazilian music, only a few places in Rio still play it. Vinicius is one of the rare venues putting on shows featuring this music 7 days a week. *Rua Vinicius de Moraes 39. ☎ 021/2287-1497. www.viniciusbar.com.br. Tickets R$25–R$35. Metrô: General Osorio. Map p 125.*

★ **Vivo Rio** CENTRO One of the city's most modern large concert stages, Vivo Rio attracts major national and international stars. Prime seats at these A-list shows come at a hefty price. *Av. Infante Dom Henrique 85 (next to the Museu de Arte Moderna). ☎ 021/2272-2900. www.vivorio.com.br. Tickets R$80–R$160. Taxi recommended. Map p 125.*

Samba Shows

★★ **Carioca da Gema** LAPA This is your best bet for a blind date with samba. Carioca da Gema takes pride in packing the small stage of this intimate venue with some of the best musicians in town. Shows usually start at 9:30pm. *Rua Mem de Sá 79. ☎ 021/2221-0043. www.barcariocadagema.com.br. Tickets R$15–R$25. Bus:433 or 464. Map p 125.*

★★★ **Centro Cultural Carioca** CENTRO Aptly named, the Centro Cultural Carioca is an excellent ambassador for local *sambistas* (samba musicians) and attracts top-notch acts. The house band, Sururu na Roda, offers a great introduction to classic samba. *Rua do Teatro 37. ☎ 021/2252-6468. www.centroculturalcarioca.com.br. Tickets R$12–R$25. Bus: 433 or 464. Map p 125.*

★★ **Mas será o Benedito?** CENTRO One of the newest venues in Lapa, this bar features three floors that include an excellent bar, pool tables, and a stage that hosts great samba music. *Rua Gomes Freire 599. ☎ 021/2232-9000. Tickets R$12–R$25. Bus: 433 or 464. Map p 125.*

A game at Maracanã Stadium.

Spectator Sports

Hipódromo da Gávea GÁVEA Every week, four horse races are held at Brazil's largest racetrack in Gávea. The public watches from the elegant 1920s grandstands and places their bets underneath the crystal chandeliers in the main lobby. *Praça Santos Dumont 31. ☎ 021/3534-9000. www.jcb.com.br. Races: Fri 5pm; Sat–Sun 2:45pm; Mon 6:45pm. Free admission. Bus: 170. Map p 125.*

★ **Maracanã Stadium** MARACANA Rio's temple of soccer is closed until 2013 to undergo major renovations to be ready in time for the 2014 World Cup. Diehard soccer fans determined to visit the legendary stadium will have to resort to a guided tour. Tours with English-speaking guides are available daily, between 9am and 5pm. *Rua Professor Eurico Rabelo, s/n, Maracanã. Entrance to Visitor Center at gate 18. ☎ 021/2334-1705. Adults R$20; children and seniors R$10. Metrô: Maracanã. Map p 125.* ●

9 The Best **Lodging**

Lodging Best Bets

Best **Old-Fashioned Glamour Hotel**
★★ Copacabana Palace Hotel $$$$ *Av. Atlântica 1702 (p 137)*

Most **Romantic Small Inn**
★★★ Casa 32 $$$$ *Largo do Boticário 32 (p 137)*

Best **Kid-Friendly Facilities**
★★★ Sheraton Rio Hotel & Towers $$$$ *Av. Niemeyer 121 (p 143)*

Most **Exclusive Hotel**
★ Rio 180 Graus $$$$ *Rua Julio Otoni 254 (p 142)*

Best **Hip Design Hotel**
★★ Fasano $$$$ *Av. Vieira Souto 88 (p 138)*

Best **Hotel Spa**
★★★ Hotel Santa Teresa $$$$ *Rua Almirante Alexandrino 660 (p 138)*

Best **Service**
★★★ Sofitel $$$ *Av. Atlântica 4240 (p 143)*

Best **Hotel for Business Travelers**
★★ Windsor Hotel Florida $$ *Rua Ferreira Viana 81 (p 144)*

Best **Ocean View**
★ Pestana Rio Atlântica $$$ *Av. Atlântica 2964 (p 141)*

Best **Hidden Gem**
★★★ La Maison $$$ *Rua Sergio Porto 58 (p 139)*

Best **Hotel Bar**
★ Marina All Suites Hotel $$$$ *Av. Delfim Moreira 696 (p 140)*

Best **Gay-Friendly Hotel**
★ Ipanema Plaza $$$ *Rua Farme de Amoedo 34 (p 139)*

Best **Digs for Art Deco Devotees**
★ Hotel Paysandu $ *Rua Paissandu 23 (p 138)*

Best **Beach Hotel**
★★★ Arena Copacabana Hotel $$ *Av. Atlântica 2064. (p 136)*

Best **Value**
★★ Portinari $$ *Rua Francisco de Sá 17 (p 141)*

Best **Budget Accommodations**
★★ Hotel Vermont $$ *Rua Visconde de Pirajá 254 (p 139)*

Best **Hostel**
★★ Leblon Spot $ *Rua Dias Ferreira 636 (p 140)*

The pool at the Windsor Hotel Florida.

Centro, Santa Teresa & Flamengo Lodging

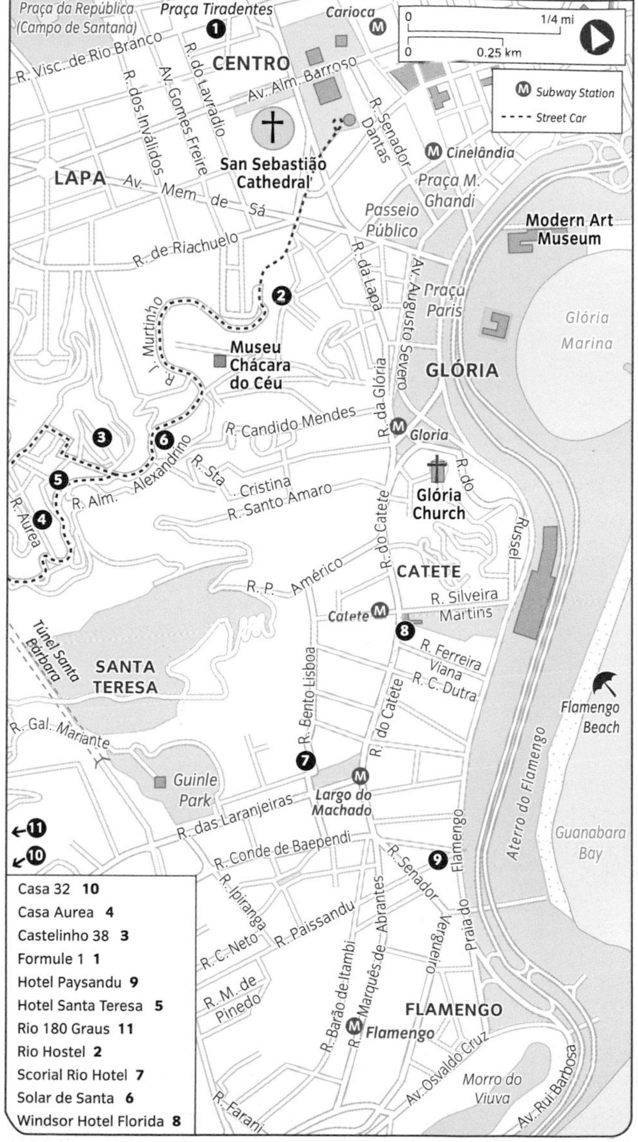
Praça da República
(Campo de Santana)
Praça Tiradentes
Carioca
0
1/4 mi
0
0.25 km
Subway Station
Street Car
R. Visc. de Rio Branco
R. do Lavradio
CENTRO
Av. Alm. Barroso
R. dos Inválidos
Av. Gomes Freire
R. Senador Dantas
Cinelândia
San Sebastião Cathedral
LAPA
Av. Mem de Sá
Praça M. Ghandi
Passeio Público
Modern Art Museum
R. de Riachuelo
R. da Lapa
Av. Augusto Severo
Praça Paris
Glória Marina
R. J. Murtinho
Museu Chácara do Céu
GLÓRIA
R. da Glória
R. Candido Mendes
Gloria
R. Alm. Alexandrino
R. Sta. Cristina
R. Santo Amaro
R. do Catete
Glória Church
R. do Russel
R. Aurea
R. P. Américo
CATETE
R. Silveira Martins
Catete
R. Ferreira Viana
R. C. Dutra
Túnel Santa Bárbara
SANTA TERESA
R. Bento Lisboa
Flamengo Beach
Aterro do Flamengo
R. Gal. Mariante
Guinle Park
Largo do Machado
R. das Laranjeiras
Guanabara Bay
R. Conde de Baependi
R. Senador Vergueiro
Praia do Flamengo
R. Ipiranga
R. Paissandu
R. C. Neto
R. Marquês de Abrantes
R. Barão de Itambi
R. M. de Pinedo
FLAMENGO
Flamengo
Av. Osvaldo Cruz
Morro do Viuva
Av. Rui Barbosa
R. Farani
Casa 32 10
Casa Aurea 4
Castelinho 38 3
Formule 1 1
Hotel Paysandu 9
Hotel Santa Teresa 5
Rio 180 Graus 11
Rio Hostel 2
Scorial Rio Hotel 7
Solar de Santa 6
Windsor Hotel Florida 8

Previous page: The Copacabana Palace Hotel.

Copacabana & Leme Lodging

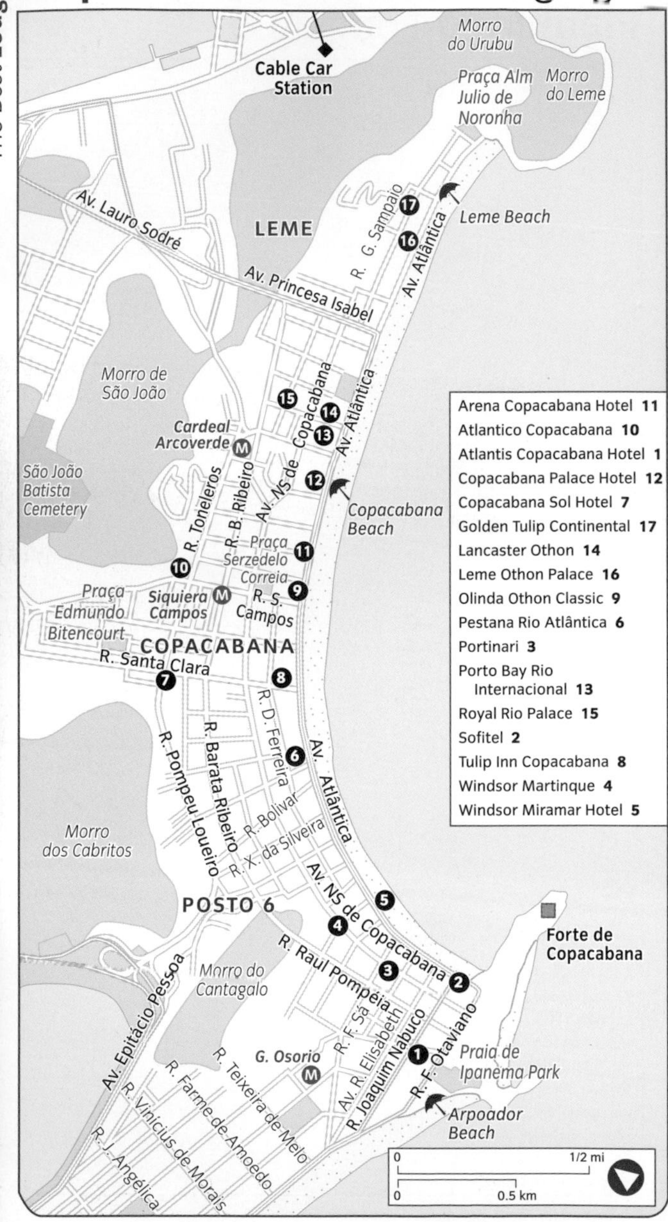
Cable Car Station
Morro do Urubu
Praça Alm Julio de Noronha
Morro do Leme
Av. Lauro Sodré
LEME
R. G. Sampaio
Leme Beach
Av. Atlântica
Av. Princesa Isabel
Morro de São João
Cardeal Arcoverde
Av. NS de Copacabana
R. B. Ribeiro
R. Toneleros
São João Batista Cemetery
Copacabana Beach
Praça Serzedelo Correia
Praça Edmundo Bitencourt
Siquiera Campos
R. S. Campos
COPACABANA
R. Santa Clara
R. D. Ferreira
R. Barata Ribeiro
R. Pompeu Loueiro
R. Bolivar
R. X. da Silveira
Morro dos Cabritos
POSTO 6
R. Raul Pompéia
Forte de Copacabana
Av. Epitácio Pessoa
Morro do Cantagalo
R. F. Sá
Av. R. Elisabeth
R. Joaquim Nabuco
R. F. Otaviano
Praia de Ipanema Park
G. Osorio
R. Teixeira de Melo
R. Farme de Amoedo
R. Vinícius de Morais
R. J. Angélica
Arpoador Beach
0 1/2 mi
0 0.5 km
Arena Copacabana Hotel 11
Atlantico Copacabana 10
Atlantis Copacabana Hotel 1
Copacabana Palace Hotel 12
Copacabana Sol Hotel 7
Golden Tulip Continental 17
Lancaster Othon 14
Leme Othon Palace 16
Olinda Othon Classic 9
Pestana Rio Atlântica 6
Portinari 3
Porto Bay Rio Internacional 13
Royal Rio Palace 15
Sofitel 2
Tulip Inn Copacabana 8
Windsor Martinque 4
Windsor Miramar Hotel 5

Ipanema & Leblon Lodging

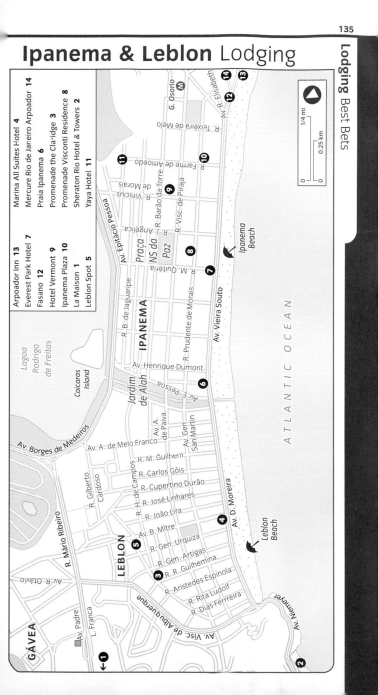

Arpoador Inn 13
Everest Park Hotel 7
Fasano 12
Hotel Vermont 9
Ipanema Plaza 10
La Maison 1
Leblon Spot 5
Marina All Suites Hotel 4
Mercure Rio de Janeiro Arpoador 14
Praia Ipanema 6
Promenade the Claridge 3
Promenade Visconti Residence 8
Sheraton Rio Hotel & Towers 2
Yaya Hotel 11

Lagoa Rodrigo de Freitas
Caicaras Island
GÁVEA
LEBLON
IPANEMA
Jardim de Alah
Praça NS da Paz
Ipanema Beach
Leblon Beach
ATLANTIC OCEAN
Av. Borges de Medeiros
Av. Epitácio Pessoa
Av. Vieira Souto
Av. D. Moreira
Av. Henrique Dumont
Av. Visc. de Albuquerque
Av. Niemeyer
Av. R. Otávio
Av. Padre
L. Franca
R. Mário Ribeiro
R. Gilberto Cardoso
Av. A. de Melo Franco
R. M. Guilhem
R. Carlos Gôis
R. Cupertino Durão
R. José Linhares
R. João Lira
Av. B. Mitre
R. Gen. Urquiza
R. Gen. Artigas
R. R. Guilhemina
R. Aristedes Espinola
R. Rita Ludolf
R. Dias Ferrreira
R. H. de Campos
Av. A. de Paiva
Av. Gen. San Martin
Av. E. Pessoa
R. Prudente de Morais
R. B. de Jaguaripe
R. M. Quitéria
R. J. Angélica
R. Visc. de Pirajá
R. Barão da Torre
R. Vinicius de Morais
R. Farme de Amoedo
R. Teixeira de Melo
Av. R. Elisabeth
G. Osorio
0 — 1/4 mi
0 — 0.25 km

Rio de Janeiro Hotels A to Z

Lodging Tips

Unless stated otherwise, all rates include breakfast and rooms feature A/C. Children under the age of 12 usually stay free, if sharing a room with their parents. Rates increase significantly for New Year's and Carnaval. Most hotels will only reserve packages with at least a 3- or 4-day stay; these often sell out months in advance, so book early. Before you book online or directly with the hotel, compare rates with a company like Brazil Nuts (p 160).

★★★ Arena Copacabana Hotel COPACABANA This beachside hotel has garnered rave reviews. The rooms are well-equipped, with modern electronics and comfortable furniture, and sound-proof windows cut down the bustle from the busy waterfront. *Av. Atlântica 2064. ☎ 021/3034-1501. www.arenahotel.com.br. 135 units. Doubles R$250–R$380. AE, DC, MC, V. Metrô: Siqueira Campos. Map p 134.*

★★ Arpoador Inn IPANEMA The ocean-view rooms at this small beachside hotel in Arpoador are the best deal in town. Unfortunately, these rooms book fast. If you find yourself left with a standard or superior room, you are better off booking elsewhere, as the rooms themselves are nothing to write home about. *Rua Francisco Otaviano 177. ☎ 021/2523-0060. www.arpoadorinn.com.br. 50 units. Doubles R$440. AE, DC, MC, V. Metrô: General Osório. Map p 135.*

★ Atlântico Copacabana COPACABANA In the heart of Copacabana's shopping district, Atlântico offers great year-round value. Rooms are pleasantly furnished and equipped with extras such as high-speed Internet, a hair dryer, and an electronic safe. *Rua Siqueira Campos 90. ☎ 021/2548-0011. www.atlanticocopacabana.com.br. 146 units. Doubles R$230–R$260. AE, MC, V. Metrô: Siqueira Campos. Map p 134.*

One of the modern rooms at the Arena Copacabana Hotel.

★★ Atlantis Copacabana Hotel COPACABANA Enjoy affordable accommodations at this government-rated five-star location between Ipanema and Copacabana. The rooms are on the small side and simply furnished, but everything is spotless. An added bonus is the free Wi-Fi, a small swimming pool, and 24-hour room service. *Rua Bulhões de Carvalho 61. ☎ 021/2521-1142. www.atlantishotel.com.br. 87 units. Doubles R$200–R$280. AE, DC, MC, V. Metrô: General Osório. Map p 134.*

Casa Aurea SANTA TERESA This small bed-and-breakfast with a leafy courtyard garden is on a quiet street within walking distance of Santa Teresa's main square. Some rooms have a shared bathroom. *Rua Áurea 80. ☎ 021/2242-5830. www.casaaurea.com.br. 12 units. Doubles with shared bathroom R$140; doubles with private bathroom R$180. No credit cards. Bus: 206. Map p 133.*

★★★ Casa 32 COSME VELHO Although I would love to keep this tip to myself, as a travel writer I have to tell you about this charming small inn, tucked away inside the idyllic leafy Largo do Boticário. With only three exquisite deluxe rooms, it never gets crowded here. The only drawback is that most attractions require a short bus or taxi ride, but coming back to this tropical refuge more than makes up for it. *Largo do Boticário 32. ☎ 021/2265-0943. www.casa32.com. 3 units. Doubles R$625. AE, DC, MC, V. Bus: 570 or 584. Map p 133.*

★ Castelinho 38 SANTA TERESA Travelers who prefer charm and character over fancy hotel amenities will be happy as a clam in this lovely neoclassical mansion in the heart of Santa Teresa. My favorite room is the master suite that boasts a fabulous view and is the only A/C unit in the house. *Rua Triunfo 38.*

A room at Castelinho 38.

☎ 021/2252-2549. www.castelinho38.com. 9 units. Doubles R$220. MC, V. Taxi recommended. Map p 133.

★★ Copacabana Palace Hotel COPACABANA Rio's most famous hotel oozes old-world glamour and style and features impeccable service. If you can afford it, avoid the rooms in the annex overlooking the street behind the hotel. *Av. Atlântica 1702. ☎ 0800/211-533 or 021/2548-7070. www.copacabanapalace.com. 225 units. Doubles R$960–R$1,170. AE, DC, MC, V. Metrô: Cardeal Arcoverde. Map p 134.*

★ Copacabana Sol Hotel COPACABANA In the heart of Copa's shopping district, this excellent mid-range hotel will leave you plenty of spending money. For an extra R$80, you can book a spacious suite with a jet tub and an extra bed. *Rua Santa Clara 141. ☎ 0800/025-4477 or 021/2549-4577. www.copacabanasolhotel.com.br. 70 units. Doubles*

The swimming pool at Fasano.

R$200–R$320. AE, DC, MC. Metrô: Siqueira Campos. Map p 134.

Everest Park Hotel IPANEMA With only 25 rooms, this unassuming hotel on a quiet side street is an excellent value, especially considering that it's less than a block from Ipanema Beach. The rooms are a little dated (think floral bedding and beige carpets), but everything is spotless and in good shape. *Rua Maria Quitéria 19. ☎ 021/2525-2200. www.everest.com.br. Doubles R$280. AE, DC, MC, V. Metrô: General Osório. Map p 135.*

★★ **Fasano** IPANEMA Designed by Philip Starck, the Fasano is Rio's hippest fashionista hotel. The best rooms are those overlooking Ipanema Beach. Accessible only to guests, the rooftop bar and swimming pool are truly spectacular. *Av. Vieira Souto 88. ☎ 021/3202-4000. www.fasano.com.br. 91 units. Doubles R$945–R$1,425. AE, DC, MC, V. Metrô: General Osorio. Map p 135.*

★ **Formule 1 Rio de Janeiro Centro** CENTRO If price matters, consider staying at the Formule 1 on the Praça Tiradentes. Cheaper than most hostels, this hotel offers spotless, modern accommodations. The location is perfect for exploring downtown Rio and Lapa's nightlife. Breakfast is not included. *Rua Silva Jardim 32. ☎ 021/3511-8500. www.formule1.com.br. 250 units. Doubles R$120. AE, MC, V. Metrô: Carioca. Map p 133.*

Golden Tulip Continental LEME If you don't mind the slightly outdated rooms and decor, this hotel offers pleasant digs in Leme, a quiet cul-de-sac neighborhood along the beach and only a 6-block walk from bustling Copacabana. *Rua Gustavo Sampaio 320. ☎ 021/3545-5300. www.goldentulipcontinental.com. 275 units. Doubles R$210–R$275. AE, DC, MC, V. Bus: 472. Map p 134.*

★ **Hotel Paysandu** FLAMENGO Architecture fans will be so charmed by this Art Deco jewel across from Flamengo Park that they can probably overlook its somewhat outdated facilities. The affordable rooms are modestly furnished and clean. *Rua Paissandu 23. ☎ 021/2558-7270. www.paysanduhotel.com.br. 76 units. Doubles R$120–R$180. AE, DC, MC, V. Metrô: Flamengo. Map p 133.*

★★★ **Hotel Santa Teresa** SANTA TERESA You may never want to leave this luxury retreat in the hills of Santa Teresa. Housed in a historic mansion, the stylish boutique hotel is tastefully decorated with Brazilian artwork and rustic local materials. Every room is unique; some have fabulous city views, some look out over the green hillside, and some feature large verandas. *Rua Almirante Alexandrino 660. ☎ 021/2222-2755. www.santateresahotel.com. 44 units. Doubles R$650–R$725. AE, DC, MC, V. Bus: 206. Map p 133.*

★★ **Hotel Vermont** IPANEMA If you just want a clean and affordable place to sleep that's in the middle of the action, look no further. Rooms are spotless and roomy (triples are available), there is Internet in the lobby, and you are only 2 blocks from trendy Ipanema Beach and prime shopping and nightlife. *Rua Visconde de Pirajá 254. ☎ 021/3202-5500. www.hotelvermont.com.br. 84 units. Doubles R$240. AE, DC, MC, V. Metrô: General Osório. Map p 135.*

★ **Ipanema Plaza** IPANEMA Right in the heart of Ipanema's gay district, this gay-friendly hotel attracts a very diverse clientele. The spacious rooms are elegantly appointed. For a top hotel, there are few amenities, except for a small rooftop pool and workout area, but you are just a block from the beach. *Rua Farme de Amoedo 34. ☎ 021/3687-2000. www.ipanemaplazahotel.com.br. 140 units. Doubles R$400–R$550. AE, DC, MC, V. Metrô: General Osório. Map p 135.*

★★★ **La Maison** GAVEA For the same price as a government-rated four-star hotel, you can stay at this beautiful house in the foothills of the Floresta da Tijuca, with a pretty swimming pool, lounge, library, and tastefully furnished guest rooms. The friendly owners of this exclusive B&B are happy to help you plan your holiday, and Leblon is only a R$12 cab ride away. *Rua Sergio Porto 58. ☎ 021/3205-3585. www.lamaisonario.com. 5 units. Doubles R$400–R$550. No credit cards. Taxi recommended. Map p 135.*

One of the luxurious rooms at the Hotel Santa Teresa.

Lancaster Othon COPACABANA One of the elegant 1940s Othon properties on Copacabana's waterfront, this hotel is in need of a makeover, but thanks to its slightly faded glory, some good deals can be had. The rooms are huge and have a separate sitting area. It's worth splurging on an oceanview room with a balcony. *Av. Atlântica 1470.* ☎ *021/2169-8300. www.hoteis-othon.com.br. 69 units. Doubles R$200–R$280. AE, DC, MC, V. Metrô: Cardeal Arcoverde. Map p 134.*

★★ **Leblon Spot** LEBLON Rio's first design hostel, Leblon Spot offers affordable and stylish accommodations in a prime location. All five private rooms are beautifully furnished and equipped with A/C. Guests also have the use of a lounge and kitchen. *Rua Dias Ferreira 636.* ☎ *021/2137-0090. www.leblonspot.com. 5 units. Doubles R$200–R$250. AE, V. Bus: 571. Map p 135.*

★★ **Leme Othon Palace** LEME Part of the Othon chain, this beachfront hotel is just off Copacabana and is perfect for those who like a bit more peace and quiet but still want to be close to the city's beach and nightlife options. The rooms are well equipped and comfortable and have recently undergone a much-needed renovation. *Av. Atlântica 656.* ☎ *021/2122-5900. www.hoteis-othon.com.br. 195 units. Doubles R$280–R$380. AE, DC, MC, V. Bus: 472. Map p 134.*

★ **Marina All Suites Hotel** LEBLON Small is beautiful; with only 39 rooms, the Marina All Suites offers spacious rooms and attentive service. A recent design overhaul has given the hotel an elegant and understatedly luxurious feel. *Av. Delfim Moreira 696.* ☎ *021/2172-1100. www.marinaallsuites.com.br. 38 units. Doubles R$765–R$1,030. AE, DC, MC, V. Bus: 474. Map p 135.*

★ **Mercure Rio de Janeiro Arpoador** IPANEMA You can't beat this location in Arpoador, a stone's throw from Copacabana and Ipanema beaches. The one-bedroom studios are spacious and modern and furnished with a separate living room and kitchen area; they're perfect for families traveling with small children. *Rua Francisco Otaviano 61.* ☎ *021/2113-8600. www.accorhotels.com.br. 56 units. Doubles R$275–R$375. AE, DC, MC, V. Metrô: General Osório. Map p 135.*

A spacious suite at the Marina All Suites Hotel.

The 1940s facade of the Olinda Othon Classic.

★★ Olinda Othon Classic COPACABANA I love this elegant 1940s building with marble floors and classic furniture. Recent renovations have given the rooms a much-needed upgrade and added modern amenities, such as Wi-Fi and flatscreen TVs. *Av. Atlântica 2230. ☎ 021/2545-9091. www.hoteis-othon.com.br. 102 units. Doubles R$250–R$325. AE, DC, MC, V. Metrô: Cardeal Arcoverde. Map p 134.*

★ Pestana Rio Atlântica COPACABANA Set in the heart of Copacabana, the Pestana is a good beachside option for people who like their amenities, such as a health club, rooftop pool and sun deck, sauna, and restaurant facilities. *Av. Atlântica 2964. ☎ 021/2548-6332. www.pestana.com. 216 units. Doubles R$400–R$550. AE, DC, MC, V. Metrô: Siqueira Campos. Map p 134.*

★★ Portinari COPACABANA Thanks to a slightly unsexy location, 1 block off the beachside boulevard, the Portinari design hotel is truly the best deal in town. Each floor features a different designer; pick your style: romantic, eco-friendly, tropical, or modern. Rooms are spacious and include queen-size beds and luxurious amenities. *Rua Francisco de Sá 17. ☎ 021/3222-8800. www.hotelportinari.com.br. 66 units. Doubles R$320. AE, DC, MC, V. Metrô: Cantagalo. Map p 134.*

★★ Porto Bay Rio Internacional COPACABANA Don't be fooled by the unassuming 1980s dark glass facade. This hotel offers

Bed & Breakfasts in Santa Teresa

If you just have a couple of nights in Rio de Janeiro, I highly recommend spending at least 1 night in a Santa Teresa bed-and-breakfast so that you can experience the bohemian, fun vibe of this charming hillside residential neighborhood. Participating homes include elegant 19th-century mansions, Art Deco houses, spacious apartments, and even a real castle. Some also feature beautiful views, lovely gardens, or a swimming pool. Room prices range between R$80 and R$180, depending on the level of luxury you choose; a scrumptious breakfast is always included. For more information, contact the **Santa Teresa Cama e Café B&B Network** (☎ 021/2225-4366 or 021/2221-7635) or browse www.camaecafe.com.br for available rooms and more information about your hosts.

pleasant, spacious rooms overlooking Copacabana Beach, a lovely rooftop pool, and friendly, attentive service. *Av. Atlântica 1500. ☎ 0800/021-1559 or 021/2546-8000. www.portobay.com. 117 units. Doubles R$460. AE, DC, MC, V. Metrô: Cardeal Arcoverde. Map p 134.*

★ **Praia Ipanema** IPANEMA This hotel straddles the border of Ipanema and Leblon. All rooms are luxuriously furnished with quality bedding and outfitted in elegant neutral tones. You can choose a room with either a full or a partial ocean view. *Av. Vieira Souto 706. ☎ 021/2540-4949. www.praiaipanema.com. 101 units. Doubles R$500–R$580. AE, DC, MC, V. Bus: 474 or 404. Map p 135.*

★ **Promenade the Claridge** LEBLON If you prefer more spacious digs (or are traveling with children), consider booking a flat. It gives you all the amenities of a hotel with the benefits of an apartment, such as a fully equipped kitchen, living room, and separate bedroom. This location is just around the corner from Rio's best restaurants. *Rua Rainha Guilhermina 156. ☎ 021/2103-2692 or 0800/702-3320. www.promenade.com.br. 24 units. Doubles R$325–R$400. AE, DC, MC, V. Bus: 571. Map p 135.*

The Promenade the Claridge's pool.

★ **kids** **Promenade Visconti Residence** IPANEMA This deluxe flat is like having your own apartment in swanky Ipanema. Choose a spacious room with a balcony or a suite (1 or 2 bedrooms). Children under age 12 stay free. *Rua Prudente de Moraes 1050. ☎ 021/2111-8600 or 0800/702-3320. www.promenade.com.br. 48 units. Doubles R$350. AE, DC, MC, V. Bus: 571. Map p 135.*

★ **Rio Hostel** SANTA TERESA If you enjoy a fun, festive atmosphere where you can make instant friends, book a room (with either a private or a shared bathroom) in this lovely hostel in Santa Teresa. Mingle with your fellow travelers by the pool or on the rooftop lounge, or join the many cultural activities organized by the front desk. *Rua Joaquim Murtinho 361. ☎ 021/3852-0827. www.riohostel.com. 10 units. Doubles R$140–R$180 with private bathroom, R$120 with shared bathroom. No credit cards. Bus: 206. Map p 133.*

★ **Rio 180 Graus** SANTA TERESA To get away from it all, splurge on this exclusive hideaway in Santa Teresa. Each room has been exquisitely decorated by a Brazilian designer. The Carnaval suite features an outdoor Jacuzzi tub with sweeping views of the city. *Rua Julio Otoni 254. ☎ 021/2205-1247. www.rio180hotel.com. 8 units. Doubles R$350–R$410. AE, DC, MC, V. Taxi recommended. Map p 133.*

★ **Royal Rio Palace** COPACABANA Location, location, location! This hotel is just 2 blocks from the beach, a block from the subway station, and right in the heart of Copacabana's shopping and dining

The Sheraton Rio Hotel & Towers.

district. The rooms are bright and decorated with a splash of color. *Rua Duvivier 82. ☎ 021/2122-9292. www.royalrio.com. 242 units. Doubles R$250–R$350. AE, DC, MC, V. Metrô: Cardeal Arcoverde. Map p 134.*

Scorial Rio Hotel FLAMENGO Those who prefer good value over location may want to consider the Scorial, an excellent government-rated three-star hotel with friendly staff and rooms that can accommodate up to four people. Just a 2-minute walk from the Largo do Machado subway, you can be on the beach within 20 minutes and still have some spending money to spare. *Rua Bento Lisboa 155. ☎ 021/3147-9100. www.scorialriohotel.com.br. 145 units. Doubles R$250. AE, DC, MC, V. Metrô: Largo do Machado. Map p 133.*

★★★ kids **Sheraton Rio Hotel & Towers** SAO CONRADO Situated right on the beach, this top hotel offers a large leisure area and pool complex, perfect for families traveling with children. The only drawbacks are that breakfast is not included in the rates and no attractions are within walking distance; it's a 10-minute cab ride to Leblon and Ipanema. *Av. Niemeyer 121. ☎ 021/2274-1122. www.sheraton-rio.com. 559 units. Doubles R$425–R$600. AE, DC, MC, V. Taxi recommended. Map p 135.*

★★★ **Sofitel** COPACABANA Looking for the best hotel in town? With its killer location, outstanding service, top-notch amenities (including two pools, a large health club, and beach service) and luxuriously appointed rooms that cost less than other five-star government-rated facilities, the Sofitel has it all. *Av. Atlântica 4240. ☎ 0800/241-232 or 021/2525-1232. www.accorhotels.com.br. 388*

A room at the Sofitel, one of the best hotels in Rio.

units. Doubles R$550–R$675. AE, DC, MC, V. Metrô: Cantagalo. Map p 134.

★ **Solar de Santa** SANTA TERESA This lovely 19th-century mansion now serves as an elegant bed-and-breakfast. Book all five rooms (which sleep up to 10 people) to have the entire villa to yourself and enjoy the large garden, pool, patio, and spectacular views from the elegant living room. *Ladeira do Meireles, 32. ☎ 021/2221-2117. www.solardesanta.com. 5 units. Doubles R$260–R$400. AE, MC, V. Bus: 206. Map p 133.*

★ **Tulip Inn Copacabana** COPACABANA This recently renovated hotel along Copacabana's waterfront offers pleasant, no-frills rooms. The standard rooms are on the small side and lack views. The best deals are the more spacious deluxe rooms with ocean views. Internet rates tend to be on the high side. Contact Brazil Nuts (p 160) to save as much as R$100. *Av. Atlântica 2554. ☎ 021/3545-5100. www.tulipinncopacabana.com. 5 units.*

The Windsor Miramar Hotel on Copacabana Beach.

Doubles R$260–R$400. AE, DC, MC, V. Metrô: Cantagalo. Map p 134.

★★ **Windsor Hotel Florida** CATETE Compared to many modern buildings, this elegant 1950s hotel has spacious rooms and a classy atmosphere. Service and amenities are top-notch, to please its core client base of Brazilian business travelers. *Rua Ferreira Viana 81. ☎ 021/2195-6800. www.windsorhoteis.com. 312 units. Doubles R$275. AE, DC, MC, V. Metrô: Catete. Map p 133.*

★★ **Windsor Martinique** COPACABANA Stretch your holiday budget by booking a hotel just off the beachside strip. For less than R$250, you get a compact room with a comfortable bed and a spotless bathroom. *Rua Sá Ferreira 30. ☎ 021/2195-5200. www.windsorhoteis.com. 116 units. Doubles R$220–R$275. AE, DC, MC, V. Metrô: Cantagolo. Map p 134.*

★ **Windsor Miramar Hotel** COPACABANA I'm a big fan of the Portuguese-owned Windsor chain. The Miramar is another excellent property; this elegant hotel boasts spacious rooms, many overlooking the beach, and excellent facilities, such as a pool, fitness area, and sauna. *Av. Atlântica 3668. ☎ 021/2195-6200. 156 units. Doubles R$240–R$320. AE, DC, MC, V. Metrô: Cantagalo. Map p 134.*

Yaya Hotel IPANEMA This simple hotel in the heart of Ipanema's gay district offers clean and affordable accommodations only a few blocks from the beach. The rooms are quite basic, but guests have the use of a TV lounge and free Wi-Fi. *Rua Farme de Amoedo 135. ☎ 021/3813-3912. www.yayario.com. 9 units. Doubles R$200 with private bathroom, R$160 with shared bathroom. AE, V. Metrô: General Osório. Map p 135.* ●

10 The Best Day Trips & Excursions

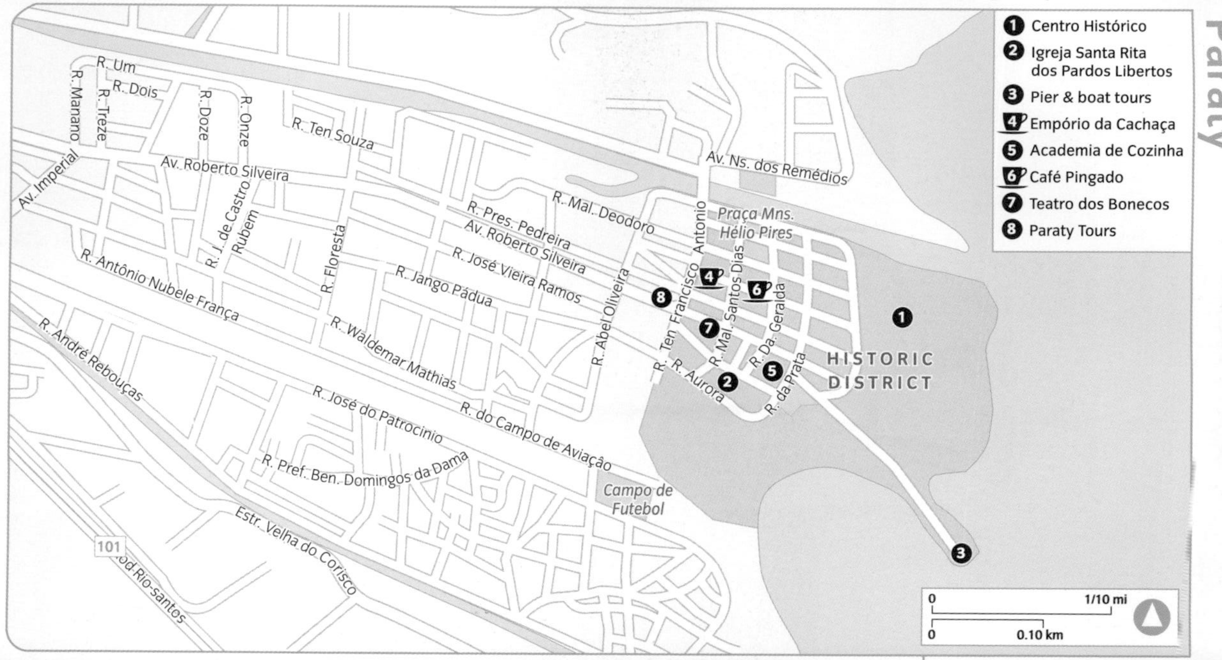
Paraty
1 Centro Histórico
2 Igreja Santa Rita dos Pardos Libertos
3 Pier & boat tours
4 Empório da Cachaça
5 Academia de Cozinha
6 Café Pingado
7 Teatro dos Bonecos
8 Paraty Tours
0 1/10 mi
0 0.10 km
HISTORIC DISTRICT
Av. Ns. dos Remédios
Praça Mns. Hélio Pires
R. da Prata
R. Da. Geralda
R. Mal. Santos Dias
R. Aurora
Antonio
R. Ten Francisco
R. Abel Oliveira
R. Mal. Deodoro
R. Pres. Pedreira
Av. Roberto Silveira
R. José Vieira Ramos
R. Jango Pádua
R. Waldemar Mathias
R. do Campo de Aviação
Campo de Futebol
R. Floresta
R. Ten Souza
R. José do Patrocinio
R. Pref. Ben. Domingos da Dama
Estr. Velha do Corisco
R. Onze
R. J. de Castro Rubem
R. Doze
Av. Roberto Silveira
R. Antônio Nubele França
R. Um
R. Dois
R. Treze
R. Manano
Av. Imperial
R. André Rebouças
101
Rod.Rio-santos

Previous page: An historic building in Paraty.

Travel back in time with a visit to Paraty, a colonial jewel wedged between lush Atlantic rainforest and turquoise ocean. Throughout the 18th and 19th centuries, Paraty served as an important export harbor, first for the gold brought from Minas Gerais, later for coffee harvested on Rio's coffee plantations. Today, Paraty is a booming tourist destination; its car-free historic center is packed with charming bed-and-breakfasts, excellent restaurants, and delightful shops and art galleries. The surrounding bay is a popular boating, snorkeling, and diving destination, and the rainforest-clad hills are a perfect playground for hikers, mountain bikers, horseback riders, and nature lovers.

A horse and buggy tour through Paraty's historic center.

❶ ★★★ **Paraty's Centro Histórico.** Half the fun of visiting Paraty is exploring its lovely colonial architecture. Pedestrians have plenty of room to stroll in the historic center since cars aren't allowed, but wear comfortable shoes for the uneven cobblestone streets. Start off at the **Praça da Matriz,** the town's main square, dominated by the impressive **Igreja Matriz de Nossa Senhora dos Remedios,** built between 1787 and 1873. The large square is a popular meeting place and often hosts events and festivals. Stroll south along Rua da Matriz or Rua

Paraty: Practical Matters

Paraty is 246km (153 miles) south of Rio de Janeiro. Bus company **Costa Verde** (☎ 021/3213-1800; www.costaverdetransportes.com.br) provides regular service from Rio's main bus station, Rodoviária Novo Rio (Av. Francisco Bicalho s/n), departing at 4, 6, 8, and 9am; noon; and 2, 4, and 8pm. The 4½-hour trip costs R$52. By car, take the BR 116, an undivided highway that winds its way down the coast. No cars are allowed within the historic city of Paraty; parking is available just outside the colonial center.

Igreja Santa Rita.

do Comercio and you'll encounter numerous art studios and galleries along the narrow cross streets. For more local artwork and an exhibit on the history of Paraty, visit the **Casa da Cultura,** the city's cultural center, on Rua Dona Geralda 117 (☎ 024/3371-2325). Also take a peek inside the recently restored **Igreja Nossa Senhora do Rosário** (Rua do Comércio and Rua Dr. Samuel Costa), built in 1757 by slaves and for slaves, who weren't allowed to worship in any of the town's other churches. The narrow lanes and alleys that run perpendicular to the main shopping streets lead to the waterfront and pier. At high tide, seawater often invades the low-lying areas, so be prepared for wet feet.

❷ ★★ **Igreja Santa Rita dos Pardos Libertos.** Paraty's most picturesque church is also the town's oldest surviving church; it was completed in 1722 for worshippers of mulatto descent and features some lovely woodwork. A small collection of religious artifacts is on display at the Museu de Arte Sacra in the back of the church. *Largo de Santa Rita s/n. ☎ 024/3371-1620. Admission R$2. Tues–Sun 9am–noon and 2–5pm.*

Where to Stay & Dine

Paraty abounds in charming bed & breakfasts *(pousadas)*. You will be in the center of the action at **Pousada do Sandi** (☎ 011/2503-0195 for reservations, ☎ 024/3371-1236 for hotel; www.pousadadosandi.com.br; doubles R$350–R$500), a lovely boutique hotel spread out over three 18th-century buildings. The interior courtyard has a beautiful garden and pool. For the ultimate pampered vacation experience, look no further than **Casa Turquesa** (☎ 024/3371-1037; www.casaturquesa.com.br; doubles R$790–R$1,200), a strong contender as my favorite *pousada* in Brazil. Everything about your stay here will be memorable, from the friendly service to the exquisite guest rooms, luxuriously furnished with local artwork to the gourmet breakfast to the stylish lounges and pool.

For an elegant meal overlooking the water, try **O Refugio,** Praça do Porto s/n (☎ 024/3371-2447). Whatever you order here, sample at least one serving of the *camarão casadinho,* a giant prawn, grilled to perfection, stuffed with a generous helping of spicy *farofa.* **Casa do Fogo** (Rua Comendador José Luiz 390; ☎ 024/9819-5111; www.casadofogo.com.br; $$) specializes in fish and meat dishes flambéed in *cachaça.* A more casual crowd flocks to **Arpoador** (Rua da Matriz 7; ☎ 024/3371-3202; $$), for its delicious *moqueca* fish or seafood stews and nightly live music.

Boats at Paraty's pier.

❸ ★ **Pier and boat tours.** A must-do excursion in Paraty is a boat trip around the Baia de Ilha Grande, one of Brazil's largest bays, dotted with hundreds of small islands. Schooners leave daily (weather permitting) between 10am and noon from this pier. A 5-hour tour, including several stops to snorkel or swim in the crystal clear water, costs about R$45 (depending on your negotiation skills). If you prefer, contact Paraty Tours to book your tour (see below).

❹ **Empório da Cachaça.** Take advantage of this pedestrian-only destination to indulge in Paraty's specialty *cachaça,* the potent firewater made from sugar cane. Empório da Cachaça stocks an impressive variety from local and national distilleries. Enjoy a sample or two, or three. *Rua Dr. Samuel Costa 22. ☎ 024/3371-6329. $.*

❺ ★★ kids **Academia de Cozinha.** Learn more about Paraty's regional history while preparing a delicious Brazilian meal from local ingredients with renowned chef and food writer Yara Castro Roberts. *Rua Dona Geralda 288. ☎ 024/3371-6468. www.chefbrasil.com. R$180 per person, including an English-language cooking lesson, recipes, dinner, and drinks. Book ahead to ensure availability.*

❻ **Café Pingado.** Paraty is packed with charming cafes, but this is one of my favorites. It serves organic coffee and a variety of delicious snacks, such as freshly made sandwiches, cookies, or desserts, any time of the day. *Rua Dr. Samuel Costa 208. ☎ 024/3371-8388. $.*

❼ ★★★ **Teatro dos Bonecos (Puppet Theatre).** Internationally renowned theater group Contadores de Estorias (Storytellers) puts on an incredible puppet show for adults, using ingenious puppetry skills and music to craft a story without words. With only 94 seats, the intimate theater sells out fast, so book ahead. *Rua Dona Geralda 327. ☎ 024/3371-1575. www.ecparaty.org.br. Wed and Fri at 9pm (more performances in high season). Tickets R$40 adults; discounts available for seniors and children 10–16. Not recommended for children under 10. Map p 146.*

❽ ★ **Paraty Tours.** Paraty's fabulous natural setting lends itself to many outdoor activities, including horseback riding, scuba diving, kayaking, rappelling, hiking, and walking tours. Stop by Paraty Tours for more information. *Av. Roberto da Silveira 11. ☎ 024/3371-1327. www.paratytours.com.br.*

Petrópolis

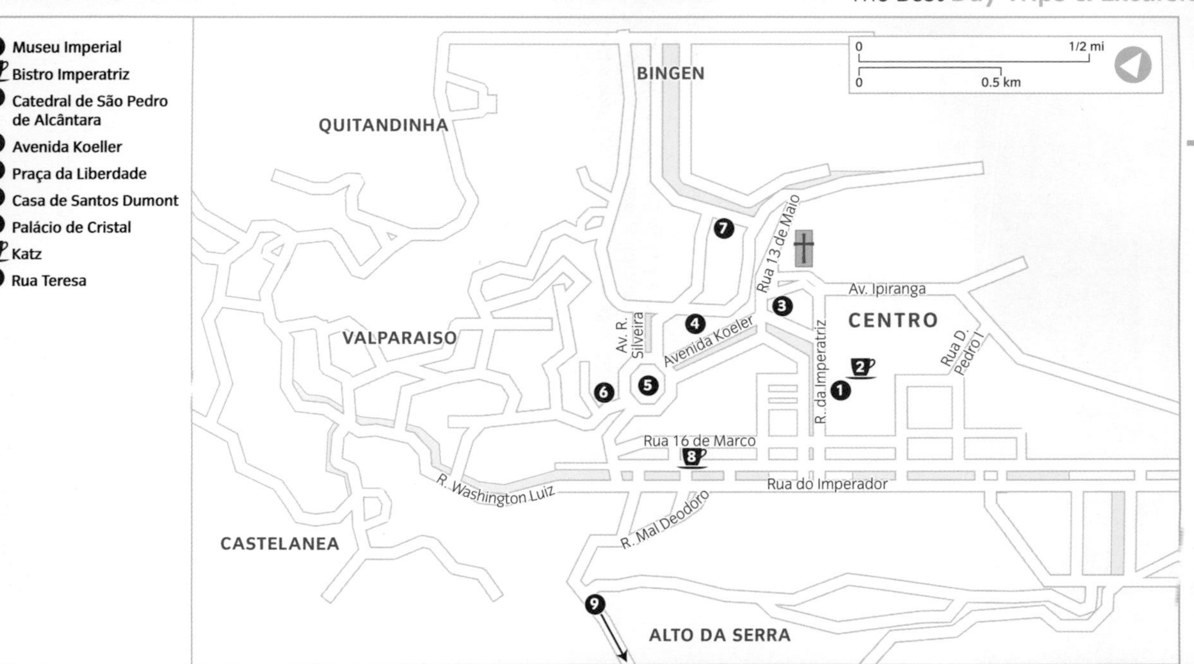
1 Museu Imperial
2 Bistro Imperatriz
3 Catedral de São Pedro de Alcântara
4 Avenida Koeller
5 Praça da Liberdade
6 Casa de Santos Dumont
7 Palácio de Cristal
8 Katz
9 Rua Teresa
0 1/2 mi
0 0.5 km
BINGEN
QUITANDINHA
VALPARAISO
CASTELANEA
CENTRO
ALTO DA SERRA
Rua 13 de Maio
Av. Ipiranga
Rua D. Pedro I
R. da Imperatriz
Av. R. Silveira
Avenida Koeller
Rua 16 de Marco
Rua do Imperador
R. Washington Luiz
R. Mal Deodoro

Follow the lead of the Portuguese royal family and head up to the lovely mountain retreat of Petrópolis, 70km (43 miles) from Rio, at an elevation of 800m (2,625 ft.). The town's main attraction is the exquisite Museu Imperial, the former summer residence of D. Pedro II, filled with magnificent antiques and crown jewels. Then take a stroll along the cobblestone boulevards lined with elegant 19th-century mansions and visit the quirky house of Brazil's pioneer inventor and aviator Santos Dumont.

1 ★★★ kids **Museu Imperial.** It was D. Pedro I who first fell in love with the cool mountain air and purchased a piece of land here in 1822. After his death, his son D. Pedro II began the construction of the imperial summer palace in 1845. This elegant neoclassical building was completed in 1862 and is now one of Brazil's most important museums and a delight to visit. All visitors must don a pair of special slippers to protect the Carrara marble and hardwood floors before embarking on a tour of at least a dozen rooms and salons, packed with 18th- and 19th-century furniture, artwork, china, and jewelry. The piéce de résistance is the Imperial crown, almost 3kg (6⅔ lb.) of gold, encrusted with 17 rubies and 19 emeralds. The former slave and servant quarters behind the palace have been converted into a carriage museum. From Thursday to Saturday, there is a nightly Sound and Light Show, a 45-minute presentation of music, waterworks, and light effects projected onto the facade of the building that tells the royal history (in Portuguese only). *Rua da Imperatriz 220.* ☎ *024/2245-5550. www.museuimperial.gov.br. Museum R$8 adults, R$4 seniors and children, R$20 family of 2 adults and 2 children. Sound and light show R$20 adults, R$10 seniors and children, R$50 family of 2 adults and 2 children. Museum: Tues–Sun 11am–6pm; gardens 8am–6pm; sound and light show Thurs–Sat 8pm. English-language audio tour R$3. Map p 150.*

The Museu Imperial.

2 **Bistro Imperatriz.** On the grounds of the Museu Imperial, you will find this lovely bistro. Enjoy a tasty hot lunch, afternoon tea or coffee, or a snack while taking in the pleasant palace grounds. *Rua da Imperatriz 220.* ☎ *024/2232-0479. www.bistroimperatriz.com.br. $$.*

3 ★ **Catedral de São Pedro de Alcântara.** Dedicated to the patron saint of the monarchy, this impressive French neo-gothic cathedral was commissioned by D. Pedro II in 1884. Built in granite, the church interior is decorated with sober marble, onyx, and bronze sculptures, lovely stained-glass windows, and exquisite jacaranda furniture. The Imperial Chapel contains the remains of D. Pedro II and Princess Isabel. Visit the church tower for a fabulous view of the surrounding region (not

Petrópolis: Practical Matters

From Rio de Janeiro, there are regular buses to Petrópolis, departing every 20 to 30 minutes from Rodoviária Novo Rio, Av. Francisco Bicalho s/n. Bus company **Única** (☎ 021/2263-8792) makes the 1-hour trip for R$16. Upon arrival at the Petrópolis bus terminal, you'll need to take a taxi or local bus into the historic center. By car, take the Linha Vermelha toward the Galeão International Airport. Then follow the signs for the BR-040. There is a toll of R$6.70 each way. For information about Petrópolis, contact the Tourist Information Center, at Praça Visconde de Mauá 305 (☎ 0800/024-1516; www.petropolis.rj.gov.br; daily 9am–5pm).

recommended for those with a fear of heights). *Rua São Pedro de Alcântara 60. ☎ 024/2242-4300. Cathedral 8am–6pm; church tower Tues–Sat 11am–5pm, Sun 1–3pm. Cathedral free, church tower R$8 adults, R$4 seniors and children under 16. No children under 10 allowed.*

4 ★★ **Avenida Koeller.** The town's most elegant boulevard is framed by lovely 19th-century mansions. Across the street from the Catedral de São Pedro de Alcântara, you will notice a lovely pink mansion (Av. Koeller 42), the former residence of Princess Isabel. The opulent yellow palace nearby at Av. Koeller 255 was built in 1889 by the Baron of Rio Negro. Later it served as the official summer residence of the president of Brazil. Toward the end of the boulevard stands another lovely neoclassical building, the elegant Solar D. Afonso (Av. Koeller 376), now a luxurious boutique hotel.

A horse and buggy tour in Petrópolis.

5 ★★ kids **Praça da Liberdade.** At the junction of the town's main boulevards lies this lovely parklike square with a children's playground, water fountains, a roller-skating rink, and a restaurant. *Praça da Liberdade s/n.*

6 ★★ kids **Casa de Santos Dumont.** Inspired by the mountains, Brazil's pioneer aviator Alberto Santos Dumont (1873–1932) built a tiny Swiss chalet. It's now a museum that reflects a great deal of the aviator's quirky and creative personality; note the space-saving stairs made with half-sized steps and the alcohol-heated shower. *Rua do Encanto 22. ☎ 024/2247-3158. Tues–Sun 9:30am–5pm. Admission R$5 adults, R$2.50 children and seniors.*

7 **Palácio de Cristal.** The glass and metal structures of this crystal palace were made in France and assembled here in 1884. The building was a present from the Conde d'Eu

Casa de Santos Dumont.

for his wife, Princess Isabel. It is now used as an exhibit space. *Praça Alfredo Pachá s/n. ☎ 024/ 2247-37721. Free admission. Tues–Sun 9am–6:30pm.*

8 **Katz.** Petrópolis's "cool" mountain air is a great excuse to indulge in the locally made chocolates and sweets at Katz, all perfectly washed down with an espresso or cappuccino. *Rua do Imperador 912. ☎ 024/2231-1191. $.*

9 **Rua Teresa.** Brazilian tourists are not only attracted by the rich history of Petrópolis, but also by its excellent bargain shopping. The region boasts an important garment industry, and you will find more than 300 stores along the Rua Teresa, selling jeans, T-shirts, dresses, and other clothing items, both for retail *(varejo)* and wholesale *(atacado)*. *Rua Teresa. Store hours Mon 2–6pm; Tues–Sat 9am–6pm.*

Horse & Buggy Tour

Why not see Petrópolis without tiring yourself out walking? Horse and buggies depart from the main entrance of the Museu Imperial, and there are two sightseeing options. The first tour costs R$60 per buggy (max. six people) and stops at the Cathedral, Palácio de Crystal, Casa de Santos Dumont, and the Palácio Rio Negro, allowing you to stop and visit each site while the buggy waits. It takes about an hour and a half. On the second, cheaper tour, you cover the same route, but you see the sights only from the outside. The cost is R$40 for up to six people, and it takes about 30 minutes. Tours run year-round, Tuesday to Sunday. Museum admission is not included in the tour prices.

Búzios

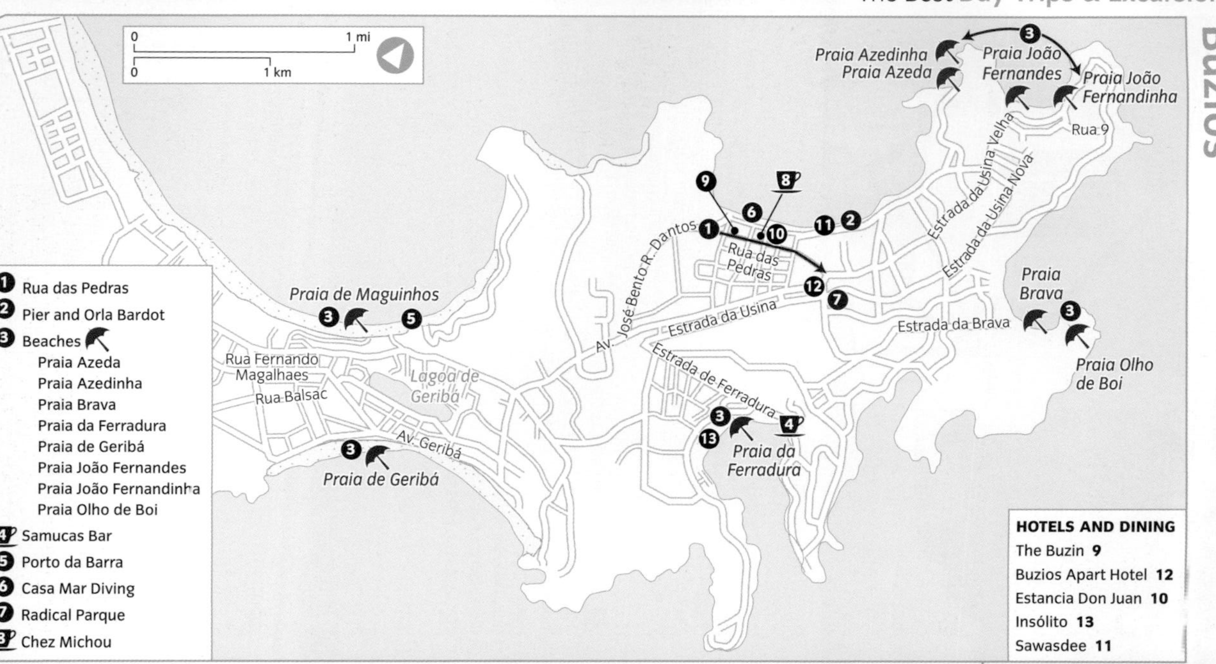
0
1 mi
0
1 km
Praia Azedinha
Praia Azeda
Praia João Fernandes
Praia João Fernandinha
Rua 9
Estrada da Usina Velha
Estrada da Usina Nova
Praia Brava
Estrada da Brava
Praia Olho de Boi
Rua das Pedras
Av. José Bento R. Dantos
Estrada da Usina
Estrada de Ferradura
Praia da Ferradura
Praia de Maguinhos
Rua Fernando Magalhaes
Rua Balsac
Lagoa de Geribá
Av. Geribá
Praia de Geribá
1 Rua das Pedras
2 Pier and Orla Bardot
3 Beaches
Praia Azeda
Praia Azedinha
Praia Brava
Praia da Ferradura
Praia de Geribá
Praia João Fernandes
Praia João Fernandinha
Praia Olho de Boi
4 Samucas Bar
5 Porto da Barra
6 Casa Mar Diving
7 Radical Parque
8 Chez Michou
HOTELS AND DINING
The Buzin 9
Buzios Apart Hotel 12
Estancia Don Juan 10
Insólito 13
Sawasdee 11

Armação de Búzios (aka Búzios) is all about the sun, sand, and sea; more than a dozen different beaches are scattered around this peninsula, perfect for swimming, boating, or simply relaxing along the shore. At night, visitors stroll the pedestrian-friendly cobblestone streets of the main village, browsing the high-end stores, dining in elegant restaurants, and enjoying the fun, festive atmosphere of this beach resort. If you like to party, the best time to visit is on weekends and during high season. To enjoy a more laid-back atmosphere, visit in the off season or on weekdays.

❶ ★★★ **Rua das Pedras.** The center of the main village is a pleasant pedestrian-only area lined with restaurants, cafes, galleries, and stores. Búzios is quite the upscale resort, so expect exclusive Brazilian and international brands and labels. More affordable purchases can be made a few blocks off this main drag.

❷ ★ **Pier and Orla Bardot.** One of the most popular day trips from Búzios is a tour of the nearby beaches onboard a wooden schooner. Boats depart from the town's pier throughout the day. Prices depend on your bargaining skills, time of day, and season; expect to pay R$25 to R$45 for a 4- to 6-hour tour, refreshments included. Boat tours will usually stop at several nearby beaches to allow for swimming or snorkeling. The seawall just beyond the pier is known as the Orla Bardot, after Brigitte Bardot (note a statue of her just beyond the first bend), who helped promote Búzios as the Saint Tropez of Brazil after her visit in the 1960s. You will find several nice restaurants, bars, and nightclubs along the oceanside boulevard.

❸ ★★ **Beaches.** Buzios' main draw is its beaches. With more than 20 different options to choose from, it's just a matter of deciding what you are in the mood for: sunbathing, swimming, surfing, fun and bustling, or secluded and quiet? Note that most of the area beaches have strong waves, ideal for surfing but not so great for inexperienced swimmers, especially for small children. **Praia de Geribá** is Búzios' trendiest beach, attracting the young and beautiful. It is also a favorite surf destination and offers some of the best waves in the region. Nearby **Praia**

Strolling along Rua das Pedras.

A schooner out on the water by Búzios.

da Ferradura, a perfect horseshoe-shaped bay, features the best beach-side bars and restaurants along this stretch. This is also the best beach for swimming on this side of the peninsula. Closer toward the point is another great beach for surfing, **Praia Brava,** more private and isolated than the other two beaches along this side of the peninsula. Just beyond Praia Brava lies Búzios' only nude beach, **Praia Olho de Boi.** It's a 20- to 30-minute walk from Praia Brava to reach this beautiful and secluded white beach. Locals love **Praia Azeda,** a pretty cove only a 10-minute walk from the village. The calm, protected waters here are great for swimming. The smaller cove just beyond is known as **Praia Azedinha,** a lovely, sheltered beach with large rocks that form natural swimming pools at low tide. Most tourists prefer action-packed **Praia João Fernandes,** a sandy beach with calm turquoise water, still within walking distance from the village. With several restaurants, bars, and watersports rentals, it's easy to spend an entire day here. To get away from the crowds, follow a short trail to the next beach over, **Praia João Fernandinho,** a small cove, almost at the point of the peninsula, which is great for snorkeling. There are also a number of beautiful beaches on the other side of the peninsula, a short drive away.

Búzios: Practical Matters

From Rio, there are regular buses to Búzios (travel time approx. 3½ hr.); buses depart at 6:30, 9:15, and 11:15am; and 1:15, 3:15, 5:15, and 7:30pm, from Rodoviária Novo Rio, Av. Francisco Bicalho s/n. **Bus company 1001** (☎ 022/4004-5001) makes the journey at a cost of R$32 each way. By car, take the Rio-Niteroi bridge (BR 1010) and follow the signs for Via Lagos (RJ 124, Região dos Lagos). There are several tolls along the way. For information, check www.buzios online.com.br or contact the Tourist Office at ☎ 022/2633-6200.

Once in Búzios, most attractions are within walking distance from the main village. Nearby beaches such as João Fernandes and Azeda can also be accessed by water taxi. Hail one from the pier or the beach, or contact ☎ 022/2620-8018.

4 Samucas Bar. Just look for the crowd gathered at a small kiosk toward the left side of Ferradura Beach (when facing the ocean); chances are people are waiting for an order of *pastel de camarão* (fried savory shrimp dumplings) or a plate of garlic shrimp. Order a fresh fruit juice or cold beer along with your snack. ***Praia da Ferradura, kiosk 2. ☎ 022/2623-4657. $.***

5 ★★ kids Porto da Barra. Set among the mangroves, this large pier features several restaurants and bars with outdoor patios overlooking the water. Especially in the evening, the lovely lit deck makes for a fun and romantic dining destination. Kids will love exploring the wooden walkway through the mangrove to look for crabs and other critters. ***Av. José Bento de Ribeiro Dantas 2900, Praia de Manguinhos s/n.***

6 ★ Diving. Búzios offers some of the best dive spots close to Rio de Janeiro. Although this certainly isn't the Caribbean, the water temperature is normally around 72°F (22°C) and visibility ranges from 10 to 15m (33–49 ft). Expect to see plenty of soft coral formations and parrotfish; sea turtles and stingrays are also often spotted. For a small fee, non-diving companions are welcome to join divers on the boat. *Casa Mar Diving, Rua das Pedras 242. ☎ 022/9817-6234. www.casamar.com.br. R$150 for two dives, including all gear.*

People using a water taxi in Búzios.

7 kids Radical Parque. If your kids are looking for more active pursuits, they can let off some steam at this outdoor adventure park. The large playground features climbing walls, paint ball, giant trampolines, and go-karts. ***Estrada da Usina 1 (next to the bus station). ☎ 022/2623-2904. www.radicalparque.com.br. Prices vary per activity, starting at R$10. Daily 9am–11pm (check for off-season hours).***

8 Chez Michou. For a quick snack, order a delicious stuffed crepe at Chez Michou. Choose from more than 50 combinations of fillings, sweet or savory. The kitchen stays open late (until 6am in high season) and is a popular late-night pit stop. ***Rua das Pedras 90. ☎ 022/2623-2169. $.***

One of Búzios's beautiful bays.

Where to Stay & Dine

To fully explore Búzios and enjoy the town's excellent nightlife, you may want to spend a night or two here. There's no shortage of restaurants or accommodations, but keep in mind that hotel prices are high and rooms fill up fast, especially on weekends and in high season.

Lodging

kids **Búzios Internacional Apart Hotel.** This Apart Hotel is a great affordable option for families or friends traveling together. Within walking distance of the Rua das Pedras, these spacious one- or two-bedroom apartments easily accommodate two to six people and include a comfortable sitting room and fully equipped kitchen. *Estrada da Usina Velha 99. ☎ 022/2537-3876. www.buziosbeach.com.br. 44 units. Doubles R$200–R$300. Extra person add R$20–R$60. AE, V.*

★★ **Insólito.** If you want exclusivity, consider staying at this hip boutique hotel with lush gardens and terraces overlooking Ferradura Beach. Each room is tastefully decorated with Brazilian artwork, furniture, and books. A free shuttle service to the main village is available. *Praia da Ferradura s/n. ☎ 022/2623-2172. www.insolitohotel.com.br. 12 units. Doubles R$700–R$950. AE, DC, MC, V.*

Estancia Don Juan.

Dining

★ **Buzin.** For a fast and affordable lunch or dinner, try this excellent kilo restaurant. The large buffet includes delicious salads, antipasto, vegetables, and seafood. The grill serves up beef, chicken, and fish, cooked to order. *Rua Manoel Turibe de Farias 273. ☎ 022/2633-7051. Entrees R$44 per kilo. AE, V. Lunch and dinner daily.*

★ **Estancia Don Juan.** A longtime crowd pleaser, this restaurant serves juicy Argentinean steaks and excellent red wine or sangria on a lovely patio overlooking bustling Rua das Pedras. Enjoy live tango shows on Tuesday nights. *Rua das pedras 178. ☎ 022/2623-2169. www.estanciadonjuan.com.br. Entrees R$34–R$52. AE, DC, MC, V. Lunch Wed–Sun; dinner Mon–Sun.*

★★ **Sawasdee.** Spice up your stay with fiery Thai cuisine at one of Brazil's top Thai restaurants. Start off with an aromatic bowl of coconut soup, followed by tangy noodles, fragrant stir-fries, or a spicy curry. *Orla Bardot 422. ☎ 022/2623-4644. www.sawasdee.com.br. Entrees R$28–R$48. AE, DC, MC, V. Lunch Fri–Sat; dinner Sun–Tues and Thurs–Sat.*

The Savvy Traveler

Before You Go

Tourist Offices

Riotur (☎ 021/2271-7000; www.riodejaneiro-turismo.com.br) operates several information booths throughout the city and provides excellent information on the city of Rio de Janeiro. Service at Tom Jobim International Airport (Terminal 1; ☎ 021/3398-4077; daily 6am–11pm) can be spotty. Your most reliable bet is the well-stocked **Riotur Information Center** (☎ 021/2541-7522) on Av. Princesa Isabel 183, Copacabana, open Monday to Friday from 9am to 6pm, or the beachside booth on the Av. Atlântica (in front of Rua Hilário de Gouveia; daily 8am–10pm). Make sure you pick up a free map and the must-have *Guia do Rio (Rio Guide)* booklet, published every 3 months. Written in both English and Portuguese, it lists all tourist attractions, events, and festivals, and has many other useful phone numbers. Riotur also operates an information line, **Alô Rio** (☎ 021/2542-8080, or 0800/285-0555), with English-speaking staff, which is open Monday to Friday from 9am to 6pm.

Useful Websites

www.rioofficialguide.com: Riotur's outstanding website has detailed information on attractions. Its useful *Rio Guide* is also available as a PDF.

www.brazil.org.uk: The Brazilian embassy in the United Kingdom has a comprehensive website with background information, including a detailed reading list on a wide range of Brazilian topics.

Previous page: The Santa Teresa streetcar.

Planning Your Trip

For expert travel assistance, contact travel agency **Brazil Nuts,** 1610 Trade Center Way, Naples, FL (☎ 0800/553-9959 or 239/593-0266; www.brazilnuts.com). The owners and staff are real Brazil experts who not only provide excellent advice and recommendations, but also offer highly competitive rates on airline tickets and hotels. It's worth checking their prices, even if you are making your own airline and hotel arrangements.

To make the most of your time in Rio, contract the services of **Soul Brasileiro,** Rua São Clemente 185/303, Botafogo, Rio de Janeiro, (☎ 021/2538-9409; www.soulbrasileiro.com). This innovative company offers personalized sightseeing itineraries to suit your specific interests. Fill out a detailed questionnaire and for a small fee (approx. R$25 per day), the knowledgeable staff will put together a unique program that goes beyond the standard tourist attractions and includes tips on nightlife, cultural events, and educational activities.

The Best Times to Go

Rio de Janeiro is a year-round destination, but there are some things to keep in mind. Situated in the southern hemisphere, Rio's seasons run opposite those in the U.S. and Europe; the hottest months are December to March. This is also high season, when Brazilians and other South Americans on their summer vacations flock here to enjoy the beach and perhaps celebrate New Year's and carnival. As a result, prices go up, way up, but at the same time the city exudes a fun holiday vibe. From April through October, temperatures are more

Escolas de Samba

The stars of Rio's Carnaval parade are the Escolas de Samba (samba schools), community-based associations that put together a parade with elaborate floats, costumes, choreography, and, of course, a captivating samba song. The league is organized into several divisions, and there are dozens of schools throughout the city. However, only the elite schools *(Grupo Especial),* or A and B divisions, parade in the Sambodromo (p 39), the official Carnaval venue. Judges evaluate the schools on their performance, creativity, costumes, and music to determine the ranking. By June or July, the schools are practicing weekly to be ready in time for Carnaval. The public is welcome to watch as musicians, and especially the percussion players, rehearse their songs (during the parade, they will perform more than 90 min. non-stop!). Most samba schools are located in poor communities or favelas; some are quite far from downtown Rio.

These events are very safe, and children are welcome. However, do keep in mind that rehearsals usually don't start until 11pm, and wear casual, light clothing. Below is a list of some accessible schools:

- Salgueiro, Rua Silva Telles 104, Andaraí (☎ 021/2238-0389; www.salgueiro.com.br)
- Mangueira, Rua Visconde de Niteroi 1072, Mangueira (☎ 021/2567-4637; www.mangueira.com.br)
- Vila Isabel, Blvd. 28 de Setembro 382, Vila Isabel (☎ 021/2578-0077; www.gresunidosdevilaisabel.com.br)

amenable (see the chart on p 163) and prices go down. One minor exception is the month of July, when North Americans and Europeans enjoy their summer vacation and Brazilians (especially those from the south) take time off for a "winter break." Rio's attractions are open year-round.

Festivals & Special Events

Your best resource for up-to-date information on special events is Riotur's English-language website www.rioofficialguide.com. Below you will find a list of the city's most popular yearly events.

JANUARY–MARCH. On January 20, the patron saint of Rio de Janeiro is honored with a lavish afternoon procession that starts in the neighborhood of Tijuca, just north of Rio's downtown, departing from the Igreja de São Sebastião dos Frades Capuchinhos (Rua Haddock Lobo 266). Thousands of believers will accompany the statue of the saint on its journey to the city's modern cathedral in downtown.

Celebrated in February or early March, **Carnaval** is Rio de Janeiro's largest event. The official kick-off occurs on Thursday night when the mayor hands the keys of the city to King Momo. The samba school parades take place on Saturday (A group) and Sunday to Monday *(Grupo Especial)*. Carnival officially ends at noon on Ash Wednesday. The results of the Carnaval parade are announced Wednesday afternoon and bring the city to a standstill.

JUNE–SEPTEMBER. Throughout the month of June, the city celebrates the so-called ***Festas Juninas*** (June Celebration), in honor of saints Anthony, John, and Peter. Celebrated throughout Brazil, this harvest festival offers country music, bonfires, hot-air balloons, and fun fairs. For details, contact Riotur (☎ 021/2271-7000; www.riodejaneiro-turismo.com.br) or Alô Rio (☎ 021/2542-8080).

Runners from all across the world compete in the **Rio de Janeiro marathon** (www.maratonadorio.com.br), usually held on the third Sunday of July. The flat course follows the city's waterfront. Half marathon and 6km (3¾-mile) fun-run courses are also available.

Fans of animated films don't want to miss the **Anima Mundi Film Festival** (third week of July), a 9-day event with over 400 animated films from all over the world. For more information, see www.animamundi.com.br.

On September 7, Brazil celebrates its **Independence Day.** Like most cities, Rio de Janeiro marks the occasion with an impressive military parade that takes place along Avenida Rio Branco and runs past the World War II monument downtown.

In late September, Rio de Janeiro holds its most important film festival, the **International Film Festival** (www.festivaldorio.com.br), showcasing Brazilian and international films. Subtitles are in Portuguese, but there is usually a good selection of international movies.

OCTOBER–DECEMBER. Rio de Janeiro hosts one of Brazil's largest **gay pride parades.** The event usually occurs in October, and the festive, colorful floats and participants parade along Copacabana Beach.

One of my favorite events takes place in Santa Teresa in October or November. The Santa Teresa **Portas Abertas** (www.chavemestra.com.br) is like a giant open-house party, when dozens of artists welcome the public to their studios and showcase their artwork.

For a tropical Christmas experience, attend the **lighting of the city's Christmas tree,** usually in the third week of November. The 85m-high (279-ft.) metal tree-shaped structure is placed in the middle of the Lagoa and inaugurated with a spectacular light and sound show.

Compared to many other religious events, **Christmas** is a relatively quiet event, celebrated on the evening of the 24th with a large family dinner at home. Most restaurants are closed.

New Year's Eve is Rio de Janeiro's largest single-day celebration. Cariocas traditionally ring in the New Year on the beach by making an offering to the Yemanjá, the Goddess of the Sea. In the days leading up to December 31, you will see people making offerings of flowers and other gifts. The city's official party takes place on Copacabana Beach. Dressed in white for good luck, crowds gather on the sand to enjoy live music and of course a spectacular fireworks celebration at midnight. Check the Riotur website for details on programming and transportation (major road closures have a significant impact on the city's traffic flow).

Weather

Rio has very hot and humid summers—100°F (38°C) and 98% humidity are not uncommon. Summer is

AVERAGE DAYTIME TEMPERATURES & RAINFALL IN RIO DE JANEIRO

	JAN	FEB	MAR	APR	MAY	JUNE
Daily Temp. (°F)	82	82	81	79	73	72
Daily Temp. (°C)	28	28	27	26	23	22
Days of Precip.	5.3	4.9	5.3	4.3	3.1	2.0
	JULY	**AUG**	**SEPT**	**OCT**	**NOV**	**DEC**
Daily Temp. (°F)	72	73	75	81	81	42
Daily Temp. (°C)	22	23	24	27	24	6
Days of Precip.	1.8	2.4	3.2	3.9	5.4	10

also the rainy season, with heavy but short showers almost every day. Rio winters are quite mild, with nighttime temperatures dropping as low as 66°F (19°C), and daytime temperatures climbing to the pleasant and sunny mid-80s (30°C), still warm enough to enjoy the beach. However, periodic cold fronts that sweep up from the south can bring colder weather and rain, so don't forget to bring a sweater.

Getting **There**

By Plane

Most major airlines, including American Airlines, United Airlines, Delta, Continental, US Airways, Air Canada, Tam, KLM, Air France, and British Airways, fly to Rio de Janeiro, sometimes with a stop or connection in São Paulo. International passengers arrive at **Antônio Carlos Jobim Airport** (☎ 021/3398-5050), more commonly known as Galeão Airport, which is 20km (12 miles) from downtown.

Getting into Town from the Airport Taxis at Galeão are a challenge. Drivers will start to hassle you the minute you step into the arrivals hall. The safer but more expensive bet is to buy a prepaid fare at the TransCoopass desk in the arrivals hall (☎ 021/2209-1555; www.transcoopass.com.br; all major credit cards accepted). Rates range from R$65 to Flamengo, and R$70 to R$90 to the beach hotels of Copacabana and Ipanema. These prepaid taxis are about 40% more expensive, but give you peace of mind; it doesn't matter if you get stuck in traffic or the driver takes the long route. On the other hand, if you know what you're doing, you can cut those prices significantly just by hailing a regular taxi out in front of the terminal. A ride to Copacabana should cost about R$50 in average traffic conditions. Unfortunately, rip-offs are not uncommon. Someone recently told me how a cabbie showed an "official" rate chart and charged him R$150 for a ride to Copacabana!

Gray Line (☎ 021/2512-9919; www.grayline.com) offers a minibus transfer service from Galeão to the hotels of the Zona Sul or Barra. The cost is R$40 one-way, with one bag free, and extra bags R$5. Buses leave once every hour on the hour. You meet the uniformed Gray Line driver by the RioTur booth in either Terminal 1 or Terminal 2.

By Bus

All long-distance buses arrive at the **Rodoviária Novo Rio,** Av. Francisco Bicalho 1, Santo Cristo (☎ 021/3213-1800; www.novorio.com.br), located close to downtown near the old port. It's best to use a taxi while traveling to or from the station, particularly with all your bags, as it's not in the best part of town. Prepaid taxi vouchers are available at the booth next to the taxi stand.

By Cruise Ship

Cruise-ship season runs from November through March and ships dock in the terminal almost opposite Praça Mauá. Downtown is an easy walk, and public transit is close by. On weekends and after dark, it's best to take a taxi.

Getting **Around**

Public Transportation

By Subway The easiest way to get around in Centro and the Zona Sul is by the Metrô (www.metrorio.com.br). If you have a choice between the bus and the subway, I highly recommend the latter as it is much cleaner, easy to navigate, and more comfortable than the bus. There are only two lines: Line 1 goes north from downtown—it's useful for going to the Maracanã and the Quinta da Boa Vista (Zoo)—while Line 2 covers most of Centro, then swings thorough Glória, Catete, Flamengo, and Botafogo before ducking through the mountain to Copacabana and Ipanema. Traveling from Centro to Copacabana takes 20 minutes, and the system is very safe and efficient. You purchase a magnetic ticket card at the entrance of the station, either from a machine or from a ticket booth. You can buy a single ride card (R$2.80), or opt for a rechargeable magnetic card, to which you then add value, which gets deducted when you swipe the card passing through the turnstile. Trains run Monday to Saturday from 5am to midnight and Sunday 7am to 11pm.

By Bus Rio's buses follow direct, logical pathways, sticking to the main streets and many of the same routes you'd take if you were driving. Figuring out which bus to take is straightforward. The route number and final destination are displayed in big letters on the front of buses. Smaller signs displayed inside the front window (usually below and to the left of the driver) and on the side of the bus list the intermediate stops. For information on how to reach a specific tourist destination or neighborhood, contact Riotur's general information number at ☎ 0800/285-0555 or 021/2542-8080.

Buses only stop if someone wants to board, so make sure you wave your hand at the driver. Have a small bill or change ready—R$2.80 to R$3.50—as you will go through a turnstile right away. Small bills are best, as operators have limited change. You pay for each ride; there are no transfers. Buses are safe during the day; just watch for pickpockets when it gets busy. In the evening, when fewer passengers ride, it is better to take a taxi.

By Taxi

Taxis are plentiful and relatively inexpensive. They're the perfect way to reach more out-of-the-way places and the best way to get around in the evening. Regular taxis can be hailed anywhere on the street. A ride from Copacabana to Praça XV in Centro costs about R$25; a ride from the main bus station to Leblon costs R$35 to R$40 in moderate traffic. Most hotels work with special, more expensive, radio taxis, so if you don't want to pay extra, just walk to the corner and hail your own regular taxi. To reserve a regular yellow cab, contact **JB Radio Taxi** at ☎ 021/2241-7107. Taxis accept cash only.

On Foot

Rio de Janeiro's downtown and southern neighborhoods are very pedestrian-friendly, and walking is an excellent way to get around and soak up the atmosphere. That said, keep in mind that the city's cobblestone streets and uneven sidewalks can be challenging for people with disabilities (p 170), strollers, or those sporting inappropriate footwear. Also take great care when crossing the street and *always* watch for motorcycles, which often zip in between parked or stopped cars, sometimes even going in the opposite direction of traffic.

By Car

Driving in Rio is not for the weak of heart. Traffic is hectic, street patterns confusing, drivers just a few shades shy of courteous, and parking next to nonexistent. A car is not required for exploring Rio; a combination of public transit gets you pretty much anywhere in the city for very little money.

You will find at least half a dozen car rental companies along Avenida Princesa Isabel in Copacabana. Reliable companies with good service include Avis, Av. Princesa Isabel 350, Copacabana (☎ 0800/725-2847; www.avis.com.br); Hertz, Av. Princesa Isabel 500 Copacabana (☎ 0800/701-7300 or 021/2275-2383; www.hertz.com.br); and Localiza, Av. Princesa Isabel 150, Copacabana (☎ 021/2275-3340; www.localiza.com). Rates for a compact car (Fiat Palio or VW Gol) with A/C start at R$75 per day.

Fast **Facts**

APARTMENT RENTALS Get more bang for your dollar (or euro or pound) by booking an apartment instead of a hotel room. Rates typically start around R$80 to R$100 per night. Most tourist flats (*temporada* in Portuguese) are found in Copacabana and Ipanema, ranging from compact studios to opulent duplex penthouses. I recommend **www.aluguetemporada.com.br**, which offers affordable options outside the main tourist areas. For a very different experience, reserve a room in a B&B in Santa Teresa. For more information, see p 141.

ATMS/CASHPOINTS The easiest way to get money in Brazilian reals is to make a direct withdrawal from an ATM. Check with your bank to make sure your debit or credit card is authorized to make international withdrawals (and don't forget to memorize your 4-digit PIN). Most international cards work with the Maestro, Cirrus, or Plus networks, most commonly found at the following banks: **Banco do Brasil, HSBC, Citibank,** and **Bradesco.** For a slightly higher fee, you can usually withdraw money from the **Rede 24 horas,** often found in convenience stores or gas stations.

BABYSITTING Most major hotels will be able to provide babysitting services for an additional fee. But before you book a sitter, it's worth noting that Cariocas are very child-friendly. Nobody will bat an eyelash if you go out for dinner with your kid(s) at 10pm.

BANKS **Banco do Brasil** has the most reliable currency exchange services. You will find branches at Rua Joana Angelica, Ipanema (☎ 021/3544-9700) and Av. N.S. de Copacabana 594, Copacabana (☎ 021/3816-5800) and numerous other locations. However, using Brazilian banks will only add unnecessary stress to your holiday, as hours for foreign exchange are limited, service is slow, and fees are high. Instead of exchanging foreign money or cashing traveler's checks, you're better off using a major credit card for larger expenses and ATM withdrawals to obtain cash.

BIKE RENTALS Bikes can be rented at **Bike e Lazer,** Rua Visconde de Pirajá 135, Ipanema (☎ 021/2267-7778) for R$60 per day or R$15 per hour.

BUSINESS HOURS Stores are usually open from 9am to 7pm weekdays, and 9am to 2pm on Saturdays. Most places close on Sundays. Shopping centers are open Monday through Saturday from 10am to 10pm. On Sundays, many malls open their food courts and movie theaters all day, but mall shops will only open from 3 to 8pm. Banks are open Monday through Friday from 10am to 4pm.

CLASSES A great way to experience Brazilian culture is by taking a course or a workshop. **Cook in Rio**, Rua Ronald de Carvalho 154, Copacabana (☎ 021/8761-3653; www.cookinrio.com; R$120 per person), offers afternoon cooking classes of Brazilian classics such as *feijoada*; it's a delicious way to learn more about local traditions and take home some excellent recipes.

If you love samba but are baffled by the fast-paced frenetic steps, take a private dance lesson with samba expert **Carlinhos de Jesus,** Rua Álvaro Ramos, 11, Botafogo (☎ 021/2541-6186; www.carlinhosdejesus.com.br; R$70 per person). Brazilian music lovers can brush up on their percussion skills or learn a new instrument with private lessons at **Maracatu Brasil,** Rua Ipiranga 49, Laranjeiras (☎ 021/2557-4754; www.maracatubrasil.com.br). Lessons start at R$60 per person.

Always wanted to learn Portuguese? Add some language lessons to your holiday and soon you will be able to converse with the *Cariocas*. **Casa do Caminho,** Rua Farme de Amoedo 75, Ipanema (☎ 021/2267-6552; www.casadocaminho-languagecentre.org), offers private lessons (R$50) or one-, two-, or three-week part-time language courses for foreigners (starting at R$170 per week), that still leave you plenty of time to explore the city.

CREDIT CARDS Credit cards are widely accepted in Rio de Janeiro, even for relatively minor purchases. Just keep in mind that you can sometimes negotiate a better discount on a room or in a store if you pay cash. The most commonly accepted cards are Visa and MasterCard. American Express and Diners Club are also often accepted.

CONSULATES & EMBASSIES **Australia:** Av. Presidente Wilson 231, Ste. 23, Centro (☎ **021/3824-4624**). **Canada:** Av. Atlântica 1130, 5th floor, Copacabana (☎ **21/2543-3004**). **U.S.:** Av. Presidente Wilson 147, Centro (☎ **021/3823-2000**). **U.K.:** Praia do Flamengo 284, 2nd floor, Flamengo (☎ **021/2555-9600**).

CURRENCY EXCHANGE If you want to exchange some cash, try the **Casa Universal Cambio,** Av N.S. Copacabana 371, loja E., Copcabana (☎ 021/2548-6696). Rates are usually lower than the official exchange rate available via bank or credit card companies, but the service is quick and hassle-free.

CUSTOMS As a visitor, you are unlikely to be scrutinized very closely by Brazilian Customs; however, there are random checks, and your luggage may be thoroughly inspected. Visitors are allowed to bring in whatever they need for personal use on their trip, including electronics such as a camera and laptop. If you are bringing in new electronic items, you may be asked to register the item to ensure that you will take it with you when you leave. Gifts purchased abroad worth more than US$500 must be declared and are subject to duties for the value over US$500. Upon arrival, you may purchase up to US$500 in the airport duty-free shop (after passport control, in the baggage claim area).

ELECTRICITY Rio de Janeiro's electric current is 110 volts. However, some hotels may also provide 220 volts or both. Most laptops and battery chargers can handle both, but when in doubt, check before plugging in. Brazilian plugs are being converted to three prongs: two round and one flat. If necessary, you can buy an inexpensive converter at any local hardware store.

EMERGENCIES For police, call ☎ **190.** To report a fire or call an ambulance, dial ☎ **193.** For the tourist police, at Av. Afrânio de Melo Franco 159, Leblon, call ☎ 021/2332-2924 or 021/2334-2885.

GAY & LESBIAN TRAVEL Gay and lesbian travelers will find a small but vibrant gay community in Rio, more often geared toward men than women, with a gay pride parade, as well as gay beach areas, bars, and clubs. However, public displays of affection are not common among gays and lesbians. One Brazilian travel agency in Rio that specializes in tours for gay and lesbian travelers is **Rio G Travel,** Rua Teixeira de Melo 16, Ipanema (☎ **021/3813-0003;** www.riog.com.br).

HEALTH Standards for hygiene and public health in Rio de Janeiro are generally high, and there are no specific vaccination requirements. Before leaving, however, check with your doctor or with the Centers for Disease Control (www.cdc.gov) for specific advisories, especially if you are visiting other destinations. Use common sense when eating on the street or in restaurants.

One health concern that affects the city periodically is dengue fever, a viral infection transmitted by mosquitoes. It's characterized by a sudden-onset high fever, severe headaches, joint and muscle pain, nausea/vomiting, and rash. (The rash may not appear until 3–4 days after the fever.) Proper diagnosis requires a blood test. The illness may last up to 10 days, but complete recovery can take 2 to 4 weeks. Dengue is rarely fatal.

The risk for dengue fever is highest during periods of heat and rain, where stagnant pools of water allow mosquitoes to breed. There is no vaccine for dengue fever. Symptoms can be treated with bed rest, fluids, and medications to reduce fever, such as acetaminophen (Tylenol); aspirin should be avoided. The most important precaution a traveler can take is to avoid mosquito bites in dengue-prone areas. Try to remain in well-screened or air-conditioned areas and use a mosquito repellent. For up-to-date information on the status of dengue fever in Brazil, consult the Centers for Disease Control website (www.cdc.gov).

HOLIDAYS The following holidays are observed in Brazil: New Year's Day (Jan 1); Carnaval (various dates in Feb or Mar); Easter (a Sun in Mar or Apr); Tiradentes Day (Apr 21); Labor Day (May 1); Corpus Christi (various dates in June); Independence Day (Sept 7); Our Lady of Apparition (Oct 12); All Souls' Day (Nov 2); Proclamation of the Republic (Nov 15); and Christmas Day (Dec 25). On these days, banks, schools, and government institutions will be closed, and some stores may be closed as well.

HOSPITALS Public hospital emergency rooms can be found at Miguel Couto, Rua Bartolemeu Mitre 1108, Leblon (☎ **021/3111-3800**) or at Souza Aguiar, Praça da Republica 111, Centro (☎ **021/3111-2600**). Private emergency rooms can be found at the Cardio Trauma Ipanema, Rua Farme de Amoedo 86, Ipanema (☎ **021/2525-1900**) and at the city's best hospital, Copa D'or, Rua Figueiredo de Magalhães 875, Copacabana (☎ **021/2545-3600**).

INSURANCE For information on traveler's insurance, trip-cancellation insurance, and medical insurance while traveling, please visit www.frommers.com/tips.

INTERNET ACCESS Wi-Fi is becoming increasingly common in Brazil. Many hotels offer it either in the lobby or in rooms, or both; usually for a fee. Wi-Fi hotspots are far less common, but the number is steadily increasing. Internet cafes (called cybercafes or Lan Houses in Brazil) are quite common everywhere. Locations include **Internet House,** Av. N.S. de Copacabana 581, loja 201, Copacabana (☎ **021/2235-3892**) and **Netty Internet,** Rua Visconde de Pirajá 281, loja 302, Ipanema (☎ **021/2513-1410**).

LIQUOR LAWS Officially, Brazil's drinking laws only allow those over 18 years of age to drink, but this is rarely enforced. Beer, wine, and liquor can be bought any day of the week from grocery stores and delis, without any form of ID. Beer is widely sold through street vendors, bakeries, and refreshment stands.

LOST PROPERTY Contact your credit card company as soon as you discover that your wallet has been lost or stolen. In Brazil, contact **American Express** at ☎ 0800/785-050, **Mastercard** and **Visa** at ☎ 0800/784-456, and **Diners Club** at ☎ 0800/784-444. If any other items have been stolen, you may also wish to file a police report. The Tourist Police in Leblon has English-speaking staff on hand to assist (see "Emergencies" above). To report any stolen documents such as a passport or ID, contact your consulate (see "Consulates & Embassies" above).

MAIL & POSTAGE Look for the yellow-and-blue sign saying *correios*. Locations are downtown: Av. Rio Branco 156, Centro (☎ 021/2240-8764); Copacabana: Av. N.S. de Copacabana 540, Copacabana (☎ 021/2256-1439); and Ipanema: Rua Visconde de Pirajá 452, Ipanema (☎ 021/2567-6197). The international airport also has a post office (☎ 021/3398-7024) that's open Monday to Friday from 9am to 9pm and Saturday from 9am to 1pm.

MOBILE PHONES International GSM cellphones work in most parts of Brazil, but charges can be high—usually US$1 to US$1.50 per minute. A better option is to buy a local SIM card, which gives you a Brazilian number and allows you to pay local Brazilian rates (about R$1 per min. for local calls, R$1.40 for long distance). There is no charge to receive calls if you are in your home area. The only Brazilian company that provides reliable service is TIM (www.tim.com.br). There are TIM kiosks in all major malls and department stores. Note that after you buy a TIM SIM chip, you will have to call and register your account; as part of its anti-crime laws, Brazil does not allow anonymous mobile phone accounts. You will need to give your name and passport number.

MONEY The official unit of currency in Brazil is the real (pronounced ray-*all;* the plural is reais, pronounced ray-*eyes*), which the Brazilian government introduced in 1994 in an attempt to control inflation. In recent years, the real has become quite strong, whereas the U.S. dollar and euro have been on a steady decline. For many travelers, this means that Brazil is still affordable, though not the bargain it was in years past. I list prices in reais (R$) that were accurate as of press time under the following exchange rates: US$1 = R$1.77; UK£1 = R$2.70; 1€ = R$2.27; C$1 = R$1.70; A$1 = R$1.57; NZ$1 = R$1.27. Real bank notes come in R$100, R$50, R$20, R$10, and R$5; and coins of R$1 and 5, 10, 25, and 50 cents. ***Tip:*** When exchanging money, keep the receipt. You will need it in case you want to change back any unused reais at the end of your trip. See **www.xe.com** online for an easy currency converter.

NEWSPAPERS & MAGAZINES Your best bet for international papers are the newsstands along Visconde de Pirajá in Ipanema. Check out the Web-based English-language Rio paper, ***The Gringo Times*** (www.thegringotimes.com). For entertainment and nightlife listings, check the cultural insert in the Friday edition of ***O Globo*** or ***O Dia*** newspaper or the weekly ***Veja*** magazine.

PASSPORTS/VISAS Nationals of Australia, Canada, and the United States require a visa to visit Brazil. British nationals (and holders of an E.U. passport) and New Zealand passport holders do not require a visa, but do need a passport valid for at least 6 months and a return ticket. Requirements and fees vary per country; American citizens pay US$100 for a standard single-entry tourist visa that is valid for 90 days. Count on at least 2 weeks of processing time. Upon arrival in Brazil, visitors will receive an entry stamp in their passport (maximum of 90 days) and a stamped entry card. Hang on to the card for dear life, as losing it will result in a possible fine and a major hassle when you leave. If necessary, the visa can be renewed once for another 90 days. Visa renewals are obtained through the local Policia Federal at the International Airport, Terminal 1, 3rd floor (☎ 021/3398-3142; Mon–Fri 8am–6pm).

For more information regarding visas and to obtain application details, contact the Brazilian consulate in New York (☎ 917/777-7791; www.brazilny.org); Los Angeles (☎ 323/651-2664; www.brazilian-consulate.org); or Miami (☎ 305/285-6200; www.brazilmiami.org). Canadians can apply through Toronto's Brazilian consulate (☎ 416/922-2503; www.consbrastoronto.org). In the U.K., more information is available at ☎ 020/7399-9000 or www.brazil.org.uk. Australians can call 02/6273-2372 or log on to www.brazil.org.au, and in New Zealand inquiries can be made in Wellington (☎ 04/473-3516; www.brazil.org.nz).

PHARMACIES Brazilians love drug stores (*farmácias* or *drogarias*), so you should have no problem finding one. A licensed pharmacist will be glad to assist you with any minor ailments. Many drugs available by prescription only in the U.S. and Canada are available over-the-counter in Brazil.

POLICE See "Emergencies" above.

SAFETY Rio retains a somewhat unsavory reputation for street violence, though things have improved significantly since their nadir in the late-'80s and early 1990s. That said, there are still several things to keep in mind to ensure that you have a safe trip. It's a bad idea to wander unaccompanied into any of the favelas (shantytowns) found in and around the city. It's also best to avoid the city center (Centro) on weekends and holidays, when this part of town is mostly deserted. Don't go down to the ocean at night; stick to the brightly lit and police-patrolled pedestrian boulevard that parallels the beach. At night, traveling by taxi is also recommended—don't rely on public transportation. Finally, as in any large metropolitan area, it's wise to observe common-sense precautions: Don't flash jewelry and large amounts of cash, and stick to well-lit and well-traveled thoroughfares.

SENIOR TRAVELERS Senior travelers can try and ask for discounts, though these are reserved for those over 60 or 65 years of age who can show a Brazilian ID. Still, it's worth asking at tourist attractions if there's a discount. The phrase to use is *"Tem disconto para idoso?"* (Is there a discount for seniors?)

SMOKING In the last few years, strict smoking regulations have gone into effect; all enclosed public areas are now nonsmoking, including malls, offices, restaurants, bars, and clubs. Most hotels have non-smoking rooms or floors.

TAXES There are no taxes added to goods purchased in Brazil. Restaurants and hotels normally add a 10% service tax. In Rio, the city also levies a 5% tax on hotels. All airports in Brazil charge departure taxes; this is usually included in the ticket.

TELEPHONES See "Mobile Phones" above for info on cellular phones. See the inside back cover of this book for information on dialing instructions.

TIME ZONE Rio de Janeiro is 3 hours behind GMT. During daylight saving time (usually late Oct through mid-Feb), Rio's time difference changes to 2 hours behind GMT.

TIPPING A 10% to 12% service charge is automatically included on most restaurant and hotel bills (including room service), and you aren't expected to tip on top of this amount. If service has been particularly bad, you can request to have the percentage removed from your bill. Taxi drivers do not get tipped; just round up the amount to facilitate change. Hairdressers and beauticians usually receive a 10% tip. Bellboys get tipped R$1 to R$2 per bag.

TOILETS Usually, restrooms are marked *mulher* or with an M for women and *homem* or with an H for men. Sometimes the door will read *damas* or D for ladies and *cavalheiros* or C for gentlemen.

TRAVELERS WITH DISABILITIES Travelers with disabilities will find Rio de Janeiro challenging, especially for those who use a wheelchair. Even as Metrô stations, hotels, malls, restaurants, and attractions are becoming increasingly more accessible, streets and sidewalks are often uneven and lack ramps. For wheelchair-accessible taxi service, contact **Coop Taxi** (☎ 021/3295-9606).

WATER The tap water in Rio de Janeiro is increasingly safe to drink. However, as a result of the treatment process, it still doesn't taste great. To be on the safe side, drink bottled or filtered water (most Brazilians do). All brands are reliable; ask for *agua sem gas* for still water and *agua com gas* for carbonated water. However, you can certainly shower, brush your teeth, or rinse fruit with tap water.

Rio de Janeiro: **A Brief History**

Not a lot is known about Rio de Janeiro's pre-colonial history. The earliest inhabitants most likely came from Asia, traveling overland via the land bridge across the Bering Sea, approximately 8,000 to 10,000 years ago. The tribes that settled on the eastern side of the Andes remained semi-nomadic; unlike the large civilizations on the western side of the Andes, little archaeological evidence of Brazil's first inhabitants has been found.

Brazil's colonial history began on April 22, 1500, when Portuguese explorer **Pedro Alvares Cabral** landed his ships in the south of Bahia and claimed the land for the Portuguese crown. Early colonial endeavors were mostly focused on exploiting the resources of this new territory. One of the coveted finds was *Pau Brasil,* a native tree that produces an excellent red dye. In 1532, sugarcane was introduced to the northeast and would become one of the colony's major cash crops. As early as 1550, Portugal began importing slaves from Africa to work on the plantations. The first Portuguese expedition to sail into Guanabara Bay, on January 1, 1502, believed it had discovered the mouth of a great river and named the location, erroneously, Rio de Janeiro or "River of January." While the Portuguese were busily expanding their sugarcane operations in Bahia and Pernambuco, the French were challenging their rule around Rio de Janeiro. Joining forces with local Indian tribes, the French managed to gain a foothold in the region, until they were expelled on March 1, 1565, by **Tomé de Souza,** who founded the city of São Sebastião do Rio de Janeiro.

The discovery of gold in **Minas Gerais** in 1665 heralded the beginning of a new era for Rio de Janeiro. Attracted by the gold rush, settlers flocked to the region, and Rio de Janeiro developed into a major port and supply center. Power gradually began to shift south from Bahia; in 1763, Rio de Janeiro became the new administrative capital of the colony.

The **Napoleonic wars** (1799–1815) in Europe completely changed Rio de Janeiro's course of history. Fearing the invasion of French troops, **Portuguese King João VI** moved his entire family and court from Lisbon to Rio de Janeiro in 1808. Almost overnight, Rio's population practically doubled, with the arrival of 15,000 new residents. No longer a colonial backwater but the center of the entire Portuguese Empire, Rio was finally allowed a printing press, universities, and a library. The crown also founded the Banco do Brasil in 1808 and developed the state's iron industry.

When the Portuguese king returned to Portugal in 1821, his son **Pedro I** remained in Brazil as a regent. Dissatisfied with losing their status as capital of the empire, Brazilians supported Pedro I by declaring Brazil's independence from Portugal and proclaiming him emperor. Pedro I abdicated in 1832 as pressure for political reforms grew. Only 5 years old then, his son, **Pedro II,** took his place as emperor in 1840, at the ripe age of 14. With growing (inter)national pressure to end slavery, Pedro II's daughter, **Princess Isabel,** passed the *Lei Aurea,* setting Brazilian slaves free. During more than 300 years of slavery, an estimated 3.6 million slaves were taken from Africa and brought to Brazil. In 1889, a liberal coup ended Pedro II's rule, and Brazil was proclaimed a republic with Rio de Janeiro as its national capital.

The city blossomed as the country's political and cultural center, until its reign came to an abrupt end in 1960. Elected as president in 1955, **Juscelino Kubitschek** had made a campaign promise to build a new capital in the center of the country. True to his word, after a 4-year construction frenzy, he inaugurated Brazil's modernist capital, Brasília, on April 21, 1960. Overnight, Rio de Janeiro lost its leading role and political support. Throughout the 1970s and 1980s, the city seemed to have lost some of its mojo; crime rates soared, and with little investment in public works or infrastructure, Rio radiated an aura of neglect. Finally, as host of the **1992 Earth Summit,** Rio de Janeiro was forced to deal with some of its most pressing issues and began to regain its sparkle and confidence.

Although no longer the political capital, Rio is still a major cultural force and the most visited destination in Brazil. In 2009, Rio de Janeiro received a major shot in the arm when it was chosen as the host of the **2016 Summer Olympics,** beating out competitors like Chicago and Madrid. In 2010, Brazilians elected **Dilma Rousseff** president. Rousseff makes history as the first female president of the largest country in South America.

Useful Phrases

Tip: The letter A in Portuguese is usually pronounced like the "a" in "car," never like the "a" in "at."

Useful Words & Phrases

ENGLISH	PORTUGUESE	PRONUNCIATION
Good morning	Bom dia.....	*Bon* jeea (j as in jive)
How are you?	Como vai?	Kohmo vi? (i as in high)
Very well	Muito bem	*Mooy*-toh beng
Thank you	Obrigado	Obri*ga*doo
You're welcome	De nada	Dee nada
Good-bye	Tchau	Tchow
Please	Por favor	*Por* fahvor
Yes	Sim	Seeng
No	Não	Naung
Excuse me	Com licença	Com *lee*sensa

ENGLISH	PORTUGUESE	PRONUNCIATION
Give me	Me dá	Mee dah
Where is . . . ?	Onde fica..?:	Ondee *fee*ka
the station	a estação	ah *sta*sowng
a hotel	um hotel	oong ootel
a gas station	um posto de gasolina	*oong poosto deh* gazolcena
a restaurant	um restaurante	oong restauranteh
the toilet	o banheir	oban-yeero
a good doctor	um bom médico	oong bong *me*dicoo
the road to	o caminho parao	o ka-*meen*-yoh para
to the right	A direita	Ah jee*ray*-tah
to the left	A esquerda	Ah eesh-kayr-dah
straight ahead	Em frente	Eng *fren*-tee
I would like	Gostaria	Gostah*ree*-a
a room	um quarto	*oong kwartoh*
Do you have . . . ?	Você tem...?	Vosay teng?
a dictionary	um dicionário	oong dee-seeyonario
How much is it?	Quanto custa?	Kwantoh *koo*stah?
When?	Quando?	Kwandoh?
What?	Quê?	Kay?
There is (Is there . . . ?)	Tem?	Teng?
What is there?	O que tem....?	Oh kay teng?
Yesterday	Ontém	Ohn-teng
Today	Hoje	Ooh-gee
Tomorrow	Amanhã	Aman-yah
Good	Bom	Bong
Bad	Mal	Mau
Better (best)	O melhor	Mel-yore
More	Mais	Mish (i as in high)
Less	Menos	Mehnos
No smoking	Proibido fumar	Proo-ee-bee-doh *foo*mar
Postcard	Cartão postal	Kartaum poshtal
Insect repellent	Repelente contra insetos	Repaylentee kontrah insetos
Do you speak English?	Você fala inglês?	Vosay falah in-*glays*?
Is there anyone here who speaks English?	Tem alguem aqui quem fala ingles?	Teng algeng akee Kem falah in-*glays?*
I speak a little Portuguese	Falo um pouco de português	Faloh oong pohkoh dee portu*gays*
I don't understand Portuguese very well	Não entendo português muito bem	Naum entendoh portu*gays* *mooy*-toh beng

Numbers

ENGLISH	PORTUGUESE	PRONUNCIATION
One	um / uma	oong/ooma
Two	dois / duas	doy sh/*doo*-ash

ENGLISH	PORTUGUESE	PRONUNCIATION
Three	tres	trays
Four	quatro	kwatro
Five	cinco	*seen*-ko
Six	Seis	saysh
Seven	sete	*seh*-tee
Eight	oito	*oy*-toh
Nine	nove	*noh*-vee
Ten	dez	deish
Eleven	onze	*ohn*-zee
Twelve	doze	*doh*-zee
Thirteen	treze	*tray*-zee
Fourteen	quatorze	katohrzee
Fifteen	quinze	*keen*-zay
Sixteen	dezeseis	deezesaysh
Seventeen	dezesete	deezay-*seh*-tee
Eighteen	desoito	deezoitoh
Nineteen	dezenove	deezay-*no*vee
Twenty	vinte	*veen*tee
Thirty	trinta	*treen*tah
Forty	quarenta	kwa-*ren*-tah
Fifty	cinquenta	sin-*kwen*-tah
Sixty	sessenta	ses-*sen*-tah
Seventy	setenta	se-*ten*-tah
Eighty	oitenta	oy-*ten*-tah
Ninety	noventa	noh-*ven*-tah
Hundred	cem	sayn
Thousand	mil	meal

Fruit

ENGLISH	PORTUGUESE	PRONUNCIATION
Banana	banana	bah-*nah*-na
Pineapple	Abacaxi	ah-bah-ka*shee*
Apple	Macã	mah-*san*
Pear	Pera	*pay*-rah
Grape	Uva	*Oo*vah
Lime	Limão	Lee*mowng*
Orange	Laranja	lah-ranja (j as in jive)
Mango	Manga	man-ga
Strawberry	Morango	moo-*ran*-goh

Vegetables

ENGLISH	PORTUGUESE	PRONUNCIATION
Tomato	Tomate	toma*tee*
Onion	Cebola	saybolah
Scallion	Cebolinha	say-bo-leen-ya
Garlic	Alho	alyoo
Ginger	gengibre	gen-geebree (g as in gesture)
Cucumber	pepino	pay-pee-noh

ENGLISH	PORTUGUESE	PRONUNCIATION
Bell pepper (green / red)	pimentão (verde / vermelho)	pee-men-*towng* (verday/vermaylioh)
Avocado	abacate	*a*h-ba-katee
Carrot	cenoura	*say*-norah
Celery	aipo	*ai*-poh
Broccoli	brocolis	*bro*-kolees
Cauliflower	couveflor	*koh*-vee flor
Collards	couve	*koh*-vee
Cilantro	coentro	koh-*en*-troh
Beans	feijao	fay-*jowng*
Green beans	vagem	*va*-jeng
Lettuce	alface	al-fa*see*
Mushroom	cogumelo	koh-goomellow
Squash	abôbora	aboh-borah
Spinach	espinafre	speenahfree

Meat

ENGLISH	PORTUGUESE	PRONUNCIATION
Meat	carne	car-nay
Beef	bife	*bee*fee
Chicken	frango	*frahn*-goh
Pork	porco	porkoh
Ham	presunto	pray-*zoon*-toh
Lamb	cordeiro	kor-*day*-roh
Turkey	chester	shester
Veal	vitela	vee-*te*-lah
Hot dog	cachorro quente	ka-showroh ken-*tee*
Egg	ovo	*oo*-voo
Tofu	tofu (quejo de soja)	too-*foo* (kayjoo dee sojah)

Seafood

ENGLISH	PORTUGUESE	PRONUNCIATION
Fish	peixe	*pay*-shee
Tuna	atum	ah-*toong*
Salmon	salmão	sal-*mowng*
Shrimp	camarão	kama-*rowng*
Lobster	lagosta	lagostah
Oyster	ostra	*oh*-strah
Mussels	mexilhão	me-sheel-*yowng*
Crab	siri	*see*-ree
Mud crab	carangueijo	ka-ran-*gay*-joo
Squid	lula	*loo*-lah

Bread & Pasta

ENGLISH	PORTUGUESE	PRONUNCIATION
French bread	pão frances	powng fran-*sayz*
(Brown) rice	arroz (integral)	arrohsh (integral)
Potato	batata	bah-*tah*-tah
French fries	batata frita	bah-*tah*-tah *free*-tah

ENGLISH	PORTUGUESE	PRONUNCIATION
Pasta	massa	*ma*-sah
Pita bread	pão arabe	powng *ah*-rabee
Cookie	biscoito	bees-*koi*-toh
Oats	aveia	ah-vay-ah

Restaurant Terms

ENGLISH	PORTUGUESE	PRONUNCIATION
Breakfast	Café da manhã	ka-*feh* da man-*yang*
Lunch	Almoço	almoh-soo
Dinner	Jantar	jan-*taar*
Appetizer	Entrada	entrada
Dessert	Sobremesa	so-bree-*mesa*
Glass	Copo	*ko*-poo
Plate	Prato	*pra*-too
Fork	Garfo	*gar*-foo
Knife	Faca	*fah*-kah
Spoon	Colher	kool-*yehr*
Napkin	Guardanapo	guarda-*nah*-poh
Cooked	Cozido	koo*zee*doo
Grilled	Grelhado	grel-*ya-doo*
Fried	Frito	*free*-too
Breaded	Empanado	em-pah-nado
Roasted	Assado	ah-*sa*-doo
Bill/check	A conta	Ah *kon*-tah
Waiter	Garçom	gar-*son*
Do you take credit cards?	Aceita cartão de crédito?	Ah-*say*-ta kar-*tong* dee *kre*-deetoh
I would like a receipt	Gostaria de um recibo	Gostah-ree-ah dee oong ray-*see*-bo

Beverages

ENGLISH	PORTUGUESE	PRONUNCIATION
Water	agua	*ah*-gwa
Coffee	café	*ka*-feh
Tea	chá	sjah
Juice	suco	*soo*-koo
Soda/pop	refrigerante	ray-*free*-gerantee

Dairy

ENGLISH	PORTUGUESE	PRONUNCIATION
Milk	leite	*lay*-tee
Cheese	queijo	*kay*-joo
Yogurt	iogurte	io-*goor*-tee
Butter	manteiga	mantayga
Ice cream	sorvete	sohr-*vay*-tee

Index

See also Accommodations and Restaurant indexes, below.

O

P

Q

R

S

Accommodations

Restaurants

Photo **Credits**

p viii: © Lisa Wiltse; p 4: © Hiroshi Higuchi/Photolibrary; p 5, top: © Lisa Wiltse; p 5, bottom: © Tim Clayton; p 6, top: © Florian Kopp/Imagebroker/Alamy; p 6, bottom: © Lisa Wiltse; p 7: © Lisa Wiltse; p 9: © Lisa Wiltse; p 10: © Lisa Wiltse; p 11, top: © Tim Clayton; p 11, bottom: © Lisa Wiltse; p 13: © Lisa Wiltse; p 14, top: © Lisa Wiltse; p 14, bottom: © Lisa Wiltse; p 15, top: © Alessandra Del Bene; p 15, bottom: © Lisa Wiltse; p 16, top: © Lisa Wiltse; p 16, bottom: © Lisa Wiltse; p 19, top: © Tim Clayton; p 19, bottom: © Lisa Wiltse; p 20: © Tim Clayton; p 21: © Tim Clayton; p 22: © Lisa Wiltse; p 23: © Florian Kopp/Imagebroker/Alamy; p 25: © Lisa Wiltse; p 26: © Lisa Wiltse; p 27: © Lisa Wiltse; p 29, top: © Alessandra Del Bene; p 29, bottom: © Alessandra Del Bene; p 30, top: © Lisa Wiltse; p 30, top: © Lisa Wiltse; p 32: © Lisa Wiltse; p 33: © Tim Clayton; p 35: © Lisa Wiltse; p 36, top: © Lisa Wiltse; p 36, bottom: © Lisa Wiltse; p 37: © Tim Clayton; p 39: © Yadid Levy/Alamy; p 40: © Bertrand Gardel/Hemis/Photolibrary; p 41: © Courtesy Carioca da Gema; p 43, top: © Lisa Wiltse; p 43, bottom: © Lisa Wiltse; p 44: © Tim Clayton; p 45: © Lisa Wiltse; p 47: © Lisa Wiltse; p 48, top: © Lisa Wiltse; p 48, bottom: © Lisa Wiltse; p 49: © Lisa Wiltse; p 51: © Lisa Wiltse; p 52, top: © South America/Alamy; p 52, bottom: © Lisa Wiltse; p 53: © Lisa Wiltse; p 55: © Lisa Wiltse; p 56: © Lisa Wiltse; p 57: © Tim Clayton; p 59: © Lisa Wiltse; p 60: © Lisa Wiltse; p 61: © Courtesy Jockey Club Brasileiro; p 63, top: © Tim Clayton; p 63, bottom: © Lisa Wiltse; p 65: © Alessandra del Bene; p 66: © Lisa Wiltse; p 70: © Alessandra del Bene; p 71: © Alessandra Del Bene; p 72: © Lisa Wiltse; p 73: © Lisa Wiltse; p 74: © Lisa Wiltse; p 75, top: © Lisa Wiltse; p 75, bottom: © Tim Clayton; p 76: © Alessandra del Bene; p 77: © Tim Clayton; p 79: © Lisa Wiltse; p 81, top: © Lisa Wiltse; p 81, bottom: © Lisa Wiltse; p 83: © Lisa Wiltse; p 84: © Balthasar Thomass/Alamy; p 85, top: © Lisa Wiltse; p 85, bottom: © Lisa Wiltse; p 86: © Tim Clayton; p 87: © Lisa Wiltse; p 89: © Lisa Wiltse; p 90: © Lisa Wiltse; p 91: © Lisa Wiltse; p 93, top: © Tim Clayton; p 93, bottom: © Lisa Wiltse; p 94: © Lisa Wiltse; p 95: © Alessandra Del Bene; p 96: © Lisa Wiltse; p 101: © Lisa Wiltse; p 102, top: © Lisa Wiltse; p 102, bottom: © Courtesy Bar d'Hotel; p 103: © Lisa Wiltse; p 104: © Lisa Wiltse; p 105: © Tim Clayton; p 106: © Lisa Wiltse; p 107: © Lisa Wiltse; p 108: © Lisa Wiltse; p 109: © Lisa Wiltse; p 110: © Lisa Wiltse; p 111: © Lisa Wiltse; p 112: © Lisa Wiltse; p 115: © Lisa Wiltse; p 116: © Lisa Wiltse; p 117: © Alessandra Del Bene; p 118: © Lisa Wiltse; p 119: © Courtesy Baronneti; p 120: © Alessandra Del Bene; p 121: © Lisa Wiltse; p 122: © Lisa Wiltse; p 123: © Tim Clayton; p 124: © Alessandra Del Bene; p 127: © Tim Clayton; p 128: © Lisa Wiltse; p 128: © Lisa Wiltse; p 129: © Lisa Wiltse; p 130: © Lisa Wiltse; p 131: © Courtesy Orient-Express Hotels, photos by Alessandro Batistessa; p 132: © Courtesy Windsor Hotels; p 136: © Courtesy Arena Copacabana Hotel; p 137: © Courtesy Castelinho38 hotel, Photos by Silvia Constani; p 138: © Courtesy Hotel

Fasano; p 139: © Courtesy Hotel Santa Teresa; p 140: © Courtesy Epoque Hotels; p 141: © Courtesy Hoteis Othon; p 142: © Courtesy Prominade The Claridge Hotel; p 143, top: © Courtesy Sheraton Rio Hotel & Resort; p 143, bottom: © Courtesy Sofitel, Photo by Fabrice Rambert; p 144: © Courtesy Windsor Hotels; p 145: © Lisa Wiltse; p 147: © Lisa Wiltse; p 148: © Lisa Wiltse; p 149: © Lisa Wiltse; p 151: © Lisa Wiltse; p 152: © Lisa Wiltse; p 153: © Lisa Wiltse; p 155: © Lisa Wiltse; p 156: © Tim Clayton; p 157, top: © Lisa Wiltse; p 157, bottom: © Lisa Wiltse; p 158: © Courtesy Estancia Don Juan; p 159: © Alessandra del Bene.

Notes